Perspectives on Curriculum Development 1776-1976

Prepared by the
ASCD 1976 Yearbook Committee

O. L. Davis, Jr.
Chairperson and Editor

Association for Supervision and Curriculum Development
Suite 1100, 1701 K Street, N.W.
Washington, D.C. 20006

Stock number: 610-76078
Library of Congress Catalog Card Number: 76-39962
ISBN 0-87120-078-3

Foreword

A HISTORICAL CELEBRATION would fall flat without its due modicum of ringing words and its recognition of valiant deeds. This Yearbook, as our Association's contribution to the Bicentennial Celebration of the American Revolution, provides both these elements in its own way. Its purpose is to celebrate the conception, birth, and growth of the idea of free public education and of a suitable curriculum for all in the schools of the United States of America, 1776 to 1976.

The six major chapters of the book are deliberately couched as *perspectives*, for they help the reader to view historical facts in relationship to the past, present, and future. The authors' topic is curriculum development, centering upon the opportunities for growth and development for all who are influenced or affected by the guidance of the school. These opportunities and activities are provided through the various forms and arrangements for instruction.

That these supportive forms and arrangements for instruction have varied through the years of our independence as a nation is evident in the several contributions included here. Curriculum development, though relatively young as a science, has nevertheless shown much vitality in schools and schooling since our founding. Even a casual look at the record shows that many curricular practices have been adopted and abandoned, *re*adopted and *re*abandoned. One value of a historical work such as this may be to help us to keep from being swept off our feet by every "new" panacea that is proposed, by making us aware that the idea has actually been tried before and has not lived up to its glowing promises.

Such a historical account should also sensitize us to the true value and worth of curricular insights and practices that were attempted and that may have been rejected or discontinued before being adequately tried and recognized. History, even that of curriculum development, has its lessons. Not all these lessons are of failure; some are records of remarkable success. The perspectives given relate to both.

A unique feature of this book is the insertion, among the major chapters, of a number of vignettes. These are brief statements bringing to today's readers an immediate sense of the feeling, thinking, experiencing, and undergoing of great persons and ideas in the historical growth of curriculum.

A second feature of the Yearbook consists of the illustrations used throughout. These are supplied from the historical files of the Library of Congress. The importance of the inclusion of these original and for the most part previously unpublished photographs is that in these pages the reader can observe, in the process of teaching and learning, the children and young people and their teachers in various periods of our history. This again is closeness and immediacy; and such closeness can be a moving and instructive experience for the reader.

The ringing words and the recognition of the valiant deeds are here in this our own celebration of the nation's Bicentennial. We hope that all persons concerned with the theory, practice, and evaluation of curriculum development will learn much from this presentation of perspectives. Only so will we be enabled to free ourselves from many of the mistakes and failures of the past and thus to move on to new and sounder planes of endeavor.

DELMO DELLA-DORA, President 1975-76
Association for Supervision
and Curriculum Development

Contents

v

Contents   vii

PUBLIC SCHOOL.

STANDARDS OF AMERIC

Prologue: Curriculum Across Two Hundred Years of Independence

O. L. Davis, Jr.

There is nothing very exciting about a foxhole full of ice water or even high explosive from shells or bombs. The only exciting things in the world are matters of high meaning. . . . There have been some exciting moments in the military history of the United States, but the long social history of the United States is much more exciting and meaningful. In that social history the progress of the American system of public education still remains for me the most dramatic story. . . . Right now, soldiers and battle heroics seem important. They are only as important as they were always—important because they are necessary consequences of badly educated human groups. The crucial and transcendant task is better education of those groups. Perhaps this sounds commonplace to you. To me, about to see very soon my seventh major engagement, it is the one belief which stirs my blood more than bugles. . . .

—Harold R. W. Benjamin, 1944.[1]

W E AMERICANS celebrate this year an event of signal importance, the two hundredth anniversary of our political independence. Our common celebration, called Bicentennial, is a joyous time. It is also a sad time. It forces remembrance. It insists on newness. Our Bicentennial pro-

---

[1] Harold R. W. Benjamin. "More Than Bugles. . . ." *The Journal of the National Education Association* 33: cover; September 1944. When he wrote this, Benjamin, a USAF major, was on leave from his post as dean of the School of Education, University of Maryland.

claims for ourselves and all the world the high value of political independence. We recognize the anniversary of our Declaration of Independence, and, as well, the continuing fulfillment of its strident assertions.

Our present national celebration is a birthday of sorts. Yet, unlike our custom with individuals, this bicentennial celebration lifts up founders, not celebrants. It calls attention to the fullness of the growth of the Republic, and the development of its related institutions. Bicentennial recognition of two centuries of a new nation among nations manifests reflection as well as rededication.

The high seriousness of the moment is attended by awe and accompanied by detraction. Both sentiment and sentimentality are known. Exaggerated claims of merit and scorn violate equally honest honed understanding and reasonable propriety. Yet American political independence has survived two hundred years and will endure its Bicentennial. We Americans probably will like the celebration and, with future generations, will continue to enjoy the benefits of independence which warm our lives.

This bicentennial celebration calls for participation joined by contribution. We think of colored flags and unfurled banners, ice cream and noisemakers, cannons firing blank but noisy charges, skyrockets, county fairs, and commemorative plates. Of special speeches, poems, books, and paintings, sculpture, songs. Of eternal American verities like apple pie, hominy grits, and fresh milk. Of races, marches, and games. We think of our jobs, our recreations, our loves. And we always wonder if what we choose to do and to give is enough. And good enough.

This book is one contribution to this year's celebration. Like its authors and its sponsor, it pretends little. It is neither minor nor grand. It is, nevertheless, seriously proffered, a result of diligent and thoughtful purpose and labor. It stands apart from the gaudy extravagance and exaggeration of artifact and act. It stands a part of the thoughtful reflection and calm deliberation of statement and life of American mind. This book is called *Perspectives on Curriculum Development 1776-1976*.

Three goals have motivated the development of this contribution to the history of American school curriculum. First, the effort adds to the general celebration; second, it adds to our understandings of the nation's schools; also, the essays in this volume present both narration and interpretations of curriculum history.

To focus this 1976 Yearbook on curriculum history must be seen as a decision both insightful and propitious. For the bicentennial occasion, the Association's Executive Council in choosing the theme recognized full well the larger rationale for the volume. In this time of reflection and honor, what was the state of the curriculum in the nation's schools during two hundred years of independence? Some curriculum workers newly interested in curriculum history had dramatized the general lack of understanding of curriculum in our nation's life by claiming that we had forgotten our history.[2] These claims jarred conscience. The Bicentennial provided a convenient and appropriate opportunity to recover that curriculum history, assertedly forgotten. Also, the commitment of a yearbook to curriculum history came at a most auspicious time. Interest in curriculum history was mounting and a yearbook could increase the momentum for serious study as well as general understanding of the field.

The claim that curriculum workers have forgotten their history, while dramatic, seems even on the surface to be exaggerated. For it to have been forgotten, that history would have to have been known. And surely there would be evidence of their having once known that history. But there is little, if any, such evidence. The early shock persists: curriculum history in this country has never been known.

To be sure, some individual workers [3] have provided helpful accounts and have suggested productive relationships. A few scholars have included in larger works summary accounts, some extended, about the history of American schools' curriculum.[4] More commonly, however, we have misconceived general history of schools as material about curriculum. We characteristically have lauded or lamented as freshly minted descriptions those excesses of hyperbole which promote rather than

[2] Herbert M. Kliebard has expressed this position in several major works. One of the first was his "The Curriculum Field in Retrospect." In: P. Witt, editor. *Technology and the Curriculum.* New York: Teachers College Press, 1968. pp. 69-84. Clearly, Kliebard merits recognition for giving the curriculum field major pushes toward finding its history.

[3] A number of sources are helpful here. Most are descriptive reports of projects undertaken. They probably yield richer lodes for study and interpretation when they include specific details and anecdotes amidst more general commentary. Examples of such useful sources are: Katherine C. Mayhew and Anna C. Edwards. *The Dewey School: The Laboratory School of the University of Chicago, 1896-1903.* New York, 1936; and Carleton W. Washburne and Sidney P. Marland, Jr. *Winnetka: The History and Significance of an Educational Experiment.* Englewood Cliffs, New Jersey: Prentice-Hall, Inc., 1963. Harold O. Rugg relates some important personal accounts about development of his social science program, albeit too sketchily, in his *Foundations for American Education.* Yonkers-on-Hudson, New York: World Book Co., 1947. Another type of useful source is: Agnes Snyder. *Dauntless Women in Childhood Education 1856-1931.* Washington, D.C.: Association for Childhood Education International, 1972.

[4] See: J. Minor Gwynn and John B. Chase, Jr. *Curriculum Principles and Social Trends.* Fourth edition. New York: Macmillan Publishing Co., Inc., 1969; Leonard V. Koos. *The American Secondary School.* Boston: Ginn and Co., 1927; Gerald R. Firth and Richard D. Kimpston. *The Curricular-Continuum in Perspective.* Itasca, Illinois: F. E. Peacock Publishers, Inc., 1973; Daniel Tanner and Laurel N. Tanner. *Curriculum Development: Theory into Practice.* New York: Macmillan Publishing Co., Inc., 1975.

describe. We have consistently seemed to talk about slogans rather than sharp realities—talk of the appearance of things rather than the things themselves.

Nevertheless, like the general history of American schooling,[5] attention has been diffused, most frequently has relied on secondary accounts, and has been directed to support a commitment. Indeed, history of curriculum seems most apparently flawed by writers' inability or refusal adequately to distinguish curriculum from other aspects of schooling. Their general failure to employ sources from differing levels of curriculum acts (e.g., individual school and pupil records,[6] district curriculum guides, statements of national commissions) has resulted in less than accurate and possibly misleading conclusions.

Perspectives Arise from Great Concepts

Even though curriculum history is not known and, clearly, problems abound, interest in historical scholarship in this field is increasing. Monographic studies are appearing. Accounts of both prominent and obscure projects are being undertaken. And, a fresh commitment to historical scholarship is obvious.[7] This volume of essays hopefully will add to the acceleration of interest and commitment.

The perspectives in this volume arise from great concepts of the Declaration of Independence. This impressive document called both for independence *from* and independence *for*. It was, therefore, unashamedly positive, future-directed, and utopian. The Declaration, with its virtues firmly and clearly worded, nevertheless quite possibly would

---

[5] The works of three individuals illustrate the major historiographic controversy over the history of American education. The point of departure clearly is the long influential book by Ellwood P. Cubberley. *Public Education in the United States.* Boston: Houghton Mifflin Company, 1919. The seminal monograph that sharpened the issues, and to which new history of education is deeply indebted, is: Bernard Bailyn. *Education in the Forming of American Society: Needs and Opportunities for Study.* Chapel Hill: University of North Carolina Press, 1960. The issues are responsibly discussed by: Lawrence A. Cremin. *The Wonderful World of Ellwood Patterson Cubberley: An Essay on the Historiography of American Education.* New York: Teachers College Press, 1965.

[6] One use of such materials is: O. L. Davis, Jr. "Textbooks Used in an Ohio District School, 1855-1859." *The Serif* 2: 27-32; March 1965.

[7] Gerald A. Ponder. "The Curriculum: Field Without a Past?" *Educational Leadership* 31 (5): 461-64; February 1974. Note, also, the major emphasis on interpretations of curriculum history in recent issues of *Curriculum Theory Network.* Attention is given to the Twenty-Sixth NSSE Yearbook in 4:4 (1975) and scientific curriculum making in 5:1 (1975). Both are enriched by reprints of major papers by George S. Counts, Harold O. Rugg, and Boyd H. Bode.

have been soon forgotten in the absence of success of arms. For a revolution is a rebellion that did not fail. Different observers than these present authors may be expected to glean different concepts from the Declaration. Independence, individuality, and inclusion, nevertheless, surely would be among those seen. Other noble concepts identified may, with little distortion, be at home in their company. These three—independence, individuality, and inclusion—stamp the perspectives shared here and aid the understanding of two centuries of confidence in American independence.

American life and American education are utopian. Characteristic of both is Browning's admonition that "a man's reach should exceed his grasp, or what's a Heaven for?" And with the poet, Americans have realized the desirability, the positive good of the discrepancy between real and ideal. For the discrepancy provides "wiggle-room," space to move out or up or in. The Puritan's errand on the land as well as the 1776 revolutionists in Philadelphia, Camden, Boston, and Williamsburg recognized the discrepancy. All in their different ways implored the desirability of the ideal, although they humanly recognized this as possibly unattainable in its fullness in their lifetime, to depart from the real toward a goal.

And so has life in America proceeded. Building turnpikes and canals. Abolishment of slavery. Restrictions of child labor. Rural electrification. Extension of the franchise. In our time, Martin Luther King captured the reality of this utopianism in his speech at the Lincoln Memorial by declaring, "I have a dream. . . ." American life has known utopianism untempered by pragmatism. Both Harmony Farm and the 1960's Free Schools expressed the wish to be in immediate Paradise, however phrased, without going through the rough and tumble and the ordinary and common realities of living. The utopianism of the Declaration was not so misled nor, like it, was most of American life.

Utopian and also rational is the Declaration. Independence to John Hancock and his fellow colonials was not freedom to do or to be anything or nothing. They desired, so the Declaration asserts boldly, the rights of Englishmen, rights they held to be unalienable but illegally withheld. Thus, independence from George III's Britain realized was restoration of Magna Charta and other English rights and liberties to once-English colonists in America, now Americans. The Declaration proclaimed independence and admitted to dependence in the same sentences. Dependence on rights. Dependence on guarantees from God through the strong heritage of common law. Independence without dependence simply was not rational to those two hundred year ago Americans.

Those early American leaders never meant to be held to the literalness of their rhetoric. The Declaration was both an insult to the crown and an appeal for common support and for unity. Language, under such circumstances, cannot be literal; it would be too feeble. In these times, the act of Declaration must be understood for what it was, both literal and symbolic. And we must distinguish the rhetoric of both. Doing this, we lend ourselves a mighty assist in understanding other aspects of language in American life, including language of curriculum.

Like those early Americans, others employ rhetoric for their purposes. The characteristic language of the New Englander is the rhetoric of understatement. The language of Black Americans sometimes constructs a rhetoric of overstatement. So also does the clever rustic, the unsophisticated, uncomplicated American of all regions; his is the language of hyperbole. Probably not many of these people on such occasions mean for themselves to be held accountable for their rhetoric.

The consideration of language is essential to understanding history. The demand is particularly insistent as we examine works of both activists and historians. Some recent historians, therefore, err in their requirement that another's rhetoric, outside the situation and audience for which the language was used, must perforce be accountable on their own criteria.[8] Language is congruent with observed reality only when the intentions are literal. At other times, language communicates symbolic meanings. Mistaking symbolic language for literal meanings is misunderstanding an ideal as a norm. This problem, at once logical as well as linguistic, plagues correct understanding in all forms of discourse in life, personal, political, religious, and educational, to enumerate only a few.

The *Cardinal Principles of Secondary Education*[9] is a case in curriculum. In no manner of understanding may these statements be known as descriptions of reality. They clearly are statements of hope about what should be, desires in search of substantiation. And they were also agreements not of the many but, rather, of an appointed few whose

[8] The comment here is not intended to discredit, even mildly, the excellent works of several revisionist historians of education. Their work has contributed much and promises to offer additional fresh insights from a variety of data sources. See: Colin Greer. *The Great School Legend: A Revisionist Interpretation of American Public Education*. New York: Viking Press, 1972; Michael B. Katz. *The Irony of Early School Reform: Educational Innovation in Mid-Nineteenth Century Massachusetts*. Boston: Beacon Press, 1968; Joel H. Spring. *Education and the Rise of the Corporate State*. Boston: Beacon Press, 1972.

[9] Commission on the Reorganization of Secondary Education. *Cardinal Principles of Secondary Education*. Department of the Interior, Bureau of Education Bulletin, 1918, No. 35. Washington, D.C.: Government Printing Office, 1918.

constituency was metaphoric in large measure. Credibility was attempted and achieved not only by the sponsorship of the Commission, but also by the frequency of remark and by the authority of the one who referred to the statements. That the Principles were useful in some measure to justify or to legitimize changes in school programs is to attest to the power of hope and symbolic language. And, also, to the logic of persuasion which employs phrases like "consistent with the Cardinal Principles." Even so, the Principles seem to have had most impact in settings some distance removed from local schools. Little evidence has been uncovered which indicates that many working teachers and local administrators knew or used the Principles. Such recognitions do not vitiate the Principles. These understandings, on the other hand, urge a caution against claiming too much for the Principles, or too little. They may provide, additionally, insights about the construction and use of language on other occasions, certainly a matter of no small curriculum consequence.

Role of Language in Curriculum Development

Language increasingly is recognized as vital to understanding and producing knowledge about curriculum.[10] Distinction between symbolic and literal meanings is clear and real. So, too, are understandings about the language of description and analysis and the special language of science.

The language of analysis and reportage seems difficult to hear and read. We are inclined to evaluate. Thus, hearing a report we assign evaluative weight to descriptions because our values are congruent with or are in opposition to what is received. So very difficult is the reception of a message without declaring for or against both it and the sender. Likewise difficult is to understand the variety of possibilities yielded by analysis and not to assign grades of merit to the assembled array. For example, "control" and "profession," used throughout several of the perspectives in this volume, are employed as descriptive terms in most cases. But these, and like-used terms and phrases, carry attendant pejorative meanings. They further carry opportunities for expansion of

[10] See: Dwayne Huebner. "Curricular Language and Classroom Meaning." In: James B. Macdonald and Robert R. Leeper, editors. *Language and Meaning*. Washington, D.C.: Association for Supervision and Curriculum Development, 1966; James B. Macdonald. "Myths About Instruction." *Educational Leadership* 22 (8): 571-76; May 1965; Edward F. Kelly. "Curriculum Evaluation and Literary Criticism: The Explication of an Analogy." In: Gerald A. Ponder and O. L. Davis, Jr., editors. *Curriculum Perspectives*. Austin, Texas: Texan House, Inc., 1976. pp. 79-119.

ideas and restrictions on excess, among other things. Some terms, like "subject matter," "process," "involvement," and "textbook" also evoke strong evaluative meanings due to tenaciously held commitments. The positions of belief convert otherwise analytic and descriptive terms to matters of ridicule or praise. To be sure, this use of our language seems intimately related to identifying villains and to extolling saints. The possibilities for distortion and logical translation are real. Recognizing this, caution is a responsible restraint.

While science in education has been recognized as very profound,[11] curriculum appears to have incorporated science and experimentalism only piecemeal. The language of science, especially, seems to have been adopted partially, still a stranger in a strange land. The point to be made here is not that the language of science should have displaced all other language in curriculum discourse. Rather, the point is that the language of science, not clearly understood, competes unwittingly for territory and, further, is used synonymously with other language in profound error.

Note samples of scientism in curriculum talk. "Research shows" (or, less accurately, "research proves") is employed in sentences of justification and attempts at persuasion. As important, in this regard, is the anti-science remark, "No matter what the research says, my experience is . . ."

And the word, "experiment." What a reference to hard-nosed, firmly grounded legitimacy, and power. The curriculum field is littered with abandoned "experiments," artifacts of someone's attempt "to try" something. Surely, the language of science has been corrupted when a "try," unfettered by the prescriptions inherent to science, is known as an "experiment." And "experiments" seem always to work, to come out "right," especially if those involved, self-styled "experimenters,"

---

[11] The literature of science in education is extensive, but the literature on science in education is weak. Examples of contributions of scientific inquiry include all the publications of the American Educational Research Association. That the scientific method has usurped other research methodologies in curriculum inquiry is a charge leveled by: O. L. Davis, Jr. "Publication of Research on Curriculum by the American Educational Research Association." *Curriculum Theory Network.* 11: 98-105. A major historical inquiry into one dimension of science in education is: Raymond E. Callahan. *Education and the Cult of Efficiency.* Chicago: University of Chicago Press, 1962. A significant biography of an early and greatly influential scientist in education, including curriculum, is: Geraldine Jonçich. *The Sane Positivist: A Biography of Edward L. Thorndike.* Middletown, Connecticut: Wesleyan University Press, 1968. Necessary to any understanding of science in education is the larger context of science and American culture. See: D. D. Van Tassel and M. G. Hall, editors. *Science and Society in the United States.* Homewood, Illinois: Dorsey Press, 1966.

want them to. And they usually want them to. The scene is motivated by belief, undiluted commitment, not by hypothesis; the result is little of science but, more, resembles alchemy. Even so, "experiment" and other of its dimensions—for example, "procedures," "variables," "tests," "analyses"—populate curriculum language, and, too often, vulgarize it. The conditions of science (e.g., validity, confidence) require universal conditions absolutely or, at least, rigorously defined (e.g., temperature, resistance) and conditions not available in schools. Thus, the language of science in schooling is another and special, as well as quite powerful approximation. Curriculum use of the language of science, and this language is often appropriate, requires care and understanding, not careless and uncritical addition to vocabulary.[12]

The language of science, as well, seems to promise too much. Conclusions never tell us what to do, even in our great hunger for direction. And description by itself is distorted when translated into prescription. Nevertheless, we yield easily to this temptation. That young children can learn some things earlier than once thought, uncharitably referred to as the St. Jerome dogma, the "can" has been translated quite illogically to "should." Consequences of unfulfilled expectations are loss of confidence, reliance on intuition, and slogan. Or, seizure of an idea advanced by charisma. Or, to do what we know is comfortable—tradition, it is called—and to persevere if not succeed in our typically commonplace way. Language, like clothes, does influence us and our perceptions.

The three great concepts derived from the Declaration—independence, individuality, inclusion—are not just labels and are not so treated in these perspectives. Each becomes more richly known when coupled with a companion concept. Together, the two concepts describe a powerful tension in American life. Independence and dependence. Individuality and conformity. Inclusion and exclusion. These three tensions provide an organizing element of the perspectives of this volume.

Recognition of tensions notes the reality of extremes and opposites. Also, this awareness acknowledges that extremes are not only present, they are helpful, even necessary. One without the other is excess, a misconception of reality, and, likely, an invitation to vigorous and maybe violent response. A common example of the excess of independence is license—unrestrained, capricious acts yielding chaos. Dependence to an

---

[12] See: Herbert M. Kliebard. "The Rise of Scientific Curriculum Making and Its Aftermath." *Curriculum Theory Network* 5: 27-38; 1975; O. L. Davis, Jr. "Myths About Research in Social Studies Education." Unpublished paper prepared for the convention of the National Council for the Social Studies, November 1975.

excess, on the other hand, is slavery whether physical or intellectual. Neither concept alone is adequate. Each is more or less attractive at times when the other appears to embody lesser or greater parity.

Conceptualization of tensions also acknowledges, at least in our land, general means of response. Excessive, unrelenting pressure at any extreme of a tension has in our history snapped the tension and produced violent reaction. The Declaration of Independence and armed revolution were such a result. So were civil war, labor strife, and several strategies of protest over civil rights and the Viet Nam war. Over the long distance, however, American response to tensions has been accommodation of both extremes to some livable position. In political terms, the response is called compromise. Tension implies, moreover, that accommodation is not likely to persist as a steady state and that continuing resolution of pressures and inconsistencies are necessary to both maintenance and growth.

Our way of living continues to recognize in tensions the existence of ambiguities, inconsistencies, nonrelevant characteristics, and aberrant notions. Their existence and, more, tolerance of their existence are marks of the success of this system. For, in this system, accommodation triumphs, not absolutism; resolution and acceptance are known, not solution.

Contrary to popular subscription and general pedagogic assent, our country really does not desire solutions, at least not literal solutions, no matter the attractiveness of the appeal. Also, our people generally realize that even if "solutions," rather than accommodations, were desired, they would occur mainly in rhetoric rather than in reality. The "Jewish problem" was not solved by Hitler's Germany; neither has the "Nazi problem" been solved by Jews or by Israel. America's China problem was not solved by an armored wall around the southern mainland of China nor support of the Koumintang remnants on Taiwan. Accommodation, over time, even accompanied by belligerence, has provided witness to the visit of American presidents to the People's Republic of China and various exchanges between West Germany and Israel.

So, too, in American curriculum matters. Reading is not the vassal of any one championing belief; other commitments are too strong for a singular capture. And reading is enriched by the several claimants, their approaches and materials. The New Mathematics stressed conceptual development, and, in de-emphasizing the computation of the old mathematics, has been attacked vigorously for "going too far." The risk of complete loss of the virtues of New Mathematics seems minimized when accommodation is a goal of curriculum process. And such accommodation is a goal in mathematics education. Both concepts and computation in mathematics appear to be winners, rather than either being lost in the resolution.

Thus, tensions are resolved by a kind of creeping moderation. Partisan rhetoric asserts "either/or," primarily as symbol, and usually expects neither alone but a portion of both. The nature of tensions reveals a considerable latitude of moderate acceptance, centrist without being a center. "Love It or Leave It," "Better Dead Than Red," "Back to the Basics," "Subject Matter, Yes; Value Clarification, No"—these and kindred slogans give the appearance of extreme positions and the points of tension move. Adjustment in society and schools, in the absence of severe upheaval, must be assessed by what really takes place in the living of lives, not only by what is said about that living. Failure to heed this proposition in knowing our history, as a people and in our schools, adds unnecessary credence to the aphorism, "The more things change, the more they remain the same."

This Bicentennial accords special recognition to a period of 200 years of national life. This reckoning of time, interestingly, begins with the Declaration, a presumptuous and preposterous essay, for the United States was then no nation but only a coalition of friendship sponsoring a rag-tag amalgam of armies. But this act of defiance, after five long years of anguish amidst few victories, was finally crowned by Cornwallis' surrender at Yorktown and the Treaty of Paris; the Declaration was sealed as the beginning of national independence.

Truly, two centuries is a lengthy tenure for survival of a political institution that has contended with wars, internal strife, subversion, and stupidity. Hardy indeed must be the ties that bind it together and give it sustenance: the sentiments shared by its citizens.

Two hundred years of nationhood, on the other hand, is not a long time for a people to know itself. The Mayas and Aztecs in the Americas were civilizations with much longer histories. And so on other continents with everyday awareness of the continuity of civilization, if not a particular government, over thousands of years of recorded and artifact history. The sense of history in the United States lacks the perspective of the fullness of time. No everyday reminders of the building of a city on foundations in a vast lake as in Mexico City. No effigies of local knights like those in Salisbury Cathedral. No shard remnants of a family vessel like those from an Israeli tell. The American substitute for perspective has been instant action and the expectation of instant success.

Two Centuries Provide a Start Toward Perspective

Reviews of institutions and ideas across these 200 years can provide a start toward perspective. Two centuries is not such a long time to have developed elevated beliefs about prominence. In this regard, we can recognize the early republican necessity to sculpt General Washington garbed in a toga as a symbolic link to wisdom, leadership, and legitimacy. But now, we require no portrait of Eisenhower as caesar but only as a man. Two centuries help to provide perspective.[13]

In the same way, two centuries is not such a long time to be unable to overcome past efforts, whether they are called successes or failures. Educational reforms in American life are tied intimately to reform of society itself. Efforts appear at the same time to have succeeded and failed. Witness the Great Society programs begun just a few years ago. But efforts will continue, if the future follows the lead of our past, efforts however haltingly undertaken and persisted in. Certainly, we need not grovel about failures to change fundamentally the human condition in only eight generations! We can continue to work. Similarly, we must be only humbly happy about contributions over such a time.

With such awareness of time in our national life, curriculum history surely should not expect a bountiful harvest of instant changes. Efforts of a term or year, even several years, may yield only scant evidence of development or movement from where one was to another, more advanced, or perhaps only different site. Slowness to change in education has been a common complaint, certainly in the past half century. But that slowness need not be seen as unqualified evil. It could be known for what it is, the careful substitution of belief and practice about what is good for children and youth for something else of matchable or increased credibility and applicability. Widening our historical perspectives on curriculum provides us with specifics and generalizations for narrative and interpretation about curriculum life over time.

This present set of perspectives on curriculum, this yearbook, claims some things and denies others. The way it is known by its committee is set within the context of this Prologue's propositions and is further made explicit by a group of *is* and *is not* statements. These

---

[13] The perspective truly assists understanding of the school books used by the nation's children. Curiosity aside, the early appearance of textbooks by Webster and Morse and others was motivated in large measure by desire to make education "American" and to strip it of particularly "English" influences. See: Ruth M. Elson. *Guardians of Tradition: American Schoolbooks of the Nineteenth Century.* Lincoln: University of Nebraska Press, 1964.

understandings served to guide the authors' preparation of their papers and should aid readers' understanding.

The yearbook is not a history by historians. It is a set of informed commentary on curriculum throughout American history by curriculumists. These individuals, primarily professionally involved in the curriculum field, are also trained in, and several have reasonable credentials in, historical scholarship.

The yearbook does not assert a consensus. Although the work of a committee, it is not a committee report like those of Rugg[14] or Bruner.[15] The points of view expressed by this yearbook's authors are similar, but far from identical. Too, some scholarly positions seemed more appropriate than others to the authors and these are clearly and properly personal. A consensus would appear particularly artificial in such a yearbook as this, a kind of "one best system"[16] that works only partially for both schools and books. On the other hand, the yearbook committee and authors assert the nobleness of the Declaration's dream through two centuries. They have tried not to glorify even when special meritoriousness, even "glory," is recognized. Neither have they, in the acknowledgment of baseness, caprice, and fraud, permitted such unfortunate motivations and consequences uncritically to control interpretations and to discredit very real accomplishment.

The volume is not a definitive history of American curriculum. It is neither text nor handbook. Indeed, as its title suggests, it is a set of historical perspectives on curriculum. It is a contribution, we hope, toward a comprehensive history of curriculum. Clearly, it has omissions—of information, ideas, events, institutions, and questions. Many of these are important and known to the committee. For example, little attention is given to specific curricular fields like English,[17] mathematics,[18] voca-

14 National Society for the Study of Education. *The Foundations and Technique of Curriculum Construction.* Twenty-Sixth Yearbook of the National Society for the Study of Education, Parts 1 and 2. Bloomington, Illinois: Public School Publishing Co., 1926. Harold O. Rugg was the chairman of the Society's committee that produced the yearbook.

15 Jerome S. Bruner. *The Process of Education.* Cambridge, Massachusetts: Harvard University Press, 1961.

16 David B. Tyack. *The One Best System.* Cambridge, Massachusetts: Harvard University Press, 1974.

17 See: Arthur N. Applebee. *Tradition and Reform in the Teaching of English: A History.* Urbana, Illinois: National Council of Teachers of English, 1974.

18 Phillip S. Jones, editor. *A History of Mathematics Education in the United States and Canada.* Washington, D.C.: National Council of Teachers of Mathematics, 1970.

tional education,[19] and sports.[20] Or to instructional technology,[21] and counseling.[22] The present task seemed impossibly large with such a desirable and tempting possibility. As well, the recognition is easy that some fields simply have little of the required spadework completed. Selectivity, of course, is the twin matter of deciding what to bring in as well as what to leave outside. And hard decisions were made. Other omissions are missed by the gaps and chasms of ignorance shared by the committee members. Choices have the intent to highlight rather than cover or ramble. And the volume is incomplete, certainly an unfinished agenda, as is all history.

Further, these perspectives on curriculum history attempt to differentiate the schools' curriculum and the curriculum field from other enterprises of schooling. School organization and reorganization, school finance, teacher education, and counseling are thus among important aspects of schooling hopefully not directly attended to. So, too, excluded deliberately were the media, family, peer culture, and religious institutions for they seem not to have direct relationship to curriculum. We recognize reasonable dissent from this position, which is really a definitional rule. The committee has suggested categories and hypotheses. They seemed to have worked, at least for this venture. We hope they are helpful. The categories and interpretations undoubtedly reflect late twentieth-century convictions, ideas, even dogmas and myths. They may not work for others and disagreement is not unexpected. Such dissent here and elsewhere in the volume should precipitate inquiry, add to the available fund of knowledge and insights, and further serious development of the field.

In addition to the general yearbook narrative, two special features are included. One is a carefully chosen set of photographs from the extensive collection of the Library of Congress. Most but not all of these exceptional photographs are from two special collections, the Frances Johnson photographs and the wide-ranging Farm Security Administration collection. The photographs selected for this volume were not

[19] See: Roy W. Roberts. *Vocational and Practical Arts Education: History, Development and Principles.* Second edition. New York: Harper and Row, 1965. For an impressive account of the conflict over the establishment of a vocational high school in St. Louis, see: Selwyn K. Troen. *The Public and the Schools: Shaping the St. Louis System, 1838-1920.* Columbia: University of Missouri Press, 1975.

[20] A refreshing and stimulating essay is: Joel H. Spring. "Mass Culture and School Sports." *History of Education Quarterly* 14: 483-99; Winter 1974.

[21] Paul Saettler. *A History of Instructional Technology.* New York: McGraw-Hill Book Co., 1968.

[22] W. Richard Stephens. *Social Reform and the Origins of Vocational Guidance, 1890-1925.* Washington, D.C.: National Vocational Guidance Association, 1970.

chosen to illustrate any part of the narratives. Quite the opposite, they were chosen because each communicated ideas about curriculum differently and with considerable dramatic power. The second feature is a set of short vignettes about some people, events, and institutions of curriculum. Some subjects of these essays are well known; others are obscure. The intent of the committee here was to illustrate the variety and range of contributions and contributors to curriculum and, while spotlighting a few, to signal the absolute need for additional illumination for many, many others.

The yearbook is a deliberate contribution to the celebration of our nation's Bicentennial. It directs attention to the compelling necessity, not curious luxury, of our understanding curriculum in American schools more and more fully. Hopefully, it provides some new ideas and fresh visions. A particular hope is that it strengthens a community of professional people and commitment through recognition of its shared past and present.

1

Education for All: The Triumph of Professionalism

Walter Doyle

Friends, educators of America, does the duty of the hour call us here in council over the conflict which rages between light and darkness? In answer to its pressing questions, does some one weighed down with the conviction of the unquestionable evils of ignorance already experienced point to the fact that five years, or a school generation, have so far been lost in the regions swept over by the late war, and the friends of education by so much put to disadvantage? Does another point to the variety of races already composing the American people, and declare that a harmony and homogeniety (sic) sufficient for national action is impossible according to all the lights of history? Does another declare that the struggle with the effete elements of European civilization has been all that we can stand, and with pallor and trembling whisper that 'tis vain to hope for success in the face-to-face encounter with the ossified civilization of the Orient . . . Does another find reason for further and irretrievable disaster in the conflict between free and papal religions, between Christianity and Paganism, the common school going down amid the hostilities of dogmas and the indifference of its friends? . . . Does not the spirit of the hour, admitting all these facts and possibilities of stern encounter, thrill us with the declaration that, whatever has been lost in the past, there is time enough yet for victory?

—General John Eaton, Jr., address to the
National Teachers' Associations, 1870

THE GROWTH OF AMERICAN EDUCATION has, in large measure, been a process of incorporating greater numbers of students within an expanded and unified system of formal schooling. Schooling emerged from being

Left: Abandoned rural school, Ramsey County, North Dakota, 1940.

17

an activity restricted to an elite few to become a major event in the lives of all Americans. In addition to this "democratizing" of learning, the schools moved from the periphery to the center of American conscious- ness. Indeed the very concept of schooling has grown to be commonly identified with the totality of education itself. From rather modest beginnings, the schools eventually became linked with social mobility, vocational success, and equality of opportunity. With rising urgency, the schools were typically assumed to be key instruments for eradicating social ills and securing national prestige and defense. In a very real sense the traditional American faith in the efficacy of schooling is reflected in the maxim: "Human history becomes more and more a race between education and catastrophe."[1]

At the same time, the modern school enterprise, with its formalized procedures and complicated technologies, has grown cumbersome and unresponsive. With rising enrollments have come an increased isolation and resistance to change. Although more people are involved in school- ing than ever before, fewer experience the ability to influence directly the decisions affecting their lives and the lives of their children. Although access to schooling has equalized considerably in recent years, the dis- parity in educational achievement among students has remained large. As a result a substantial portion of students remains excluded from social and occupational opportunities which require school success as a condition of entry. Sensitivity to these apparent "failures" of schools has produced disillusionment and a major alteration of confidence in the promise of schooling.[2]

The problem at this juncture in American history is to interpret both the aspirations for and the disaffection with schooling. In the pres- ent context it is especially important to discover the meaning of these events for the history of the curriculum and the development of the curriculum field. In the past, educational historians saw the expansion of schools and the linkage of schooling with social and vocational bene- fit as evidence that the public school was necessary to ensure democracy and equality for all. Recent historians have substantially revised this "legend." In their view, the growth of schooling is equivalent to the rise of an educational bureaucracy which accentuates differentiation and specialization, standardization and efficiency, mindlessness and immobil- ity. This schooling bureaucracy also embodies middle-class biases and

[1] H. G. Wells. *The Outline of History*. 3rd edition. New York: Macmillan, 1921. p. 1100.

[2] See: Joseph Adelson. "Battered Pillars of the American System: Education." *Fortune* 91: 140-45; April 1975.

protects elite self-interests at the expense of providing effective educational experiences for all youth, especially the children of the poor.[3]

Regardless of one's point of view, the bureaucratic model, as a framework for interpreting American educational history, has contributed much to understanding the nature and mechanisms of the public schools. The present analysis, however, is based on the premise that the bureaucratic approach is insufficient for comprehending and analyzing the distinctive quality of the transformation which affected American schooling since 1776. As Hays notes, bureaucratization was a general process permeating the fabric of American institutions during the building of an organizational society in the late nineteenth and early twentieth centuries.[4] The schools, especially in urban centers, were to share in this organizational metamorphosis; they did bureaucratize. In addition, however, schools professionalized. And it is this professionalization process which establishes a framework for explaining the dual tendencies within schooling of including more and more diversity in population and curriculum while excluding public access to the centers of decision making and influence.

In the context of the present Yearbook, the professionalism model is especially relevant to analyzing and interpreting the history of curriculum and events in the curriculum field. Self-conscious manipulation of curriculum content and form accompanied the growth of the curriculum field as a functional speciality within schooling. Curriculum experts, emerging in the early decades of the twentieth century, assumed a technical focus and specialized in methods for selecting and arranging content.[5] Differentiation and specialization were consistent with the

---

[3] See: Michael B. Katz. *Class, Bureaucracy, and Schools: The Illusion of Educational Change in America.* New York: Praeger, 1971; Colin Greer. *The Great School Legend: A Revisionist Interpretation of American Public Education.* New York: Viking Press, 1972; and Joel H. Spring. *Education and the Rise of the Corporate State.* Boston: Beacon Press, 1972. For an insightful review of the revisionist approach, see: Marvin Lazerson. "Revisionism and American Educational History." *Harvard Educational Review* 43: 269-83; May 1973. The bureaucratic model is central in: David B. Tyack. *The One Best System: A History of American Urban Education.* Cambridge, Massachusetts: Harvard University Press, 1974. See also: Vernon F. Haubrich, editor. *Freedom, Bureaucracy, and Schooling.* 1971 Yearbook. Washington, D. C.: Association for Supervision and Curriculum Development, 1971.

[4] Samuel P. Hays. "The New Organizational Society." In: Jerry Israel, editor. *Building the Organizational Society: Essays on Associational Activities in Modern America.* New York: The Free Press, 1972. pp. 1-15. See also: Robert H. Wiebe. *The Search for Order, 1877-1920.* New York: Hill and Wang, 1967. pp. 133-63.

[5] See: Mary Louise Seguel. *The Curriculum Field: Its Formative Years.* New York: Teachers College Press, 1966 for a summary and analysis of the works of several key early curriculum professionals. The history of curriculum is reviewed

Artist's impression of a schoolroom in 1776.

bureaucratic movement of the times. Being as close as it was to the core technology of schooling, however, the curriculum field played a key role in the professionalization process by which schooling became the dominant educational agency—a matter to be considered in greater detail shortly. Indeed professionalism was the functional ethic around which developments in educational program and the curriculum field took place. The particular character of the curriculum field and the direction and fate of various curriculum reform movements are therefore most interpretable within a professionalism framework.

Before detailing the argument and its implications, a brief overview will serve to orient the reader and integrate the discussion. The analysis begins with a consideration of the process of professionalizing, its relationship to bureaucratization, and, especially, the applicability of the model to schooling. This primarily analytical section is followed by a discussion of a more historical nature focusing on the growth of professionalism in schooling. The purpose of this second section is to describe the general stages in the professionalization of schooling and to illustrate

in: J. Minor Gwynn and John B. Chase, Jr. *Curriculum Principles and Social Trends.* 4th edition. New York: Macmillan, 1969. pp. 1-32, 141-92; and Daniel Tanner and Laurel Tanner. *Curriculum Development: Theory into Practice.* New York: Macmillan, 1975. pp. 147-395. Much useful information is contained in: Raymond E. Callahan. *Education and the Cult of Efficiency.* Chicago: University of Chicago Press, 1962.

the often striking parallels with the development of other professions. The section also concentrates on the broad impact of professionalism and the particular implications of this occupational transformation for assigning meaning to events in the curriculum field. The final section contains a brief assessment of professionalism in the face of contemporary contingencies and expectations, many of which run counter to traditional perceptions of the glory of schooling.

The overall character of the paper is intended to be broadly occupational. That is, the analysis focuses on the relation of the enterprise of schooling to the larger occupational and social context—in modern terms, the interface between schooling and society. Details of internal mechanisms and disputes are considered only insofar as they illuminate more general questions of occupational image and status. In addition, the discussion is highly selective, concentrating on delineating an interpretive framework rather than telling a complete story. Finally, the interpretation offered is intended to be considerably more tentative and hypothetical than the exposition will at times suggest. Efforts to secure a point should not be mistaken for proof or even conviction. The task here, rather, is to define and apply an interpretive model which may have sufficient power to merit further attention.

The Professionalization of Schooling

To the extent to which the objectives outlined herein are adopted as the controlling aims of education, to that extent will it be recognized that an extended education for every boy and girl is essential to the welfare, and even to the existence, of democratic society.

—Cardinal Principles of Secondary Education, 1918

The term "profession," unfortunately, is applied within the field of education to widely different phenomena, more often than not to aggrandize and persuade rather than describe and analyze. The significance of the present investigation, however, rests on a clear and specialized conception of the nature of a profession. Given the obscurity of meaning associated with such a ubiquitous term, it is necessary at the outset to consider the matter of definition.

The Concept of Profession

As traditionally used, the term "profession" is invoked to describe an occupation whose members are reputed to possess high levels of skill, commitment, and trustworthiness.[6] Freidson contends, however, that emphasis on the personal attributes of the members of a profession overlooks the distinctive character of a professionalized occupation and hence lacks analytical utility. Professionals may or may not be morally and intellectually superior, but a profession, as distinct from other occupations, does enjoy a "preeminence" in the division of labor. A profession, in other words, is a special kind of occupation "which has assumed a dominant position in a division of labor, so that it gains control over the determination of the substance of its own work."[7] Ultimately the profession secures the power to transform, in keeping with its own occupational perspective, the social reality bounded by the professional domain. The social meanings attached to health and sickness, for instance, are defined and validated in large measure by the medical profession itself.[8]

As evidence of its dominance in a division of labor, a profession gains a legal monopoly within its sphere. Freidson describes the case of medicine as follows:

> Medicine's position today is akin to that of state religions yesterday—it has an officially approved monopoly of the right to define health and illness and to treat illness.[9]

Although a professional monopoly is never complete (chiropractors and osteopaths still manage to practice), a profession is largely free of substantial competition within its own area and no other *occupational* group is in a position to establish, independently, policy with respect to the profession's work.[10] Here again, the case of medicine is illustrative.

The achievement and maintenance of this extraordinary position of professional dominance and monopoly involve a long and often complicated sociopolitical process designed to secure acceptance of an occupation's claims to technical and moral superiority. All occupations make

[6] See, for example: Myron Lieberman. *Education as a Profession*. Englewood Cliffs, N.J.: Prentice-Hall, 1956; Morris L. Cogan. "Toward a Definition of Profession." *Harvard Educational Review* 23: 33-50; Winter 1953; and William J. Goode. "Encroachment, Charlatanism, and the Emerging Professions: Psychology, Sociology and Medicine." *American Sociological Review* 25: 902-14; December 1960.

[7] Eliot Freidson. *Profession of Medicine: A Study in the Sociology of Applied Knowledge*. New York: Harper & Row, Publishers, Inc., 1970. p. xvii. The entire discussion of professionalization in this paper is indebted to Freidson's seminal analysis (see pp. 71-84 and 185-201 especially). Although Freidson concentrates on medicine as an illustrative case, his analysis is intended to and does achieve wider applicability.

[8] *Ibid.*, pp. 205-331 especially.

[9] *Ibid.*, p. 5.

[10] The point here is not that professions are totally free of outside influence.

such claims; a profession is simply an occupation whose claims are in fact believed by the general public—or at least by influential segments of that public—and, importantly, by the public government. The key to professional status is not the existence of such claims or even the empirical validity of the assertions, but rather the acceptance by important social segments and agencies of the legitimacy of the occupation's claims. The professional ethic, which asserts exemplary skill and virtue, serves, therefore, not to define a profession but to aid in the processes of "establishing, maintaining, defending, and expanding the legal or otherwise political advantage of the occupation." [11]

The professionalization of an occupation also depends upon the presence of two additional beliefs. First, the work of the occupation must be seen as having significant, far-reaching, and proximal social consequences. Second, dominant social groups must perceive the general public as being either incapable or unwilling to conduct or evaluate adequately the available options within the particular social sphere. Convinced of the dignity and the moral and technical superiority of an occupation and perceiving a lack of competence by the public, "the state may exclude all others and give the chosen occupation a legal monopoly that may help bridge the gap between it and laymen, if only by restricting the layman's choice." [12]

A profession, then, is an occupation which has assumed a central decision-making posture with respect to a significant social function. This particular definition, by focusing on occupational structure rather than personal qualities, emphasizes the features of *dominance* and *monopoly* associated with the professionalization of an occupation. It is in this sense that the professional model will be used as an analytical and interpretive framework for the present inquiry into the curriculum field.

Government is both used by and influences professions, although this influence is frequently consistent with the interests of the profession and is largely exercised in indirect ways. See: *Ibid.*, pp. 23-46 especially; William J. Goode. "Community within a Community: The Professions." *American Sociological Review* 22: 194-200; April 1957; and Corinne Lathrop Gilb. *Hidden Hierarchies: The Professions and Government.* New York: Harper and Row, 1966. The lay public also exercises influence, both through government and by personal boycott, although, again, this influence is indirect and tends to be individualistic and unorganized. The key consideration in the present context is that a profession is free from major competition (a potentially powerful source of influence) and from direct control by other *occupations* in the division of labor.

[11] Freidson, *Profession of Medicine*, p. 200.

[12] *Ibid.*, p. 74. The process of professionalizing is obviously not instantaneous. The stages in the growth of professionalism will be treated in greater detail later in the present discussion.

The focus on professionalization departs from the practice by contemporary educational historians of stressing the bureaucratization of schools. This is not to say that historians have neglected entirely the question of professionalism. The tendency, however, is to equate professionalism with expertise rather than occupational dominance and to view professionalization as a minor theme subordinate to the process of bureaucratizing.[13] Given the present departure from convention, it is necessary to outline briefly a rationale for emphasizing professionalization in the growth of American schooling.

The question here is not one of any fundamental incompatibility between professionalization and bureaucratization. Both processes operated simultaneously in schools during the nineteenth and twentieth centuries. Bureaucratization, however, refers primarily to the internal organization of work adopted by a given occupation. This framework contributes little to an understanding of the status of an occupation or the degree of monopoly it might enjoy. The professionalization approach, therefore, brings into focus process dimensions which are simply neglected by the bureaucratic framework. Furthermore, bureaucratization, as a process common to nearly all American institutions, simply fails to describe the distinctive character of the development of American schooling. As noted earlier, the present inquiry is based on the premise—to be elaborated and justified shortly—that the schools did in fact professionalize, that the professional model is applicable to schooling. The growth of the common school is not just a matter of internal organization but also the transformation of an occupation's status in a domain of considerable social importance. *The question, therefore, is not one of how schools became organized, but how schooling came to dominate education.*

Applying the Professional Model to Schooling

Application of the professional model to the enterprise of schooling has been impeded by at least two interrelated factors: (a) the view that bureaucracy and professionalism are incompatible; and (b) exclusive focus on the teacher in discussions of the profession of schooling. Since school systems are obviously organized bureaucratically and teachers are obviously subject to bureaucratic control, it would seem to follow that education is not yet a profession or is at best a semiprofession.[14]

---

[13] For a bureaucratic emphasis, see especially: Katz, *Class, Bureaucracy, and Schools*. Tyack, in particular, deals with the phenomenon of professionalism as well as bureaucracy. See his *One Best System*.

[14] See: Lieberman, *Education as a Profession*; Oswald Hall. "The Social Structure of the Teaching Profession." In: Frank W. Lutz and Joseph J. Azzarelli, editors. *Struggle for Power in Education*. New York: Center for Applied Research in Educa-

The implication is that bureaucratization somehow places an absolute limit on the possibility of professionalizing. More recent scholarship suggests, however, that the distance and conflict between these two processes are not as great as had been assumed. In order to consolidate power and to unify members in the face of considerable geographical and ideological diversity, the professions, in keeping with the general organizing movement in society beginning about 1890, adopted the bureaucratic model of internal organization. As Freidson notes, "a formal table of organization for the medical division of labor could be drawn which is quite comparable to those conventionally drawn for corporate enterprises or other obvious 'organizations.' " [15]

The point here is, however, that professions, although bureaucratized internally, are not subject to *externally imposed bureaucratic regulation* within the domain of the substance of their work.[16] This is simply another way of saying that a profession has achieved dominance in a division of labor and enjoys a monopoly within its sphere. If one equates the enterprise of schooling with the occupation of teaching, then it is clear that teachers are subject to bureaucratic regulation and hence are not professionalized, i.e., do not dominate the division of labor. Teaching and schooling are not, however, synonymous enterprises. Indeed, teachers are perhaps the least powerful functionaries within the school structure. Focusing on a professional subgroup (e.g., physicians) in isolation from the structure of the occupational enterprise (e.g., medicine) is potentially misleading. Physicians may have considerable pres-

---

tion, 1966. pp. 35-48; Amitai Etzioni, editor. *The Semi-Professions and Their Organization.* New York: The Free Press, 1969; and Robert Dreeben. *The Nature of Teaching.* Glenview, Illinois: Scott, Foresman, 1970.

[15] Freidson, *Profession of Medicine,* p. 200. On the process of bureaucratizing in the professions, see: Gerald E. Markowitz and David Karl Rosner. "Doctors in Crisis: A Study of the Use of Medical Education Reform To Establish Modern Professional Elitism in Medicine." *American Quarterly* 25: 83-107; March 1973; and Daniel H. Calhoun. *Professional Lives in America.* Cambridge, Massachusetts: Harvard University Press, 1965. See also: Hays, "The New Organizational Society."

In another context, Freidson argues that professional authority is a form of institutionalized expertise and hence clear distinctions between bureaucratic authority and professional authority are difficult to make. See: Eliot Freidson. "The Impurity of Professional Authority." In: *Institutions and the Person: Papers Presented to Everett C. Hughes.* Chicago: Aldine, 1968. pp. 25-34. The institutionalized dimension of professional authority is developed further in: Walter Doyle. "A Professional Model for the Authority of the Teacher in the Educational Enterprise." Unpublished doctoral dissertation. Notre Dame, Indiana: University of Notre Dame, 1967.

[16] On this point, see: Freidson, *Profession of Medicine,* pp. 23-46. See also: Goode, "Community within a Community"; and Howard M. Vollmer and Donald L. Mills, editors. *Professionalization.* Englewood Cliffs, New Jersey: Prentice-Hall, 1966. pp. 265-97.

tige in the general society, but they also dominate the division of labor in medicine. Teachers are simply not in a position to dominate schooling, regardless of the degree of public recognition.

Given the peculiar structure of American public schooling, superintendents clearly dominate the division of labor and are the occupational subgroup which is virtually free from external, direct, non-government regulation. This attempt to draw a parallel between superintendents and other professional groups will be treated more completely throughout the remainder of the analysis. At this juncture it is necessary to emphasize that superintendents are in fact the dominant professional group within the enterprise of schooling such that other school-related occupations, including teaching, are subordinate to it. In achieving this dominance, superintendents certainly used bureaucratic measures. In this regard, however, the professionalization of superintendents did not differ substantially from that of other professions.

Not only did superintendents come to dominate schooling, but schooling grew to dominate education. Herein lies the heart of the process which resulted in the professionalization of schooling.[17] In the terms of the present discussion, schooling achieved a virtual monopoly in the domain of education. The fact that the terms "schooling" and "education" have become so closely identified in both educational and popular literature is certainly testimony that a schooling monopoly does exist. More importantly, schooling has largely displaced other competing educative agencies—family, church, community [18]—in the sense that education in these alternate settings fails to "count" for most social and vocational purposes. In a manner remarkably similar to medicine's relation to illness, schooling has transformed the substance of its work so as to define in its own terms the very meaning of "educated."

The schooling dominance and monopoly become especially prominent when elementary and secondary schools are contrasted with the

[17] Implicit in this discussion are a number of distinctions among the concepts of occupational subgroup (e.g., physicians), occupational enterprise or collective (e.g., medicine), and the domain of occupational work (e.g., health). Physicians dominate an occupational enterprise and are, strictly speaking, the professionals. The professionalization of physicians does, however, professionalize the entire enterprise in the sense that the enterprise comes to dominate the work domain and achieves a virtual monopoly. Because of the broadly institutional intent of the present analysis, the discussion will focus on the professionalization of schooling rather than merely the superintendent group.

[18] On the substitution of schooling for family functions in the history of American education, see: Bernard Bailyn. *Education in the Forming of American Society.* Chapel Hill: University of North Carolina Press, 1960. The question of the displacement (vs. substitution) of the family in education will be treated in more detail later in the present study.

situation prevailing in higher education. The American higher education "system," such as it is, can hardly be seen as being monopolized by any single institution. Rather, it is more a collection of distinct colleges and universities which share a similar internal bureaucratic structure, but which are indeed diverse in affiliation and governance. Some individual universities may well enjoy considerable prestige and set a pattern in the field, but they hardly exercise direct dominance over other institutions. At the elementary and secondary level, in contrast, the public schools enjoy a competitive advantage which virtually excludes other institutions. Alternative schools and school systems do, of course, operate [19] but they enroll a minuscule portion of the total population. Moreover, the relationship between public schools and alternative schools is akin to that between physicians and chiropractors rather than freely competing independent practitioners in an open market. Like chiropractors, alternative schools operate under a set of state regulations which often reflect the interests and preferences of the dominant system. By including more and more educational functions under its direct control, the public school system has effectively eliminated serious competition.

Although more details remain to be considered, it seems clear that schooling has achieved a degree of dominance and monopoly which suggests that professionalization, and not just bureaucratization, has occurred. It would seem legitimate, therefore, to use the professional model as a framework for interpreting both the nature of the relationship of schoolmen to the society and the significance of events and practices in the curriculum field.

The Growth of Professionalism

The Government of a republic must educate all its people, and it must educate them so far that they are able to educate themselves in a continued process of culture, extending through life.... A free, self-conscious, self-controlled manhood, is to be produced only through universal public education at public cost, and as this is the object of our Government, it is proper for our Government to provide this means and at the cost of the people.

—William T. Harris, address to the
National Educational Association, 1871

There are, indeed, three critical factors in the educative process: the

---

[19] For an excellent discussion, with historical perspectives, of alternative school movements, see: Daniel L. Duke. *The Re-Transformation of the Schools.* Chicago: Nelson-Hall, 1975.

child, contemporary American society, and, standing between them, the school curriculum.

> —*Harold Rugg, Twenty-Sixth Yearbook,*
> *National Society for the Study of Education, 1926*

Having established the analytical potential of the professionalism model, it is now necessary to explore the stages in the process whereby the professionalization of schooling occurred. After some preliminary comments on the basic ingredients of this process, the discussion turns to the growth of professionalism in education. This developmental analysis contributes to a greater understanding of the applicability of the professional model to schools, the nature of the schooling monopoly, and the impact of professionalization on curriculum.[20]

Symbol manipulation in education. As indicated in the previous attempt to define professionalism, the achievement of professional status involves manipulating symbols in order to achieve acceptance of occupational claims. Of the many symbols available, language plays a key role. In the case of education, rhetoric concerning the dignity and social significance of schooling as well as the virtue and competence of schoolmen has followed a consistent pattern from the early 1800's to the present. At various stages in its history, schooling has been promoted as an instrument for eliminating sin and corruption, securing urban tranquility, assimilating and Americanizing diverse peoples, conferring occupational and social mobility, extending equality of opportunity, eradicating racial strife, and defending national prestige and honor. Through this "rhetoric of intentions," schoolmen did in fact construct what Greer has called the "great school legend." [21] The widespread acceptance, until recently, of this legend attests to the degree of professionalization which has occurred in schooling.

---

[20] The growth of professionalism was not necessarily as self-conscious, rational, or deliberate as a retrospective analysis might imply. Especially in the case of schooling, the professionalizing process appears to have been less self-conscious than is typically perceived in medicine and law. There is, hence, a need to avoid, as Lazerson suggests, "a clarity of decision-making, a finality and rationality that oversimplifies the ambiguities, incompleteness, and irrationality of historical events." See: Lazerson, "Revisionism and American Educational History," p. 282.

[21] Greer, *The Great School Legend*, pp. 1-7 especially. Early histories of American education played a major role in building the school legend. It is commonplace to cite the use of these histories in normal schools and teachers colleges as a reason for the inspirational and pedagogical character they assumed. These early histories were certainly not (nor were they necessarily intended to be) descriptive or analytical. But they were not simply pedagogical. Whether intentionally or not, these histories served the same function as general schooling rhetoric, viz,

That the schools did not always accomplish their mission is not surprising; given the exalted nature of the goals, it could hardly be otherwise. Promulgation of such goals did, however, serve professionalism purposes. By associating grand designs with the work of schools, these hyperbolic claims fostered belief in the dignity and social significance of schooling. Furthermore, the criteria professionals used to judge "success" did not always correspond to the achievement of the goals defined by schooling rhetoric. More often than not the magnitude of the effort became a convenient substitute for evidence concerning actual goal accomplishment. This particular selection of criteria supported an expansive mentality with respect to schooling and, hence, stimulated extraordinary growth of the enterprise itself.

The school curriculum eventually became a key element in symbol manipulation to achieve and maintain professionalism. The curriculum concretized school rhetoric and the symbols of professional "success." The magnitude of curriculum endeavors was, in other words, a critical component in legitimizing the schools' claim to superior competence in meeting the challenge of educating American youth. This theme of "curriculum as symbol" is of special importance in the following analysis of professional development in education.

Professionalizing schooling: historical perspectives. The purpose of the following sections is to describe key events in the evolution of the profession of schooling. The discussion is a broadly historical and highly selective approach to the topic. The intent is to illustrate stages of professional growth rather than depict an entire chronology.[22] For interpre-

---

helping to ennoble schooling and justify and legitimize the dominance of schooling in the field of education. From the professionalism perspective, the historiographical question is not merely one of poor scholarship, but also one of the symbolic role of history in the sociopolitical mechanisms of professionalizing.

[22] The field of American educational history has experienced a veritable renaissance in recent years and, as a result, several excellent sources are available for the reader interested in greater detail than is possible in the present context. In addition to the sources cited in Footnote 3, see: Michael B. Katz. *The Irony of Early School Reform: Educational Innovation in Mid-Nineteenth Century Massachusetts.* Boston: Beacon Press, 1968; Carl F. Kaestle. *The Evolution of an Urban School System: New York City, 1750-1850.* Cambridge, Massachusetts: Harvard University Press, 1973; and Marvin Lazerson. *Origins of the Urban School: Public Education in Massachusetts, 1870-1915.* Cambridge, Massachusetts: Harvard University Press, 1971. See also: Robert H. Wiebe. "The Social Functions of Public Education." *American Quarterly* 21: 147-64; Summer 1969. Some useful material on American faith in schooling is presented in: Henry J. Perkinson. *The Imperfect Panacea.* New York: Random House, 1968. The present analysis draws upon these works for both interpretive and illustrative material. In the interest of clarity and continuity, it has not been possible to document explicitly each direct contribution to the present investigation. The author acknowledges, however, indebtedness to these sources.

tive purposes the sections also draw upon parallels between schooling and other professional groups. As will be seen, there are a number of remarkable parallels between the evolution of professionalism in schooling and in other occupations. At the same time, schooling acquired distinctive features which necessarily flow from the particular character of the enterprise. Finally, in order to demonstrate the power of the model to clarify curriculum issues, selected events from the curriculum fields are integrated into the discussion.

Foundations of Professionalism

During the seventeenth and eighteenth centuries, schooling was neither a unified nor a central ingredient in American life, and schools, from a professionalism standpoint, "did not have a monopoly on the skills they taught." [23] Schools existed but a given "school" was often equivalent to a single, and often transient, teacher. The prevailing pattern of schooling was essentially informal, localized, fragmentary, and unstable. Schooling, in other words, consisted of a discontinuous collection of independent school units, each of which tended to have a denominational and a provincial character. Schooling was therefore "bought on the open market" and schools shared the domain of education with family, church, community, and the experience of living. Of key importance was the fact that schooling as an enterprise was, at the time, simply not viewed as a matter of general public policy. As Kaestle notes: "Common schooling prompted little group support and no community-wide decisions." [24]

The factionalized and localized character of schooling by the end of the eighteenth century was not substantially different from the condition of most modern-day professions at that time. Both Freidson and Gilb note that, prior to industrialization and urbanization, professions operated as collections of disconnected, individualistic practitioners all oriented to a common domain. There was little governmental or associational regulation and certainly no occupational dominance. The times simply did not support or require the degree of occupational self-consciousness and specialization necessary for professionalism. [25]

Emerging ideology. Although in practice, schooling during the

[23] Kaestle, *Evolution of an Urban School System*, p. 1.

[24] *Ibid.*, p. 27. On the denominational and provincial character of American colonial education, see: Lawrence A. Cremin. *American Education: The Colonial Experience, 1607-1783.* New York: Harper and Row, 1970. pp. 359-479 especially.

[25] Freidson, *Profession of Medicine*, pp. 5-22; Gilb, *Hidden Hierarchies*, pp. 9-34 especially.

colonial and revolutionary ages continued according to a fragmented and incidental pattern, some progress was made in the development of the ideology of schooling.[26] Some of this ideology was directly school related, as in the works of men like Franklin and Jefferson, but the core principles appear to have emerged from the general social and experiential conditions of the time. Regardless of the source, this ideology helped in unifying schooling during the nineteenth century.

One major theme which influenced the development of schooling in often surprising ways was that of the uniqueness of the American experience. This uniqueness operated in at least two ways. First, the special character of the daily experience of Americans was a source of new knowledge as well as new methodologies for acquiring knowledge. This experience gave rise to new disciplines, such as a natural history, which eventually opened cleavages between classical and modern schooling. In addition, common access to this experience and the knowledge flowing from it served to democratize learning in the newer disciplines. Second, awareness of the uniqueness of experience provided special motivation to retain this distinctive quality of life in building American institutions. Initially the uniqueness of the American experience impeded the rise of schooling because of the discontinuity between traditional school-related learning and the daily task of living. In the nineteenth century, however, nostalgia for the distinctive quality of America became a latent theme in the common-school crusade.

Part of the uniqueness of the American experience was an abundance of opportunity to acquire land and pursue diverse occupations. This abundance demanded versatility which further created discontinuity between formal schooling and educational requirements. Eventually, however, abundance contributed to a break with elitist class systems based upon circumstances of birth. This resulted in a general popularization and diffusion of culture and knowledge, conditions which encouraged interest in common education. Cremin, in particular, has emphasized the theme of popularization in culture and schooling in the colonial period.[27]

In addition to these general themes of uniqueness, abundance, and popularization, there emerged, during the revolutionary and early na-

---

[26] For relevant documents, see: Rena L. Vassar, editor. *Social History of American Education: Colonial Times to 1860.* Chicago: Rand McNally, 1965. Vol. I, pp. 3-150; and David B. Tyack, editor. *Turning Points in American Educational History.* Waltham, Massachusetts: Blaisdell, 1967. pp. 83-118. For material on themes in colonial America, see: Daniel J. Boorstin. *The Americans: The Colonial Experience.* New York: Random House, 1958; and Merle Curti. *The Growth of American Thought.* 3rd edition. New York: Harper and Row, 1964.

[27] Cremin, *American Education,* pp. 561-63 especially.

tional periods, specific proposals for the expansion of schooling. Of particular significance to the evolving ideology of schooling were the proposals of Franklin and Jefferson. Franklin, in his own life, epitomized much of the versatility and discontinuity with classical tradition which the circumstances of the day required. More important for the present context, he envisioned an interconnection between schooling and occupational and social mobility, in what Tyack suggests was an attempt "to smooth the steepness of ascent and create through schooling a more comfortable path into occupational and social roles which were becoming discontinuous between the generations."[28] Obviously this view of schooling as a path to occupational and social status emerged again in the evolution of schooling in education.

Jefferson's legacy in the ideology of American schooling was substantial.[29] In the first place, Jefferson linked schools with the survival of democracy and hence established the social function of schooling. Second, he introduced into conceptions of schooling the notion of meritocracy, of the "natural" aristocracy of the talented. Schooling therefore became linked to sorting and validating functions in society. With Jefferson schooling acquired a kind of actuarial notion to the effect that, while some will experience deprivation, the overall enterprise will survive. In other words, although not all will achieve everything that schooling can offer, the nation itself will benefit. This actuarial notion of the social, rather than personal, uses of schooling became the central focus of educational criticism with the rise of sensitivity to equality of educational output in the mid-twentieth century.

Regardless of the eventual impact of these proposals, schooling in the pre-urbanization era did not flourish as a unified, dominant part of education. The family continued to play a major role in occupational and social access. Moreover, the concept of schooling as an instrument for sorting or certifying workers (even in the fields of medicine and law[30]) was simply not relevant to a society characterized by localism, autonomy, and a demand for versatility. In addition, the economic impediments to a large-scale schooling enterprise in the colonial period were substantial.[31]

[28] Tyack, *Turning Points*, p. 58.

[29] For a collection of Jefferson's writings, see: Gordon C. Lee, editor. *Crusade Against Ignorance: Thomas Jefferson on Education.* Classics in Education, No. 6. New York: Bureau of Publications, Teachers College, Columbia University, 1961. For a summary and analysis of Jefferson's contributions, see: Robert D. Heslep. *Thomas Jefferson and Education.* New York: Random House, 1969.

[30] Gilb, *Hidden Hierarchies*, pp. 9-14.

[31] See: Bailyn, *Education in the Forming of American Society*, on economic factors as related to colonial schooling.

Curriculum issues. Given the generally informal and discontinuous nature of schooling in the period, curriculum theory or practice was hardly an issue of major significance. With the notable exception of Franklin's proposals, there was little conscious attempt to manipulate the curriculum. There was some break with tradition, due to the discontinuity of the American experience, but the curriculum remained dedicated to the classical goals of "piety, civility, and learning."[32]

One aspect of the colonial experience which would seem to have had considerable significance for curriculum thought related to the development of language in America. Boorstin notes that American linguists were obsessed with the need to standardize language, as indicated in Webster's campaign for standard spelling of English words. This standardization, which influenced language teaching in schools, appeared to result eventually in a democratization of language. Regardless of social-class origins, it was possible for a person to learn the "proper" grammatical form for speaking and writing. Language, therefore, lost its value as a sign of class distinction. This same connection between standardization and accessibility diffused through other avenues of American life, e.g., clothing.[33] The interrelations of standardization, diversity, and access to educational opportunity and benefit formed the substance of curriculum deliberation at the end of the nineteenth century.

The Dignity of Schooling

One condition for the achievement of professional status is a belief that the functions performed by an occupation have fundamental social consequences affecting the very fabric of community life. During the nineteenth century this belief in the basic importance and dignity of schooling (as an agency of education) was established. In response to the particular circumstances and fears of the time, influential government and private groups as well as schoolmen themselves moved toward the view that schools could be more than they had been, that schooling could become an instrument for solving social problems of utmost significance. Schooling, therefore, became an issue of community-wide deliberation and a matter of public policy.

Belief in the dignity of schooling encouraged occupational self-consciousness which paralleled a growing sense of national self-identity as well as developments in other professions. Occupational self-consciousness, in turn, stimulated efforts to upgrade the quality of professional practice. The creation of normal schools, a professional

32 Cremin, *American Education*, pp. 27-106.
33 Boorstin, *The Americans*, pp. 284-301.

literature, and occupational associations was indicative of this effort to improve services. In addition, professional leaders, identified with the enterprise of schooling and active in public and governmental affairs, appeared. These leaders played key roles in the professionalization of schooling at the turn of the century.

Belief in the dignity of schooling and occupational self-consciousness had a far-reaching impact on the growth of professionalism. One of the most important consequences was the institutionalization of schooling itself. Kaestle contends: "The central, transforming, institutional development in the history of American education was the creation of a common, uniform school system in the nineteenth century."[34] This was the era of the "graded" school and numerous books, chapters, and articles were written on plans and procedures for achieving this organizational ideal. Although the focus was primarily on elementary education and enrollments never approached their potential, the creation of an inclusive, K through 12 system of schooling was accomplished in principle if not in fact. This movement culminated in the 1890's with the linking of common schooling to college education.

It is important to note that the profession of schooling does not, during the nineteenth century, achieve dominance in an occupational domain. Belief in the dignity of schooling stimulated efforts to establish schools by various private, philanthropic, and denominational groups, often in direct opposition to each other. Moreover, schooling remained largely a matter of local or regional concern, with little sense of national cohesion. The development of occupational identity and efforts to include within the auspices of a single institutional framework a continuous stream of common, free, public schooling from early childhood to college did, however, pay important dividends. In addition to providing positions for leadership, the emerging organizational character of schooling helped convince influential segments of society that schoolmen possessed the necessary competence and resources to handle the affairs of education.

The nineteenth century, therefore, represented a major stage in the growth of professionalism in schooling. After 1890 the pace quickened, but the direction was already charted.

The uses of schooling. During the middle decades of the 1800's, substantial changes were wrought in the ideological foundations of schooling. These changes were part of a general reaction among champions of Protestant middle-class culture to the social upheaval of the day. The following is a brief overview of this situation.

[34] Kaestle, *Evolution of an Urban School System*, p. vii.

For most of the nineteenth century the social climate was one of relative stability and consensus. It was, in Wiebe's terms, a "distended society" resting on the primacy of local autonomy and initiative.[35] In part because of the decentralized, localized, and agrarian nature of America, denominational and regional conflict—or, for that matter, co-operation—was at a minimum. National identity was largely symbolic and linked to a sense of belonging associated with community life and religious affiliation. In such a setting, schooling remained a minor theme in social discourse. This relative tranquility was shattered by the beginnings of industrialization, urbanization, and immigration—three inter-related developments which altered permanently the fabric of American life. By threatening orthodoxy and local autonomy, these forces elicited deep-seated and agonizing reactions from dominant groups and activated mechanisms to forge a new social consensus. Under these new circumstances, the school moved into the center of public consciousness primarily as an instrument to restore local autonomy and values.

The disruption associated with industrialization, urbanization, and immigration occurred on several fronts. The size, composition, and primary location of the population shifted dramatically. From small, decentralized rural enclaves, the pattern of American life was transformed into large, heterogeneous, concentrated cities. Urbanization inspired images of poverty, crime, disorganization, moral decay, and disintegration, and immigrants threatened the ethnic and religious solidarity of middle-class Protestantism associated frequently with national identity. Although initial efforts to combat these pernicious influences often concentrated on expanding existing private and philanthropic agencies, the magnitude and complexity of the problems called for more decisive action. A localized society, however, lacked mechanisms to achieve effective large-scale action and tended to adopt a "single solution" logic for the analysis of these emotional issues. Reformers, using a fiery rhetoric attuned to a growing sense of fear, constructed, often without conscious intent, organizations to mediate change and preserve the social structure.[36]

In this move toward an organizational ethic, the idea of the common school, of free, universal, public schooling, soon provided a focus for the reformer's zeal. Wiebe has captured some of the flavor of the common-school crusade:

[35] Wiebe, *Search for Order*, pp. 1-43.

[36] *Ibid.*, pp. 44-75. This description also relies on: Timothy L. Smith. "Protestant Schooling and American Nationality, 1800-1850." *Journal of American History* 53: 679-95; March 1967. The notion that organization became the primary mediator

In the spirit of the 19th century evangel, the reformers crusading for common schools in the 1830's and 1840's preached a ritualistic sermon of sin, promise and salvation. The American experiment—perhaps all humanity—had entered a critical phase, they began, with dangers threatening on every side. The truths and traditions that only a generation ago had cemented society were disintegrating before the rush of the masses.[37]

This strident tone and spirit permeated the "great school legend" throughout the nineteenth and twentieth centuries and helped to inspire American faith in the instrumentality of schooling, regardless of the ill to be cured.

Given the urgency and anxiety associated with social disruption, the ideology of schooling was understandably an ideology of social control. To counter urbanization and the immigrant, the primary functions of schooling were to be assimilation and stabilization. Influenced by the industrial economy as well as the organizing ethic, schools also reflected a commitment to order, punctuality, obedience, and universal standards.[38]

If the idea of free, universal, public schooling was to generate a broad base of support, in terms of both finances and enrollment, it was necessary to change the restrictive images which had become associated with this particular mode of schooling. Free schooling had, to a large extent, meant pauper or charity institutions. Schooling had also followed denominational lines, with separate schools embodying particular sectarian views. The common school was to be free, but universal; common schooling was to be neutral schooling.

The supposed "neutrality" of schooling certainly had a special connotation, at least as viewed from modern perspectives. Neutrality hardly meant that schools were to be value free. The idea of schooling separated from religion and strong doses of middle-class morality was inconceivable to the nineteenth-century reformer. The words "crusade" and "revival" have an especially descriptive utility in connection with the evangelical spirit and intent of the common-school movement. In

---

between social change and social structure is the basic theme in Katz's analysis. See his *Class, Bureaucracy, and Schools*, and his *Irony of Early School Reform*. The term "bureaucracy" is avoided in the present discussion of organizational changes in the mid-nineteenth century to avoid confusion with the subsequent bureaucratic movement which occurred at the turn of the century. This practice differs from Katz's usage, but it would seem justified by the differences between these two organizational upheavals. See: Tyack, *One Best System*. On the initial use of private agencies and the eventual turn to public schooling, see: Kaestle, *Evolution of an Urban School System*, for a discussion of the situation in New York City.

[37] Wiebe, "The Social Functions of Public Education," p. 147.

[38] *Ibid.*, p. 149. See also: Tyack, *One Best System*, pp. 72-77 especially. Katz (*Irony of Early School Reform*, pp. 49-50) notes the ambivalence in the attitudes of schoolmen toward industrialization.

keeping with Mann's compromise which called attention to a common biblical heritage, neutrality was to be founded on an interdenominational Protestant consensus. Indeed the common-school crusade itself played an important role in forging this new consensus. That this interdenominational consensus excluded Catholics, Jews, and even some Protestant sects did not seem to be a particularly troublesome point.[39]

Inherent in the interdenominational consensus within which the common school prospered was a fundamental contradiction which, over the next one hundred years, brought a decline in its own dominant role in American education. The middle-class, Protestant ideology excluded precisely those religiously and ethnically different immigrants whose children were the special targets of school reform. Evangelical zeal and confidence in their own efficacy also encouraged schoolmen to extend schooling to include all children under school influence, even by compulsory means.[40] This exclusionist, elitist mentality did not survive the more expansionist drive during the 1900's to gain custody of the entire school-age population.

Out of the complex interplay of forces operating in the nineteenth century, the ideal, if not the fact, of free, universal, public schooling was vindicated. This vindication rested in part on a shift in the willingness of the dominant and concerned segments of the society to rely on informal mechanisms of education. Given the urgency of sentiment and the perceived divergence of basic values, confidence in these mechanisms declined sharply during this period. This was especially true with respect to trust in the ability and/or the desire of the family to foster approved educational outcomes. ⌐Faith in education, which probably existed from the beginning of colonial settlement, became, in the nineteenth century, faith in schooling. Accompanying this fundamental change was a permanent relocation of the position of education in society. Education became, perhaps for the first time, an issue of public policy and schooling a matter of governmental action. Katz summarizes the overall pattern of development: "Essentially, the reformers looked to a parental state to sponsor education that would help build modern

---

[39] See: Smith, "Protestant Schooling and American Nationality." Emphasis on the Protestant, ethnocentric, middle-class bias of early school reform movements is basic to most recent histories of American education. See, especially: Katz, *Irony of Early School Reform*, as well as Tyack, *One Best System*. For a special emphasis on the role of the middle class in the common-school movement, see: Charles E. Bidwell. "The Moral Significance of the Common School." *History of Education Quarterly* 6: 50-91; Fall 1966. Horace Mann is discussed in great detail in: Jonathan Messerli. *Horace Mann: A Biography*. New York: Knopf, 1972.

[40] On compulsory attendance in the nineteenth century, see: Tyack, *One Best System*, pp. 68-71.

industrial cities permeated by the values and features of an idealized rural life."[41]

Schooling achievements. From a professionalism standpoint, the nineteenth-century achievements in schooling were primarily ideological. The period was characterized by an early reaction to the beginnings of urbanization, industrialization, and immigration. The tone was cultural, moral, and religious, and the rhetoric was strident. But, aside from the drive to organize, the implementation of concrete actions to accomplish lofty goals in the face of formidable obstacles was considerably less fruitful. Katz, in particular, maintains that "At its core the ideology was soft; the threads . . . were woven of the flimsiest logic."[42] Confident in the truth and righteousness of their cause, common-school reformers simply did not ask the questions of technique or procedure which were to occupy educationists at the turn of the century. Aside from the inherent rural-urban contradictions in the ideology itself, the evangelical religious roots of the school crusade diverted attention from methodological issues. It was faith, not works, which achieved the miracle of salvation. And the schoolman's faith was strong enough to allay any doubts about efficacy. Moreover, the organizational form of schooling did begin to emerge and, in a manner quite similar to the approach in later periods, the existence of the form became a convenient proxy for the existence of intended results.

Given these basic attitudes, the common-school movement did not effect mass education or even an overall system of American schooling. Although the organizing ethic permeated individual units, the general picture of schooling remained fragmented and localized. Moreover, opposition to common schooling, both because of the traditional pauper image as well as the irrelevance of school experience to employment, continued throughout the period. Enrollments increased, but retention of pupils beyond a few years was exceedingly rare; the per capita amount of schooling was more appropriately calculated in days rather than years. The dominant pattern in schooling was essentially one of autonomous village schools.

Growing belief in the social significance, or dignity, of schooling was, however, a crucial stage in professionalization and resulted in some concrete developments which eventually promoted occupational dominance. As suggested earlier, several specific events occurred which had long-range consequences. For example, normal schools were founded,

[41] Katz, *Irony of Early School Reform*, pp. 49-50.
[42] *Ibid.*, p. 156.

"The Public School Question," *Harper's Weekly*, August 30, 1873.

a professional literature emerged, and, due to consolidation and system-atization, the positions of principal teacher and of superintendent were established, positions which were platforms for key leadership in the professionalization of schooling. Two developments would seem, how-ever, to have had special significance from the professionalism perspec-tive. The first involved the connection between education and the state. Mann and others in different locales were able to link schooling to public government and, importantly, to secure government support for free, universal, public schooling. This financial base provided the necessary resources to make possible the building of a common-school system. The supposed "neutrality" of the school played a part in this achievement, but it would appear to have rested primarily on acceptance among powerful social groups of the central, "life and death" importance of schooling. Although the spirit is difficult to capture today, it would seem that the nineteenth-century belief in the dignity and crucial social consequences of schooling was equivalent to the twentieth-century belief in the dignity of medicine.

The second major development of the period involved the connec-tion between schooling and extra-schooling opportunities. The common-school movement was focused almost exclusively on primary and elementary schooling. At the same time, however, the public high school began to emerge as a significant institution and, indeed, was a central mechanism for organizing and controlling the collection of discrete elementary schools which still represented different sections of the cities or regions of the countryside. This effort to extend schooling by including more and more levels culminated in the linkage of common schools to college entrance. The culmination was symbolized most clearly by the Report of the Committee of Ten issued in 1894. Membership on the Committee was dominated by college representatives who also had a deep interest and direct involvement in common-school developments.

The Report defined the high school curriculum in terms of a modernized set of college entrance requirements and presented arguments for the view that preparation for college was the best contribution which the school could make to preparation for life. The Committee maintained that "this close articulation between the secondary schools and the higher institutions would be advantageous alike for the schools, the colleges, and the country." The members, therefore, sought "to make all the main subjects taught in the secondary schools of equal rank for the purposes of admission to college or scientific school." Furthermore, the members strongly supported the view "that every subject which is taught at all in a secondary school should be taught in the same way and to the same extent to every pupil so long as he pursues it, no matter what the probable destination of the pupil may be, or at what point his education is to cease."[43] Given the middle-class and often elitist character of the common-school movement, it was fitting that the initial extra-institutional linkage of schooling was with the colleges and universities.

The linkage of schooling to college entrance deepened the conviction that schooling could become a preparatory experience not just for general social participation and citizenship but also for specific institutional expectations and requirements. The full implications of the placement and sorting functions of schooling were acted upon more completely in the 1900's. At this stage the connection between schooling and employment remained, for the most part, indirect in the sense that the schools' preoccupation with order, punctuality, obedience, and universally

---

[43] *Report of the Committee of Ten on Secondary School Studies, with the Reports of the Conferences Arranged by the Committee.* New York: American Book Company for the National Educational Association, 1894. Vol. 17, pp. 52-53. For an extended discussion of the Committee of Ten, including both the Report itself and associated activities and influences of the members, see: Edward A. Krug. *The Shaping of the American High School.* New York: Harper and Row, 1964. pp. 18-122.

applied standards was compatible with the urban discipline required by an industrialized economy.[44]

In terms of professionalism, the achievement of state support and the linkage with college entrance had a massive impact on occupational dominance. Opposition to common schooling, whether for religious, intellectual, or cultural reasons, encouraged the founding of an array of alternate and competing schools, the most obvious and enduring example of which were the Catholic schools. The allocation of state funds, however, placed the competitors at a definite disadvantage since few had the necessary resources to match those of the public school system. Moreover, options other than schooling became less functional as schooling was established as the path to academically-based careers. The full brunt of these developments was not felt before the 1900's, but, to an ever increasing extent, the public school engaged in the dual process of excluding optional modes of education while striving to include more and more units and functions under its own domain.

Parallels. Nineteenth-century parallels between the occupational development of schooling and that of other modern-day professions were notable. As in the case with schooling, there was an increased occupational self-consciousness among various professional groups. This self-consciousness was reflected primarily in the creation of professional associations to upgrade the quality of the services performed.[45] Such associations typically represented a very small portion of the total number engaged in the occupation. The National Teacher Association, precursor to the National Education Association, was founded in 1857 with 43 members, a pattern similar to that in other professions such as law and medicine. The early professional associations were also exclusionist in character—often consciously so—especially with respect to women and ethnic, religious, or racial minorities. These small, exclusive, and elitist groups engaged in self-conscious reform in the name of the total occupation, but the direction of influence was clearly from the top down. In this connection, the Committee of Ten paralleled many of the characteristics of early professional groups both in composition and in mode of influence.

Freidson, in particular, has noted the key role of the state and powerful segments of the society in establishing professional dominance. Professionalization is, at its roots, a political process.[46] The founding

[44] On the concept of urban discipline, see: Tyack, *One Best System*, pp. 28-77, 234-35; and Katz, *Class, Bureaucracy, and Schools*, pp. 28-33.

[45] This description of the development of professional associations is based on: Gilb, *Hidden Hierarchies*, pp. 27-34 especially.

[46] Freidson, *Profession of Medicine*, pp. 23-26, 70-72.

members of the early professional associations were usually persons with links to governmental positions and elite social groups. The leaders of the common-school movement as well as early superintendents and schooling spokesmen shared a similar pattern of stature and affiliation.

In spite of these early efforts at occupational identity and organization, the achievements of early professional groups were minimal. Each occupation continued to be fragmented and localized with several competing groups operating within the same domain. Exclusionist attitudes and practices militated against a broad professional impact. The methods of unifying and upgrading also depended in large part on idealism and inspiration in the absence of effective means of enforcing a common code of behavior. It is interesting to note that the crusading rhetoric of the common-school movement also characterized reformist movements among other groups of professionals.[47]

Curriculum in the nineteenth century. According to Cremin, use of the term "curriculum" had nineteenth-century origins.[48] And the era contained some important foundational developments for the curriculum field. It was a time of increasing self-consciousness about curriculum. Given the general lack of immediate concern among common-school reformers for technical details, however, the curriculum field lagged behind in the process of securing an identity. The crusaders faced the urgent task of organizing a common-school system to counter what they saw as urgent and serious social dangers; there was little time to be overly concerned with the specifics of what went on within these institutions. They accepted what was already there, in large part precisely because it reflected tradition and stability. It remained for others, who, at a later date, were more concerned with the influence of specific curricular elements, to begin major efforts to manipulate the curriculum.

The factors of industrialization, urbanization, and immigration did, however, have an impact on both the scope and uses of curriculum. School reformers established the premise that schools could be used to meet identifiable problems. In reaction to the problems associated with these particular disruptions of the social scene, the curriculum became an instrument for teaching restraint, for replacing lower passions with

---

[47] Markowitz and Rosner, in connection with medical reform in the 1890's, observe: "When one reads [the *Journal of the American Medical Association*] and the state medical journals of the day, it is clear that the reform of medical education was almost a passion or a crusade." See their "Doctors in Crisis," p. 92.

[48] Lawrence A. Cremin. "Curriculum-making in the United States." *Teachers College Record* 73: 207-20; December 1971.

Left: Map study, Washington, D.C., *ca.* 1900. F. B. Johnston, photographer.

Below: Chemistry class, Western High School, Washington, D.C., *ca.* 1900. F. B. Johnston, photographer.

higher virtues. The moral tone was clear. Moreover, as indicated earlier, the curriculum, with its emphasis on punctuality, obedience, and order, taught an urban discipline compatible with the demands of industrialization. The urban pedagogy was, however, a soft pedagogy based on an almost mystical faith in the efficacy of "atmosphere." To compensate for urban blight and industrial inhumanity, the school was to construct a model environment which embodied the truth, morality, and gentility of an idealized rural Protestant ethic.[49]

[49] See: Katz, *Irony of Early School Reform*, pp. 115-60; Wiebe, "The Social Functions of Public Education," pp. 149-51; and Barbara J. Finkelstein. "The Moral Dimensions of Pedagogy: Teacher Behavior in Popular Primary Schools in Nineteenth-Century America." *American Studies* 15: 79-89; Fall 1974.

In spite of the rise of graded schooling and the organizing spirit of the era, curriculum development procedures stayed at an informal, incidental level. Curriculum decision making was, in all probability, determined by teacher preference and textbook availability. This situation was no doubt a cause for conflict among school personnel and a source of considerable frustration for the newly-appointed school administrators. Some insight into nineteenth-century curriculum development is reflected in the following excerpts. Clifford quotes from a September 1865 entry in a teacher's diary:

> Perused Morris' Grammer in the morning. It still continues to please me. I am so taken with it that I feel I am doing wrong to teach any other and would if I had books make the substitution immediately.[50]

In contrast to these sentiments, William Payne in 1875 warned his fellow superintendents that it was their duty to enforce compliance to official texts and courses of study.

> Nonconformity in either case ... can not be tolerated without great danger to the system; and ceaseless vigilance should be exercised against the encroachments of this evil. Two things should be absolutely forbidden: the use of any textbook not in the prescribed list, and the study of any subject not included in the prescribed course. To allow either of these things to be done is to sanction the gradual disorganization of a graded-school.[51]

This gap between official directives and individualistic teacher preferences has persisted in institutionalized schooling throughout its history.

Summary. By the early decades of the 1900's, the curriculum moved into the center of discourse on schooling and the curriculum field was born. The actions of the various national committees before the turn of the century called attention to the curriculum as a component in the burgeoning school enterprise. With the Committee of Ten and linkage of schooling to college entrance, widespread interest was stimulated in questions of curriculum.[52] Having established belief in the dignity of schooling, professional schoolmen turned to the task of promulgating their special qualifications for managing the educational affairs

---

[50] James Appleton Blackshear, as quoted in: Geraldine Jonçich Clifford. "Saints, Sinners, and People: A Position Paper on the Historiography of American Education." *History of Education Quarterly* 15: 257-72; Fall 1975.

[51] William H. Payne. *Chapters on School Supervision.* Cincinnati: Wilson, Hinkle, 1875. p. 53.

[52] On the impact of the various national committees on curriculum, see: Tanner and Tanner, *Curriculum Development*, pp. 147-93.

of society. In this new task, curriculum eventually assumed a dominant place.

The Dominance of Schooling

The decades between the 1890's and the 1920's defined a period of fundamental bureaucratic and professionalistic reformation of schooling in America. During this period the internal operation of school systems became centralized, rationalized, and standardized as the result of vigorous bureaucratizing energies. At the same time, schooling achieved professional dominance in a division of labor and a monopoly in a newly enlarged domain of education. Although not without opposition, schoolmen built the "One Best System."[53] These developments had an especially powerful impact on the curriculum field which, in many ways, was a product of the professionalization of schooling. Curriculum became, as never before, an instrument to be manipulated in expanding the scope and clientele of the schools. In turn, the curriculum was subjected to complex and potent forces which accompany the inclusion and retention of a larger and more diverse pupil population.

Many of the specific features of school reform in this period were distinctly "Progressive." But these developments at the turn of the century did not necessarily represent a sharp break with the ideology and spirit of the common-school movement. Commenting on the links between Protestantism and Americanism during the common-school crusade, Smith notes:

At the end of the century the alarmed reaction of Josiah Strong to the problems of an industrial age and the fervor of "progressive" educators like Francis W. Parker and Nicholas Murray Butler denoted a desire to preserve the substance if not the explicit Protestant form of this older basis of nationality in the face of rapid change.[54]

The times called for more concentrated and decisive action, but faith in the mysterious power of schooling continued to inform the dignity of the enterprise.

The "progressive" period in American schooling was especially eventful and no attempt can be made here to deal adequately with even a part of the total array of activity and development. Given the sheer bulk of material, the following discussion must necessarily be highly selective in nature. After some general comments on the organizing

[53] The phrase is Tyack's; see his *One Best System: A History of American Urban Education*.

[54] Smith, "Protestant Schooling and American Nationality," pp. 680-81.

thrust of the times, the analysis concentrates on three themes, viz, alliances, efficacy, and custody, which appear to define the central dimensions of the twentieth-century professionalizing process as it relates to schooling and to the curriculum field. Fortunately there are a number of excellent works devoted to this period of progressive reform of American education which fill the many gaps left in the present narrative.[55]

Organizing schooling. Efforts to render organizational solutions to pressing social and educational problems did not emerge fresh in the 1890's. As already seen, the organizing response characterized much of the common-school crusade. In the nineteenth century, however, schoolmen sought organization to *establish* a universal system of free schooling which was presumed to accomplish its objectives. In the twentieth century, schoolmen organized to *increase* the efficacy and *extend* the reach of schooling. The incomplete organizational structure of the earlier period was systematized into a consolidated and efficient organ of mass education.

The intensification of bureaucratic efforts was, at its core, a response to the intensification of industrialization, immigration, and urbanization, factors which had already contributed to the initial drive to school society. Industry transformed the economic structure and completed the movement from an agrarian to an urban society. Immigration transformed the labor market and expanded dramatically the size and the diversity of the population. Urbanization transformed the island village communities and altered permanently the character of city life. For the dominant native elites, these transformations instilled images of sin, decay, and disintegration and incited fear and helplessness. Horrified by urban conditions and offended by immigrant religion and culture, these dominant segments took positive action to reassert traditional faith and ideals, to "Americanize" society once again. The magnitude and complexity of these new threats to stability and order demanded a more decisive and less symbolic program of social control. Since traditional agrarian values could no longer be assumed to prevail over such formidable opposition, the control mechanisms were to be considerably more tangible and efficient, embodying in concrete procedures the fire of common-school rhetoric.

The bureaucratizing of schools at the turn of the century was not an isolated phenomenon. Rather, it was part of a more general search

---

[55] See, especially: Tyack, *One Best System*, pp. 126-268; Lawrence A. Cremin. *The Transformation of the School: Progressivism in American Education 1876-1957.* New York: Knopf, 1961; and Marvin Lazerson, *Origins of the Urban School.*

for order through which a distended society based on autonomy of isolated local communities became an organized society characterized by bureaucratic administration and a new sense of occupational identity. Administrative "progressives" emphasized managerial rationality and consolidation of power, specialization and segmentation of the work force, conscious environmental manipulation to achieve specified social and personal ends, and an expansionist ideology to extend control and influence into all levels of society. The effects of these reforms were especially evident in the emergence of technical systems which reflected a commitment to science and empirical control, a coordination of differentiated and specialized workers, and an expanded scope of interest and operation. Technical systems were most immediately apparent in the growth of functional relationships among segments in society, relationships which transcended island communities by drawing on congruence of interests and specialization among peoples of widely separated geographical locations. Once set in motion, these new bureaucracies, although activated by specific historical events, gained a momentum of their own which sustained them beyond the contingencies of immediate social climate. They began, in other words, to create, rather than simply respond to, social reality.[56]

The emergence of technical systems and functional relationships, as well as the expansionist spirit, were certainly key ingredients in the drive to professionalize. Abandoning the loosely structured, elitist approach of the nineteenth century, professional associations adopted a more practical and aggressive professionalism oriented toward consolidating power and expanding membership and influence. The bureaucratic form of organizing was quite compatible with these new objectives and was therefore incorporated into the internal operation of most professional groups. The professions, however, emerged from the organizing movement as the legitimized monopolies. To secure this special status, professions appeared to take advantage of a variety of opportunities to enlarge their domains and extend their influence. Although it is difficult to identify with confidence cause and effect relationships, it is clear that professionals became both opportunists as well as instigators in their respective fields of action.[57]

In building the organized society, schooling emerged as an especially important institution. In the distended society of autonomous local units, few mechanisms of mass action existed or were even necessary. Hence power to meet the crises of industrialization, urbanization,

56 Wiebe, *The Search for Order*, pp. 11-195; Hays, "The New Organizational Society," pp. 1-15.

57 Gilb, *Hidden Hierarchies*, pp. 27-52.

and immigration was not readily or widely available.[58] The school was particularly visible as a mechanism to have the required mass impact. Schooling, then, flourished as a major instrument to counter impending dangers and recapture the lost experiences of living in an idealized rural community. Indeed it would appear that the core meanings of "family" and "community," terms which permeate educational discourse today, were forged out of the spirit of schooling rhetoric at the turn of the century.

The bureaucratic reformation of schooling manifested itself in a number of concrete developments. Of particular importance was the creation of a centralized, inclusive, standardized, hierarchical administrative structure. Payne, one of the early superintendents, exhorted his colleagues to adopt the graded pattern of organization as a fundamental law of society:

> It is an application to the work of instruction of the great law of the division of labor. By this means a teacher's time, talent, and attention are concentrated on a prescribed range of duties, which become easy by repetition, and hence are likely to be performed in a thorough manner . . . The work of teaching thus follows the law which prevails in all well-regulated industries. This general movement is characteristic of a growing civilization.[59]

This rationalized approach to schooling assumed special significance as a device to counter the ward pattern of school governance which tended to dominate urban centers. The ward pattern reflected the island community structure of early cities, relied on local autonomy and initiative, and tolerated idiosyncratic customs and practices. Such a pattern obviously impeded the centralization and dominance of a self-conscious professionalism. Schooling professionals, by emphasizing corruption and the evils of patronage, succeeded in replacing the ward pattern with a consolidated system under the unitary control of a single superintendent and a small, elite school board. In the manner of a chess master, the administrative progressives sought to simplify school governance and increase control by reducing sources of surprise. The public high school, at the top of the schooling pyramid, became an especially important vehicle for gaining control over reluctant ward boards by establishing standards for admission to secondary schooling for all elementary students in a region.

It is difficult to overestimate the significance of the bureaucratizing of schooling. The analysis of professionalizing influences in schooling seems, however, to account for several distinctive aspects of the rise of

---

[58] Wiebe, *The Search for Order*, pp. 11-43.

[59] Payne, *Chapters on School Supervision*, pp. 83-84.

schooling in American education. As indicated earlier, professionalism is especially useful in understanding the expansionist thrust of school-men and the combined operation of inclusion and exclusion tendencies in the school enterprise. In an effort to delimit the range of possible considerations relevant to the professionalization of schooling, the present analysis is integrated around three central themes: viz, (a) the alliances schoolmen formed with various interest groups in society; (b) the concern for efficacy which characterized much progressive reform; and (c) the drive for custody of all youth which permeated school policy and had important implications for curriculum.

The alliances of schoolmen. In keeping with the pattern of aggressive professionalism, schoolmen at the turn of the century formed a series of intricate relationships with various segments of American society. The dominant theme of these alliances, which could hardly have been avoided in the complex pattern of the age, was one of control for the professional group. The control element therefore determined to a large degree the nature and duration of these various affiliations.

At its roots, the professionalization process is political. It is not, however, a matter of marketplace politics. Rather it is a political process aimed specifically at elite and influential segments of society. Professionalizing, in other words, involves the use of dominant groups and government licensing to secure occupational dominance and monopoly.[60] The elitist nature of professionalizing was certainly reflected in the events and activities associated with nineteenth- and twentieth-century schoolmen. Tyack, in particular, has noted the existence of an "interlocking directorate" composed of college presidents, school superintendents, and university professors who played a central role in the bureaucratization of schooling.[61] This directorate also defined the level at which the professionalization of schooling occurred. Men such as Nicholas Murray Butler, W. T. Harris, William Maxwell, William Payne, Charles W. Eliot, and Francis Parker were key figures in the achievement of professional dominance. Indeed the Committee of Ten, far from being an example of college dominance over common schools, was in fact a celebration of the very "directors" who had a vital and direct interest in the affairs of schooling. Since the directorate consisted mostly of rural-born, native Americans, membership admittedly excluded women, Catholics, blacks, and a host of other "different" minorities.

[60] See: Freidson, *Profession of Medicine*, pp. 23-46, 71-84; Gilb, *Hidden Hierarchies*, pp. 3-81.

[61] For a discussion of the interlocking directorate, see: Tyack, *One Best System*, pp. 129-47.

There was little reason to believe that the new profession of schooling, although inclined to speak for the educational concerns of the total society, would necessarily represent or reflect the interests of those excluded from the main decision-making network.

The elitist nature of the politics of professionalism was reflected especially in the drive, in which most professions participated, to depoliticize those activities which professionals defined as uniquely their own. In the case of schooling this drive took the form, for example, of attempting to crush the power of ward boards representing localized regions of the cities, reducing the size and changing the composition of city-wide boards, and consolidating governance in the position of a single, system-wide superintendent. This campaign to "take the schools out of politics" was, at its progressive best, aimed at correcting the abuses of the patronage system which dominated decision-making in employment and other areas of school management. It is clear, however, that the drive to remove politics also served to concentrate political power in the hands of the professional directorate itself at a time when the control of city politics was becoming increasingly difficult for elite Americans. At its worst, then, the depoliticizing of schooling served special interests by diverting attention from the fundamentally political nature of school governance.[62]

The successful campaign to separate politics and professional interests reduced considerably the significance of direct lay influence in professional decisions. The movement did not, however, lead to total lay exclusion, but rather to a redefinition of the posture of laymen with respect to the professional group. This emerging alliance between professional and lay groups was especially apparent in the anti-tuberculosis campaign in the early 1900's. Lacking a specific cure and convinced of the value of both changing the health practices of the masses and treating individual patients to eliminate sources, physicians launched a mass movement of social reform. Anti-tuberculosis societies gained considerable lay support and participation, and the apparent successes of the movement in reaching millions and in reducing the threat of the disease set the pattern for Progressive-era health reform.[63] In addition

---

[62] Tyack, in particular, has discussed the ramifications of "taking the schools out of politics." See: *Ibid.*, pp. 78-176. On the parallel situation in medicine and in other professional groups, see: Freidson, *Profession of Medicine*, pp. 71-84; Markowitz and Rosner, "Doctors in Crisis," pp. 98-107; and Gilb, *Hidden Hierarchies*, pp. 135-40.

[63] See: John C. Burnham. "Medical Specialists and Movements Toward Social Control in the Progressive Era: Three Examples." In: Jerry Israel, editor. *Building the Organizational Society: Essays on Associational Activities in Modern America.* New York: The Free Press, 1972. pp. 19-30. An interesting, and largely neglected,

to helping medicine gain client acceptance, the movement cast the layman in the role of supportive agent in a "good" cause under the benevolent leadership of dedicated physicians. Such movements would seem to have contributed directly to popular acceptance of the distinctive competence and virtue of professions, an acceptance which fostered occupational dominance.

There are numerous examples of attempts, both successful and unsuccessful, by professional groups to affiliate with public government, with powerful social segments, with the prestige of university-based training, and even with the rationality and efficiency embodied in the corporate model. Nonetheless, professions tended to establish uneasy affiliations with outside interests and organizations. Although schoolmen, as other professionals, clearly adopted the corporate model and the language of business efficiency, the push was in the direction of a pragmatic alliance designed to advance the profession's own occupational status. Once the purposes of the relationship were achieved, the profession typically moved toward isolation from external influence, toward drawing more clearly the boundaries between professional interests and those outside the occupational domain. Indeed, the professionalization process itself can be viewed in part as a middle-class reaction against corporate and governmental power and influence.[64] The tendency toward isolationism in schooling was especially apparent in the composition of the Commission on Reorganization of Secondary Education which issued the famous *Cardinal Principles of Secondary Education* in 1918 and of the Committee of the Twenty-Sixth Yearbook of the National Society for the Study of Education, a publication devoted exclusively to curriculum building.[65] In both instances the groups were dominated by members with specific professional ties and interests. This entire process of establishing an independent identity altered in basic ways the structure of alliances which impinged upon the profession of schooling. Schaefer laments the fact that schooling, prior to 1925, became isolated from

---

connection between schooling and the antituberculosis campaign took place in the form of "open-air schools." Such schools were located either in separate buildings or on top floors of regular buildings and operated mainly by opening all doors and windows, regardless of weather conditions. Especially large windows and doors were often provided to maximize the "open" effect. A compilation of some 1,900 photographs and related material is available in the Photographic Collection of the Library of Congress.

[64] See: Gilb, *Hidden Hierarchies*, p. 111 especially. See also: Wiebe, *The Search for Order*, pp. 111-32.

[65] Both of these publications are discussed in greater detail in subsequent sections of this chapter.

academic and social influences,[66] but this development would seem to have been a sign of the degree of professional maturity which schooling reached during the early decades of the twentieth century. From this latter perspective, the achievement of a separate identity was remarkably rapid.

The efficacy of schooling. With the decline of an explicit Protestant rationale for common schools and the growth of anxiety over social disruption, the efficacy of schooling was no longer self-evident. The construction of an efficient bureaucratic organization was an obvious manifestation of this concern for efficacy. Progressive reformers also became preoccupied with the technical details of school program, with curriculum and teaching effectiveness. In the process they forged a new and, as might be expected, an uneasy alliance with the modern religion of democracy—science. This was not, however, a science devoted to speculation and theory-building. Rather it was empiricism harnessed to serve explicit social ends, to gain direct control over environmental variables.

Programmatic concerns gave direct impetus to the curriculum field. By the end of the era, attention shifted from the superintendent and purely managerial considerations to the professor of education and curriculum issues. In the place of Butler, Harris, Maxwell, and Eliot, men such as Dewey, Thorndike, and Bobbitt assumed positions of leadership in the profession. Whereas the former group enshrined corporate structures and practical business acumen, the new directorate concentrated on analyzing procedural alternatives with a confidence founded on scientific exactitude and problem-solving techniques.[67]

With rising scientific sensibilities, occupational dominance depended more and more on the ability to find a technical solution to pressing problems, on the discovery of a "cure." Markowitz and Rosner[68] point

---

[66] Robert J. Schaefer. "Retrospect and Prospect." In: Robert M. McClure, editor. *The Curriculum: Retrospect and Prospect.* The Seventieth Yearbook of the National Society for the Study of Education, Part I. Chicago: University of Chicago Press, 1971. pp. 14-19.

[67] For an analysis of the men who contributed to the formation of the curriculum profession, see: Seguel, *The Curriculum Field.* For a study which places greater emphasis on administrative and business dimensions of schooling, see: Callahan, *Education and the Cult of Efficiency.* For a general discussion of scientism in curriculum making, see: Tanner and Tanner, *Curriculum Development,* pp. 281-94.

[68] Markowitz and Rosner, "Doctors in Crises," p. 92. For a similar emphasis on the significance of an empirically based technology for professionalization, see: Freidson, *Profession of Medicine,* pp. 5-22.

to the impact of the discovery in 1895 of diphtheria antitoxin, an event which ensured the dominance of "germ-theory" physicians and increased faith in medicine's curative power. Possession of a "cure," i.e., a demonstrably effective technology, conferred considerable power on an occupational group, especially with regard to achieving a monopoly. Of special importance were the technical trappings which accompanied "cures." Such trappings made direct lay participation less feasible and militated against the effective operation of a political patronage system in the professional domain.

The search for a "cure" certainly occupied a central place in schooling and would appear to account in large measure for the preoccupation with scientism in the profession during the progressive era. The emergence of educational psychology, the search for criteria of effective teachers, the concern for testing and statistical descriptions of populations, and the use of scientific criteria for including or excluding curriculum content, are just a few examples of the commitment to finding empirical solutions to schooling problems. The scientific approach of men such as Bobbitt, Charters, and Barr to problems of curriculum, instruction, and supervision virtually epitomized the scientific spirit of the day.

The search by professions for scientific cures was obviously not always successful and this was especially true in the case of schooling. Nonetheless, affiliation with science in language and manner, with the symbols of science, provided an almost equivalent effect. On the basis of a general rise in confidence in scientific solutions and a few notable successes, reformers were able to convince others that science would eventually achieve victory. In the meantime, reformers, caught up in the mass character of Progressive social reform, focused attention on quantitative factors which appeared to have a close association with empirical success. More often than not reformers, including schoolmen, cited the number of persons served, the number of units founded, the number of laws passed, or the number of campaigns launched to document "success."[69] In other words, information concerning the amount of action taken served as a convenient proxy for data on the actual

---

[69] On occasion it was possible to take credit for effects which may have had little direct connection with a particular reform movement. An excellent example of both the focus on "growth" as a substitute for "effects" and the opportunism of professionals is provided by the anti-tuberculosis campaign discussed earlier. In this instance, reformers assumed responsibility for the decline of the disease when the general improvement of living conditions, resulting from improved economic circumstances, probably accounted for most of the results obtained. See: Burnham, "Medical Specialists and Social Control," pp. 29-30.

Playground in New York City, *ca.* 1890. Jacob Riis, photographer.

impact of schooling on pupils. And, from the viewpoint of the profession itself, these factors were indicative of growing dominance in the educational domain. This emphasis on what are now called "process" rather than "product" variables, a matter of special concern in recent analyses of the impact of schooling, has characterized much of the actual scientific practice in the profession.

In addition to the peculiar uses to which science was put by schoolmen, the alliance with science itself was marked by considerable ambivalence. In a comprehensive study of the impact of research on teaching practice, Clifford found little evidence of direct application of scientific research to school practice, but did find considerable distrust and skepticism among practicing schoolmen with regard to the usefulness of educational research.[70] Freidson suggests that this discontinuity is a natural result of fundamental differences between practitioners and scientists in daily experience, work environments, and types of problems encountered. On this basis he distinguishes sharply between "academic" professions and "consulting" professions.[71] Schoolmen, like most consulting professionals who attempt to apply knowledge to the practical affairs of man, desired the benefits conferred by an association with science; they

[70] Geraldine Jonçich Clifford. "A History of the Impact of Research on Teaching." In: Robert M. W. Travers, editor. *Second Handbook of Research on Teaching.* Chicago: Rand McNally, 1973. pp. 1-46.

[71] Freidson, *Profession of Medicine*, pp. 158-84. Callahan explains schoolmen's adoption of business efficiency practices, which he considers unfortunate, on what appears to have been an abiding sense of "vulnerability." See his *Education*

did not necessarily feel compelled to follow the dictates of scientific inquiry in managing the "realities" of schooling.

The custody of youth. The evangelistic spirit of the common-school crusade in the nineteenth century reflected a confidence in the efficacy of schooling to overcome social turmoil and, in turn, nurtured a desire to bring all youth into the fold, especially those who were in greatest need of hearing the message. Most often this basic thrust has been viewed as a noble attempt to extend the blessings of universal education to all American youth. The movement can also be seen as an expansionist drive to gain custody of the nation's children. This same desire for custody informed the self-conscious professionalism of the twentieth century, but, given the technical attitude which prevailed, the approach became more pragmatic and more directed toward concrete programs to increase the attractiveness and holding power of the schools. In the 1800's, the campaign for custody was spirited but fell short of its goal. In the 1900's, the effort was equally spirited, but this time schoolmen marshaled the resources necessary to include and retain more students and hence legitimize their claim to offer education for all.

The drive for custody was one of the most important events in the growth of professionalism in schooling. Indeed most of the mechanism and the effects of professionalization converged on the custody issue. The size of enrollments was not only a symbol of efficacy to early professionals but also became the basis for financing schools. The inclusion of a larger and more diverse population of pupils had a tremendous impact on the curriculum itself and ultimately served to define the central issues and problems of the curriculum field. In the end, achievement of virtual custody of all youth expanded the content and marked the acceptance of the schooling monopoly.

Every profession faced the problem of getting clients to make use of its services, especially those clients the professionals felt needed the service the most. The existence of a monopoly certainly played a major role in this regard, as did a belief in the dignity and special qualifications of the profession. Nevertheless, to sustain these beliefs as well as enlarge the total number of clients, professions engaged in specific

---

and the Cult of Efficiency. Freidson notes, however, that, because of the multiple contingencies of practice environments, vulnerability is a common condition of work faced by all "consulting" professionals. The recent controversy over malpractice suits in medicine certainly underscores this dimension of professionalism. It is undertandable, then, that schoolmen would seek to adopt procedures which, at the time at least, appeared to reduce the possibility, or perhaps the consequences, of error.

activities, usually of a persuasive nature, to secure client cooperation. Schooling was unique among the professions in that client use was eventually required by law. All professions achieved a monopoly in a domain; only in the case of schooling was client use of that monopoly compulsory.[72]

The issue of compulsory attendance has recently received a great deal of attention and contemporary scholarship has shed considerable light on the unique dimensions of such legislation. It is obviously not possible here to review this burgeoning literature on compulsory attendance. It is necessary, however, to point out tentative conclusions which seem to emerge from these reanalyses of the issue.[73] First, contrary to the custody—and even incarceration—rhetoric surrounding compulsory attendance, the laws were simply not enforceable when originally passed. Part of the reason that the early laws were not implemented is that no effective mechanisms or, for that matter, popular support for enforcement existed. More important, the schools of the day simply did not have the room to accept all of the available pupils, even those who were already trying to gain admission. In most major cities, large numbers of pupils were turned away because of lack of room. Second, compulsory laws appear to have been aimed at specific target groups, mostly Southern European immigrants, who were especially offensive to dominant classes and who were, for a number of reasons, prone to see little relevance in schooling. A large majority of those who attended schools appear to have done so for reasons unrelated to direct compulsion.

The issue of compulsion in schooling obviously involves more than these two dimensions. The key point, however, is that compulsory attendance legislation was not the only approach used by schoolmen to persuade clients to accept schooling. Moreover, such laws were of

[72] It is necessary to point out that other professions do enjoy some form of legal compulsion with regard to client use of their services. In medicine, for example, certain inoculations are required by law. Moreover, the compulsory use of schooling is not limited to public school attendance and is not total. There are *legal* exceptions as well as failures to enforce the laws in some instances (e.g., with regard to the Amish in several states).

[73] These conclusions are drawn primarily from the recent studies of David Tyack. See his *One Best System*, pp. 66-71; "Why Aren't You in School: Thoughts on the History of Compulsory Schooling." Paper at the American Historical Association Meeting, 1974; and "Compulsory School Attendance and Progressive Reform in the Nineteenth and Twentieth Centuries." Paper at the American Educational Research Association Meeting, Washington, D.C., 1975. The first compulsory attendance legislation was passed in Massachusetts in 1852. By 1900, 33 states had enacted such laws, the major exceptions being the southern states. By 1918, all states had such laws and efforts were made to extend the coverage of the laws to include high school years.

doubtful instrumentality in the actual achievement of custody. In many ways compulsory attendance laws were symbolic acts, similar to anti-spitting laws of the tuberculosis societies, which served as concrete evidence of the "successes" of the custody campaign. Of greater significance to actual success was the degree of public acceptance and support which made the mechanisms of enforcement unnecessary for the vast majority of students. Acknowledging the impact of popular support, Woltz has noted: "If because of changing public opinion education should cease to be voluntary on the part of most, I doubt very much that it could actually be made compulsory, whatever provision the law should make."[74]

Schoolmen implemented a number of programs, in addition to compulsion, which appear to have been directed toward broadening the base of popular support for schooling, and hence contributed to the campaign for custody. Two such programs are of particular importance in the present context: viz, (a) a shift in the rhetoric used to describe the functions of schooling, and (b) a conscious manipulation of the image and content of the curriculum. Before discussing these programs in detail, the following *caveat* is warranted. Increases in enrollments did in fact accompany the program to secure custody. It is tempting to draw rather straightforward cause-and-effect inferences from this correlation, inferences concerning the victory of schoolmen over forces opposed to universal education. Unfortunately the issue is considerably more complex than such conclusions would suggest. More students went to and stayed in school for a variety of reasons, some of which—e.g., changes in the ability of the labor market to absorb as many illiterate workers—had little to do with the direct appeals of schoolmen. Nonetheless, changes in the image and the content of schooling, matters over which schoolmen did have influence, certainly made the school option more attractive and more instrumental in gaining better employment in the future. This would seem to be another example of professionals operating as both instigators of specific effects as well as opportunists taking advantage of events for which direct responsibility was merely assumed. A similar pattern emerged with respect to the curriculum: changes in curriculum functioned to attract more students to school but, at the same time, dramatic increases in enrollment necessitated modification of traditional curricular patterns. Regardless of the causes, however, the results quickly inspired in schoolmen, including curriculum specialists, a sense of personal confidence in their ability to

[74] Charles K. Woltz. "Compulsory Attendance at School." *Law and Contemporary Problems* 20: 22; Winter 1955.

control variables and gain command of situations and served to bolster claims to special competence and commitment.

One of the best descriptions of the persuasive program to gain custody of all youth is contained in the 1918 Report of the Commission on the Reorganization of Secondary Education entitled *Cardinal Principles of Secondary Education.*[75] There is little doubt from the text of the Report that the authors were committed to the principle of education for all. The Report also reflects the view that reaching this objective depended ultimately on the willingness of parents and youth to accept the value and utility of school attendance. This realization of motivational dimensions in school attendance was related especially to the "dropout" and underscored the need to increase the fundamental attractiveness of schooling in order to gain custody of more youth for longer periods of time.

From the viewpoint of rhetoric, the Commission's Report represented a departure from nineteenth-century practice. Although the Commission was not unmindful of the impact of industrialization and urbanization and of the relation of schooling to social need, the language of the Report was less explicitly oriented toward control of the masses and more reflective of a concern for individual differences and for helping each pupil achieve maximum potential. The rhetoric, in other words, was less antagonistic and more solicitous and inclusive toward clients. It was the language of child-centered progressivism rather than that of explicit social control. Vallance, in an insightful analysis of the origins of the "hidden" curriculum, has noted a general shift in rhetoric from the colonial and national periods to the Progressive era. She explains this shift, however, by reference to the fact that social control rhetoric had served its purpose by supporting the creation of institutional structures and procedures which embodied social control functions. Hence further reference to social control was no longer necessary.[76] There was no need, in other words, to fight for what had already been accomplished. This explanation would seem to have considerable merit and heuristic power. It does not, however, explain with complete satisfaction the selection of a specifically child-centered language to replace control rhetoric. The present explanation is based on the premise that social control rhetoric, while perhaps helpful in bureaucratizing schooling, was simply not instrumental in gaining custody of youth. This

    [75] See: U.S. Bureau of Education Bulletin 35. Washington, D.C.: Government Printing Office, 1918.

    [76] Elizabeth Vallance. "Hiding the Hidden Curriculum: An Interpretation of the Language of Justification in Nineteenth-Century Educational Reform." *Curriculum Theory Network* 4: 5-21; 1973/74.

latter function, which became more salient during professionalization in the 1900's, required a more inclusive language to attract and retain clients. The language of child-centered progressivism was available and especially useful for this purpose.

Aside from the question of rhetoric, the Commission's Report recommended concrete changes in the image and content of curriculum in order to make the school more attractive and more immediately useful to pupils. Herein lies one of the fundamental reformations of schooling which occurred during the early decades of the twentieth century. This reformation rested on the acceptance of the principle of *differentiation* in content and in outcomes as a solution to the problems of schooling in a modern industrial society. Acknowledging that the holding power of the school was not strong, the Commission recommended that content first be differentiated into that which was simpler and immediately applicable (for inclusion in early secondary grades) and that which was advanced and academic (for higher grade levels). This concession to reality does not, however, define the limits of the Commission's optimism. The Report also contains the recommendation that the entire curriculum be differentiated to allow for greater matching between the individual "needs" of pupils and the program of the school. In this way the school would have utility for all pupils, regardless of their particular place in the social system. This plan was also considered more realistic because a complex industrialized society required a variety of specialized workers performing different functions according to their particular inclinations and talents. In this light, differentiation became a uniquely appropriate solution since it enabled schooling to meet simultaneously the needs of society and the needs of all youth.

In many ways the 1918 Report served as an endorsement of a variety of movements which had already begun to influence American schooling in the twentieth century, all of which emphasized individual differences in ability and career potential and which stressed direct social utility as a central function of schooling. The testing movement made it possible to invoke the prestige of science to classify pupils according to aptitudes and interests, and hence legitimized the differentiation solution to schooling problems. Of particular importance, however, was the industrial education movement which provided much of the content for differentiated programming. Industrial education had several distinct advantages and therefore served as a rallying point for a number of special interests. First, an industrial curriculum provided a way of dealing with pupils who were already attending school in greater numbers but who did not necessarily share traditional academic aspirations. At the same time, schooling could be made more attractive to more youth by seeming to connect with and improve opportunities for employment, the one major competitor in the drive for custody. In addition, the interests of labor, wanting to reduce competition for a decreasing number of jobs, and industry, wanting a more literate and specialized work force to adapt more readily to emerging technologies, converged in support of more years of schooling. Given such commonalities, it was only a matter of time before the "new" education unseated the traditional view, expressed, for instance, by the Committee of Ten that the school served best by offering a common college-preparation curriculum for all. This shift in emphasis from a uniform program to a differentiated program had profound implications for the nature and uses of schooling.[77]

As indicated earlier, it is difficult to identify with confidence the direction of cause and effect in the custody-differentiation relationship. Differentiation was in many ways both a response to a larger and more diverse student body and a factor attracting more pupils to the schools. It is clear, however, that differentiation as a solution to custody problems stimulated a vast range of activity in the curriculum field. Indeed, as both Cremin and Kliebard have observed, the question of differentiation provided one of the key defining themes around which the curriculum field took form and the differentiation issue continues to permeate curriculum discourse.[78] The work of Charters and Bobbitt in attempting to define curriculum in terms of life activities, which presumably were to be different for different groups of pupils, was but one notable example of the influence of the differentiation principle in curriculum thought. Recent enthusiasm for and animosity against "career education" suggests that the differentiation question persists.

Regardless of causality, differentiation, especially along industrial lines, made custody possible. More important, however, was the final effect of differentiation and custody on the schooling monopoly. By gaining custody of all youth and by doing so in distinctly vocational terms, schooling became directly connected to immediate employment. This linkage between schooling and the world of work completed the monopoly of schooling. By the end of the nineteenth century, schooling was perceived as the path to college and academic careers. By 1920, the

---

[77] Sol Cohen. "The Industrial Education Movement, 1906-1917." *American Quarterly* 20: 95-110; Spring 1968.

[78] Cremin, "Curriculum-making in the United States," pp. 207-20; Herbert M. Kliebard. "Historical Scholarship: Persistent Curriculum Issues in Historical Perspective." In: Edmund C. Short, editor. *A Search for Valid Content for Curriculum.* Toledo: University of Toledo, 1970. pp. 31-41.

view was established that schooling was the pipeline to the labor market. Given the diversity of students enrolled in schools and the growth of a differentiated, specialized, bureaucratized labor market, schooling now assumed the role of gatekeeper and central sorting agency for society, "the arbiter between the economy and the future worker." [79] Ultimately perception of the continuity between schooling and life led to the acceptance of school completion as a prerequisite for all extra-school opportunities. As schooling assumed more and more of these sorting and certifying functions, alternate modes of *education* were further devalued, making the schooling monopoly even more extensive. Indeed it was now possible to say that schooling dominated the division of labor in education. Education for all was a personal and social necessity; professionalism was triumphant.

The legacy of progressive reform. In the decades between the 1890's and the 1920's schoolmen, dedicated to professionalizing, faced the challenge of securing acceptance of schooling as the principal means of educating youth. In keeping with the professionalism model, they met this challenge by increasing the attractiveness of schooling as an option in the educational domain. Increasing occupational attractiveness involved two basic operations. First, schoolmen sought to improve the images of organizational and technical *competence* through an association with bureaucracy, efficiency, and science. Second, they endeavored to increase *client utilization* by using a child-centered rhetoric and by differentiating curricula to enhance the utility of school attendance. It is clear that much of this movement toward occupational dominance consisted of symbolic content embodied in the rhetoric of professional claims.

The Twenty-Sixth Yearbook of the National Society for the Study of Education stands as a monument to the professionalism ethic as expressed in the curriculum field. It is a spirited document reflecting a broadly inclusive and expansive conception of curriculum and curriculum-building methodology. The Yearbook Committee, or at least its chairman, Harold Rugg, sought a synthesis in curriculum content and among curriculum workers and consultants with a vast array of interests and specializations. The curriculum was clearly viewed as an instrument for comprehensive personal and social goals and for increasing the efficacy

[79] Kaestle, *Evolution of an Urban School System*, p. viii. An attempt to blend college preparation and new modes of differentiating and structuring curriculum to increase school attractiveness is reflected in the Eight-Year Study of the Progressive Education Association. See: Ralph W. Tyler. "Curriculum Development in the Twenties and Thirties." In: Robert M. McClure, editor. *The Curriculum: Retrospect and Prospect.* Seventieth Yearbook of the National Society for the Study of Education, Part I. Chicago: University of Chicago Press, 1971. pp. 26-44.

of schools and teachers. In all of this, science was the fundamental wellspring for curriculum substance and curricular decision making.[80]

In the last decade it has become increasingly popular to criticize schoolmen's preoccupation with "efficiency," "scientism," and "professionalism" and their efforts to differentiate curricula on the basis of predictions about the probable destiny of students.[81] Due to the fact that the curriculum field, which took form during this period, embraced these doctrines, it has been the primary target for such strictures. Criticism of the progressive reform legacy appears to be based on at least two issues: (a) the failure of science and bureaucracy to achieve the promise of efficacy and fulfillment contained in the rhetoric of advocacy; and/or (b) the incompatibility of scientism and efficiency with today's value commitments and preferences. The present analysis suggests, however, that the progressive legacy must be viewed within the context of a larger movement toward occupational dominance and monopoly. Scientism, efficiency, and differentiation provided the substance for the profession's claims to possess the necessary competence to manage the educational affairs of the nation. Such a perspective is especially useful in comprehending the events and issues in the curriculum field. In establishing an image of expertise and in securing client utilization, the curriculum became one of the major symbols to be manipulated in order to enhance the acceptability of the schooling monopoly. Although it eventually assumed its own identity, the curriculum field was launched and shaped within the larger drive to professionalize schooling. One may regret this development, but it is hardly surprising that curriculum specialists adopted the professionalism ethic.

---

[80] Guy Montrose Whipple, editor. *The Foundations and Technique of Curriculum-Construction.* Twenty-Sixth Yearbook of the National Society for the Study of Education, Parts I and II. Bloomington, Ill.: Public School Publishing, 1926. Harold Rugg, as chairman of the Yearbook Committee, played a major role in organizing and producing this yearbook. For an excellent commentary on the Twenty-Sixth Yearbook, see: Decker F. Walker. "The Curriculum Field in Formation." *Curriculum Theory Network* 4: 263-80; 1975.

[81] See, for example: Callahan, *Education and the Cult of Efficiency;* Schaefer, "Retrospect and Prospect," pp. 9-12 especially; Herbert M. Kliebard. "Bureaucracy and Curriculum Theory." In: Vernon F. Haubrich, editor. *Freedom, Bureaucracy, and Schooling.* 1971 Yearbook. Washington, D.C.: Association for Supervision and Curriculum Development, 1971. pp. 74-93; Herbert M. Kliebard. "The Rise of Scientific Curriculum Making and Its Aftermath." *Curriculum Theory Network* 5: 27-38; 1975; Tyack, *One Best System,* pp. 182-216; Katz, *Class, Bureaucracy, and Schools,* pp. 121-23. Of recent critics, Walker appears to be most aware of the extent to which science and claims to expertise were symbols in the struggle for dominance in the curriculum field. See: Decker F. Walker. "Straining to Lift Ourselves." *Curriculum Theory Network* 5: 3-25; 1975.

The Limits of Professionalism

Some children spend their entire school life under a regime *that would make criminals of harmless mollusks. . . .*

—*Adele Marie Shaw, in* World's Work, Vol. 7, 1903

The period between 1920 and 1960 appears, from current perspectives, as one of what might be called "normal" professionalism. It was a period, in other words, in which adjustments occurred in perceptions of the schools and the content of the schooling monopoly, but no serious threats to the dominance of schooling emerged. The "great school legend" prevailed in educational discourse and developments were most often simply a matter of working out in fact the custody of all youth and fulfilling the promise of education for all. Nevertheless, the seeds of confrontation were planted during this time and grew to become, after 1960, the source of a radical challenge to the fundamental bases of professionalism. The intent of the following remarks is to review, briefly and selectively, the events of the decades of normal professionalism and to contrast the climate of this period with current efforts to redefine the functions and the consequences of schooling.

The Schooling Monopoly

After 1920, the content of the schooling monopoly, defined largely in terms of access to extra-school opportunities, remained fairly constant. There were, however, several events which appear to have refined perceptions of both the extent and the relative significance of the components of the school's monopoly. The following is an attempt to delineate this refinement process in terms of the relation of schooling to education, democracy, success, and, finally, national honor.

School and education. One of the clear consequences of the professionalizing of schooling was a decline in the independent instrumentality of alternative modes of education, such as that provided by family, community, and church. This is not say that these agencies ceased to have an effect in the total educational sphere. But these agencies gradually and systematically lost the ability to certify that a person had achieved educational competencies. As a result they were no longer sufficient sources of education. Professionalization, in other words, served to limit the formal impact of other means of educating; their informal influence may not necessarily have been affected.

A common example used to illustrate the decreasing impact of nonschool agencies of education is the decline of the family. In some ways this so-called "decline" of the family has been a manifestation of schooling rhetoric and appears to justify the primacy of schooling in the educational domain. One suspects that the educative influence of the family, both positive and negative, has remained fairly constant. What changed, however, was the willingness of dominant segments of society to trust that family education would automatically produce outcomes congruent with their interests. Professionalization, rather than being a response to the decline of the family, is perhaps more accurately viewed as a development which *displaced* the family as an agency sufficient to certify educational accomplishment. As a result of the professionalizing of schooling, the family is required to depend upon schools of one form or another to secure the advantages of education for its children.[82]

An interesting perspective on the relation of schooling of the family is contained in Cohen's anthropological analysis of education. Cohen suggests that the displacement of the family and its particular mode of influence (socialization) is a natural consequence of the rise of a nation-state. Socialization in the family context emphasizes particularistic values and orientations, whereas the nation-state is dependent upon universalistic values and preferences fostered by formal modes of education. It is not that the family mechanisms fail to work, but that the family produces outcomes which are not necessarily compatible with the demands of the nation-state. Cohen also emphasizes that schooling provides a means for the child to gain independence from the provincialism of the family and therefore makes a broader range of choices possible.[83]

[82] The relation between family and school is central in Bailyn, *Education in the Forming of American Society.*

[83] Yehudi A. Cohen. "The Shaping of Men's Minds: Adaptations to the Imperatives of Culture." In: Murray L. Wax, Stanley Diamond, and Fred O. Gearing, editors. *Anthropological Perspectives on Education.* New York: Basic Books, 1971. pp. 19-50; and "Anthropology and the Study of Compulsory School Attendance." Paper presented at the Annual Meeting of the American Educational Research Association, Washington, D.C., 1975. In response to an audience question during the 1975 AERA session at which the above paper was presented, Cohen maintained that in no culture with which he was familiar was the child considered to be owned exclusively by the family. In this regard Woltz has commented that compulsory attendance laws "are the tangible expression of the accepted belief that the state has a paramount interest in the education of its citizens, to which interest the claims of parents and their right to control of their children must yield." See: Woltz, "Compulsory Attendance at School," p. 21.

All of this suggests that the relationship of schooling to the family and other agencies of education is a complex issue meriting careful and continuing attention. It is clear, however, that during the period of normal professionalism, few attempts were made to challenge seriously the extent of the schooling monopoly with respect to alternate modes of educating.

Schooling and democracy. One of the dominant themes reflected in educational writings of the Progressive era was that schooling had both personal and social consequences and therefore could be an instrument of both child development and social betterment. The child-centered rhetoric which characterized much of this writing functioned to "personalize" schooling. During the time of normal professionalism, this personalized rhetoric functioned to increase the significance of a personal-benefit conception of schooling. In relation to the refinement of the schooling monopoly, however, the social dimensions of Progressive rhetoric were also noteworthy. The following is a very brief analysis of the significance of this social position.

The concepts associated with the social functions of schooling were broadly inclusive, especially as represented in the works of men like Counts and Rugg. These progressives and others were key figures in that branch of Progressivism known as social reconstructionism, a body of thought based on the premise that the school should not only maintain existing social arrangements but, even more important, should become an instrument for changing the social order. To accomplish this reconstruction of society the school was to play a deciding leadership role in the basic governance processes of the community. Indeed the school and the teacher were presumably to operate in a quasi-political way to forge a new consensus and hence provide direction for reconstructing the social order. In defining authority, for instance, reconstructionists adopted the model of the teacher as "pedagogical vicar of the community," a definition more appropriate to a bearer of political authority than to one possessing, as does the teacher, authority based on a claim to expertise.[84]

---

[84] On progressivism and social reconstructionism in American education, see: C. A. Bowers. *The Progressive Educator and the Depression.* New York: Random House, 1969; and Cremin, *The Transformation of the School.* The concept of the teacher as "pedagogical vicar" received full development in: Kenneth C. Benne, *A Conception of Authority: An Introductory Study.* Teachers College Contributions to Education, No. 895. New York: Bureau of Publications, Teachers College, Columbia University, 1943. For a critical analysis of this definition of teacher authority together with an alternative view, see: Doyle, "A Professional Model for the Authority of the Teacher."

In the present context social reconstructionism is significant in that it appeared to define the limits of professionalism. There is little evidence that the conscious and deliberate use of schooling to build a new social order, especially one contrary to dominant social interests, has ever been a widely accepted or approved idea. Society appears to have been willing to grant schooling a monopoly over social-access functions, but has simply not viewed schooling as a mechanism for direct and radical social change. Social reconstructionism, then, represented an attempt to extend the schooling monopoly beyond the boundaries which society perceived as legitimate for the profession. As such it was the understandable thrust of any professional group. With respect to modern times, however, the degree to which a given proposal for the use of schooling involves drastic social revision gives little reason to expect that such a proposal will gain widespread support. Schooling is to reflect rather than make society.

Schooling and success. The linkage of schooling with extra-school opportunities and the elevation of personal-benefit conceptions of schooling would seem to have led inevitably to the perception of a fundamental connection between schooling and life success. Awareness of the potential power of schooling to determine success in life became a basic element in a growing sensitivity to disparities in the distribution of educational services throughout the nation. In 1939 Edwards argued, for example, that: "If formal educational attainments condition entrance to some economic and social spheres, and if great opportunities for educational advance are open to some groups while the educational facilities for others remain meager, it is obvious that education becomes an instrument of social stratification and of regional and racial inequality." [85]

Concern for equality of access to educational opportunity as well as the impact of schooling on success culminated in 1954 with the landmark Supreme Court decision on school desegregation, *Brown* v. *Board of Education of Topeka.* Basic to the decision was the view that schooling is a prerequisite for success:

Today, education is perhaps the most important function of state and local governments. Compulsory school attendance laws and the great expenditures for education both demonstrate our recognition of the importance of education to our democratic society. It is required in the performance of our most basic public responsibilities, even service in the armed forces. It is the very foundation of good citizenship. Today it is a principal instrument in awakening the child to cultural values, in preparing him for later professional

[85] Newton Edwards. *Equal Educational Opportunity for Youth: A National Responsibility.* Washington, D.C.: American Council on Education, 1939. p. 152.

training, and in helping him to adjust normally to his environment. In these days, it is doubtful that any child may reasonably be expected to succeed in life if he is denied the opportunity of an education. Such an opportunity, where the state has undertaken to provide it, is a right which must be made available to all on equal terms.[86]

In the history of education there were few better statements of the basic American faith in schooling. As will be seen, there were few decisions which have played a greater role in fostering a fundamental reconsideration of the ability of schooling to extend its benefits to all American youth.

Schooling and national honor. The ideology underlying the *Brown* decision was a logical extension of the linking of schooling with extra-school opportunity. As such, the decision refined the content of the profession's monopoly and confirmed the basic significance of schooling in American society. During the 1950's another event took place which elaborated even further the degree of American confidence in what schooling could be. The launching of the Russian satellite *Sputnik* in 1957 threatened the American sense of national pride and world leadership, and energized a number of forces to combat the perceived weaknesses responsible for this embarrassing turn of events. Schooling rapidly became both a cause of American honor in international affairs and a logical solution to the problem of restoring American leadership in the space age. A spirited controversy surrounded the substance of schooling and fundamental reforms of the curriculum were proposed and eventually implemented on a large scale and according to a surprisingly rapid schedule. In all this controversy, schoolmen appeared to be eager to admit past sins, at least those of omission, and to accept the challenge to make schooling an instrument of national defense and international prestige.

The drive for professionalism, initiated in the nineteenth-century school crusades, culminated, then, in the identification of schooling with the destiny of the nation in a space age and a complex world power network. Although some disagreed about the best way in which schooling would fulfill its promise to the nation, few doubted that its goals could be reached. Schooling had indeed completed the transition from a self-conscious occupation to a self-confident profession. Prospects seemed unlimited.

---

[86] U.S. Supreme Court. Brown *v.* Board of Education of Topeka, 1954. Quotation from text as reprinted in: Daniel J. Boorstin, editor. *An American Primer.* Chicago: University of Chicago Press, 1966. Vol. II, pp. 906-907.

Schooling and Equal Opportunity

Schooling achieved professionalization in part because of an inclusive rhetoric which stresses the importance of extending the benefits of school attendance to all American youth. Acceptance of this rhetoric served to link schooling with future opportunity and to extend the custody of the profession over its primary clients. In spite of an inclusion rhetoric, it is clear that professionalism actually excluded several identifiable groups. At the general level, increased professionalism worked to exclude direct lay influence over decisions the profession considered to be its own. Within the profession itself, women were excluded, first from membership, and then from active power positions in the National Education Association. This same exclusion mentality made it difficult for women to secure key administrative posts in school systems even though women constituted the majority of practicing teachers. The superintendency and the principalship were and still are "male" positions. A similar pattern of male expectation affected most other professions. Finally, the "one best system" of schooling excluded several minority groups. The reasons for exclusion from schooling were admittedly complex. Some, such as Catholics, Amish, and atheists, found the Protestant character of public schools intolerable. Others, such as migrant workers, faced language and life-style barriers which made school attendance difficult if not impossible. And some, especially blacks and many Indians, were required, either by law or by administrative practice, to attend separate schools because their inclusion was unacceptable to dominant mores and sensibilities. Regardless of the particular reasons involved, the end result was a consistent and systematic exclusion of many from participation in an institution dedicated to education for all.[87]

In important ways the exclusive character of schooling was a direct reflection of patterns of inclusion and exclusion in the larger society. In addition, the value of alliances with dominant power centers in the formative processes of professionalizing tended to orient early professionals away from the concerns and interests of powerless minorities. The intent here is not to excuse exclusionary practices but to attempt if possible to understand factors contributing to this tendency in schooling.

The promise of schooling. In spite of the exclusiveness of schooling at the time professionalization was achieved, it is clear that during

---

[87] For an excellent discussion of minority exclusion from schooling, see: Tyack, *One Best System*, pp. 59-65; 104-25; 217-29; 255-68.

the period of normal professionalism the exclusive character of schooling gradually diminished. Of particular importance was the *Brown* decision in 1954 which, by attacking directly a dual system of education, focused public attention on questions of inclusion and exclusion of minorities from schools. As a result of this and other developments, the ideology of equal access to schools was firmly established by 1960 and the rate of school attendance began to approach the reality promised by universal schooling. There were, however, two important developments which accompanied this movement toward inclusion and which ultimately combined to reform conceptions of the nature and functions of schooling. The first of these developments was an increased awareness of and commitment to a personal-benefit conception of the use of schooling. As indicated earlier this personal-benefit view was one of the major legacies of the period of normal professionalism and it became a central motivating factor in determining expectations for schooling in the 1960's. The second development, for which the profession had less direct responsibility, was a rising sense of minority self-identity and assertiveness. As more and more minorities gained access to schools, this self-consciousness sensitized minority-group spokesmen to the effects of schooling as related to minority interests and aspirations.

The convergence of a personal-benefit conception of schooling and increased minority-group identity had important implications for popular perceptions of the significance of school rhetoric. As indicated, the rhetoric of schooling has, from the early school crusades in the nineteenth century, reflected an evangelical and inflated tone. Throughout the history of American education, schoolmen adopted a language of advocacy designed more to defend and persuade than to analyze or describe. In the 1960's more people were inclined to take schooling at its word, to expect the individual school to meet the claims made in its behalf. In this process, a language of persuasion was converted into a language of description and the rhetoric of schooling became a contract. The implications of such a conversion are massive.

With the experience of universal schooling, it soon became evident that there were serious discrepancies between the promise and the outcomes of schooling. Although barriers to school attendance diminished, the benefits of schooling, defined by achievement, job opportunities, or social mobility, were distributed unequally. It soon became apparent that schooling worked for some more than others.

Schooling not only appeared to benefit some more than others but did little to compensate for initial achievement differences which children brought with them to school. Indeed schooling apparently did more to increase disparity in achievement than to reduce it.[88] Historical analyses of schooling effects, with special reference to immigrant groups, support similar conclusions. Contrary to popular conceptions of the contribution of schooling to occupational and social mobility in the past, the record indicates that some immigrant groups achieved substantially more than others. Moreover, the extent to which a particular group showed gains in school achievement appears to have depended more on (a) the congruence between immigrant values and aspirations and those of the school; and (b) the prior gaining of social mobility and status by the immigrant group. From this perspective, immigrant school achievement appears to be a symptom rather than a cause of social mobility. For the vast majority of the children of the poor, the school seems powerless to confer, in any substantial way, the benefits so confidently promised by its spokesmen and so widely assumed by its clientele.[89]

Equality of outcome. Evidence that schooling fails to confer its benefits equally among all children is not necessarily a cause for concern if one adopts a purely social-benefit view of schooling. Indeed this social-benefit model appears to have prevailed in perceptions of American schooling from its early founding through the age of professionalization. In the language of the Jeffersonian rationale, schooling is to be made available to all children so that they may achieve a common level of literacy necessary for intelligent citizenship. Beyond this common level the outcomes of schooling are expected to be unequal because of the "natural aristocracy among men," an aristocracy grounded in "virtue and talents." Of utmost importance to society is the identification and

---

[88] The Coleman Report supplied documentation to support this view of the efficacy of schooling. For a useful summary, see: James S. Coleman. "Equal Schools or Equal Students?" *The Public Interest* 4: 70-75; Summer 1966. See also: Christopher Jencks, *et al. Inequality: A Reassessment of the Effect of Family and Schooling in America.* New York: Basic Books, 1972; Frederick Mosteller and Daniel P. Moynihan. *On Equality of Educational Opportunity.* New York: Random House, 1972; *Harvard Educational Review* editors. *Equal Educational Opportunity.* Cambridge, Massachusetts: Harvard University Press, 1969; and Andrew Kopan and Herbert Walberg, editors. *Rethinking Educational Equality.* Berkeley, California: McCutchan, 1974.

[89] On immigrants and schooling in American educational history, see: Tyack, *One Best System,* pp. 248-55 especially; Timothy L. Smith. "Immigrant Social Aspirations and American Education, 1880-1930." *American Quarterly* 21: 523-43; Fall 1969; David K. Cohen. "Immigrants and the Schools." *Review of Educational Research* 40: 13-27; February 1970; and Michael R. Olneck and Marvin Lazerson. "The School Achievement of Immigrant Children: 1900-1930." *History of Education Quarterly* 14: 453-82; Winter 1974. Cohen contends that "education *per se* is not a vehicle of mobility in a system of social stratification.... In these terms, the opening of schools to groups who had previously been barred from them is a by-product—not a cause—of social mobility." See: Cohen, "The Shaping of Men's Minds," p. 46.

training of those who possess this natural talent regardless of their class origins. Universal schooling provides a mechanism whereby the natural aristocracy can be "raked from the rubbish" to furnish leadership for society. With the growth of the schooling monopoly in the domain of education, the schools became virtually the only avenue to personal success. Personal-benefit conceptions, therefore, began to assume equal if not greater significance in comparison with the social-utility model of schooling. From the personal-benefit perspective, claims to efficacy based on overall social effects are no longer satisfactory and equality of access is no longer a sufficient condition for equality of educational opportunity. The circumstances demand equality of results.[90]

The issue of equality of opportunity assumed added meaning when it became evident that the differential outcomes of schooling corresponded rather closely to social-class and ethnic distinctions in the larger society. This correspondence has prompted some critics to charge that schooling is an instrument which dominant classes use, consciously and deliberately, to secure benefits for their own children, exclude unwanted competition for status and wealth, and maintain the relative balance of rich and poor in society. The rhetoric of schooling, with its emphasis on past successes, equality of opportunity, and universalistic standards of merit, is seen as simply a way to hide the intended, but implicit, purposes of schooling.[91]

Regardless of the validity of these arguments, it is clear that the demand for equality of results, indicative of what Daniel Bell calls the "revolution of rising entitlements," [92] represents a serious attack on the roots of professionalism in schooling. The campaign for equal outcomes suggests a rejection of the schooling profession's claims to efficacy. To question such claims is to challenge the very legitimacy of professional dominance and monopoly. Carried far enough, this rejection can find expression in public resentment toward dependency on professional judgment and a decline in willingness to tolerate professional autonomy,

---

[90] The quotations are from Jefferson's letter to John Adams, October 28, 1813, and "Notes on the State of Virginia" reprinted in: Lee, *Crusade Against Ignorance*, pp. 162 and 94 respectively. For an informative discussion of the doctrine of quality in schooling, see: Arthur Mann. "A Historical Overview: The *Lumpenproletariat*, Education, and Compensatory Action." In: Charles U. Daly, editor. *The Quality of Inequality: Urban and Suburban Public Schools.* Chicago: University of Chicago Center for Policy Study, 1968. pp. 9-26. See also references cited in Footnote 88, above.

[91] See, especially: Greer, *The Great School Legend*; and Katz, *Class, Bureaucracy, and Schools.*

[92] Daniel Bell. "The Revolution of Rising Entitlements." *Fortune* 91: 98-103 + ; April 1975.

that is, to allow a profession freedom from outside interference in determining its affairs. Along these lines, the dramatic increase in malpractice litigation in medicine and the recent Supreme Court decision affecting fee schedules for legal services are signs that the antiprofessionalism movement is not limited to schooling. One consequence is apparent: the time is ripe for a fundamental restructuring of the relation of professions to society.

For those who retain interest in maintaining schools at all, the commitment to equal outcomes denotes an ironic combination of a profound lack of confidence in the assumed effectiveness of schooling as an instrument of education and an abiding faith that schooling, if sufficiently transformed, can become an instrument of true social equalization. But neither the nineteenth-century presumption of efficacy nor the twentieth-century substitution of activity measures for effectiveness data represents an acceptable approach to sustaining a professional monopoly. In the past, schoolmen were concerned with securing resources to make schools what they knew they could be. The contemporary question is whether the schools can ever live up to the faith Americans continue to place in them.

Curriculum and Power

A good deal of utopian spirit has permeated most discourse on schooling and continues to be an important dimension in the modern age of criticism. Schooling professionals obviously took advantage of this utopian spirit and contributed to the tradition by making elevated claims concerning the potential dignity and power of their enterprise. It became easy, in this climate, to assume that, since schooling appeared to be associated with social success for some students, schooling could cause social opportunity and mobility for everyone. This same utopian attitude led most to believe that inclusion of a larger and more diverse population in schools would have limited impact on the institutional arrangements, technical mechanisms, and the outcomes of schooling. It comes as a shock, then, to discover that perhaps schooling is much less "powerful" than American faith has always presumed it must be.

The degree to which doubt in the potency of schools has shocked American sensibilities is reflected part by the diversity and complexity of reaction to the realization of possible limitations of schooling. Among radical critics, the components of the issue seem clear: the problem is a failure of schooling to fulfill its promise; the cause is directly related to middle-class dominance and bias which infuse the basic structures and processes of schooling. The solutions, however, become considerably more clouded. To some, schooling is an instrument of cultural imperialism hopelessly linked to the vested interests of the corporate structure and hence needs to be abandoned completely. To others, with equal outrage at the failures and the linkages of schooling, schools can, if radically revised in terms of assumptions and mechanisms, become useful tools for achieving important social goals. Even here, however, there is no necessary agreement on procedures. Some argue that schooling is too differentiated and hence fails as an instrument of social mobility. Others contend that the school curriculum is not differentiated enough to be an instrument of cultural pluralism.[93]

If agreement does exist within the modern rhetoric of school criticism, it would appear to center on the need to construct instruments, whether through schooling or not, to grant the dispossessed, the poor, a means of gaining access to the wealth and advantage which are now restricted to a privileged few. The campaign, in other words, is for a radical redistribution of wealth, status, and social influence in American society. From the professionalism perspective, however, it seems clear that the schooling solution to social crises, at least as that solution has been traditionally known, is simply not one which involves a radical realignment of wealth and social power. If the previous analysis of social reconstructionism has any validity, a fundamental alteration of the social order is beyond the domain of schooling, regardless of claims to the contrary. This is not to say that the efficacy of schooling need not or cannot be improved. It does suggest, however, that there are indeed limits to the power of schooling and that these limits flow not from technical deficiencies but rather reside in the basic mandate upon which schooling rests.

The curriculum as instrument. Can schooling be transformed sufficiently to meet the sense of rising entitlements? Whatever the answer to this question, experience indicates that any systematic effort to render schooling more effective will involve curriculum considerations. One conclusion which emerges with considerable clarity from the history of schooling is the basic stability of curriculum, especially in the structural sense. Admittedly the language of change has traditionally been associated with the curriculum field. It is also true that the curriculum has, at various times, been the target of efforts to expand its scope and increase its degree of differentiation. Nevertheless, the fundamental structure appears to have predated the widespread existence of

---

[93] See, especially: Spring, *Education and the Rise of the Corporate State;* Ivan Illich. *De-schooling Society.* New York: Harper and Row, 1971; Katz, *Class, Bureaucracy, and Schools;* and Edgar G. Epps, editor. *Cultural Pluralism.* Berkeley, California: McCutchan, 1974.

schooling. The curriculum is a "given" of schooling and has survived nearly all proposals to redefine the basic organizing principles upon which it is built. Indeed in the modern curriculum literature questions of curriculum structure or design are seldom raised at all.

The very stability of the curriculum would seem to have contributed to the validity of claims that the schooling profession possessed the tools necessary to achieve approved educational outcomes. This situation suggests that, from a professionalism perspective, the curriculum has had primarily symbolic functions. The symbolic nature of curriculum was especially apparent in the Progressive era when it became an instrument to be manipulated to enhance the attractiveness and custody of schooling. Even in a bureaucratic sense, however, the curriculum is for all practical purposes a symbol. In the organization of schooling, the curriculum is a blueprint for action which supposedly functions to integrate the independent efforts of a vast number of specialists. As a control mechanism, however, the curriculum itself is dependent upon the existence of an extensive supervisory support system, which, in the case of schooling, is notoriously weak if not altogether absent. In reality, the curriculum controls by normative and symbolic means rather than by direct power.

Given the symbolic meaning of curriculum, it is hardly surprising that the curriculum is unable to confer power or that the benefits derived from schooling depend for the most part on the kinds of meanings and strategies children bring to school with them. Schooling, at the level of its core technology, remains fundamentally weak and unable to function independent of other more powerful forces in society. This situation is not necessarily different in other professions. Medicine is least successful, both with respect to cures and the distribution of medical services, where it is most needed. In the case of psychotherapy, Howard and Orlinsky observe that the dominant form of treatment, viz, talk therapy, is used more often and is most successful with those who can afford to pay the fees to gain access to the private practitioner's office. This selection factor no doubt contributes significantly to the "effectiveness" of the treatment. Others without these independent resources must take their chances with institutionalized forms of treatment which are typically less genteel or even humane.[94]

That schooling shares with other professions a basic weakness in its core technology is certainly not an adequate excuse. It does suggest, however, that increasing the power of schooling is a task of considerable magnitude and one which may well involve radical changes in the basic

---

[94] Kenneth I. Howard and Donald E. Orlinsky. "Psychotherapeutic Processes." *Annual Review of Psychology* 23: 615-68; 1972.

arrangements and regularities of schooling. Given the vested interests which have grown up around conventional school practices, it is reasonable to expect that the more readily available alternative of blaming the victim and his teachers will continue to characterize school rhetoric.

Summary

The present discussion represents an attempt to integrate and interpret a number of events and issues which have contributed to American faith in and dissatisfaction with schooling as an agency for educating youth. The approach is intentionally selective and subsumptive. The professionalism model, around which the analysis is structured, would seem, however, to be especially useful in casting new light on persistent questions in the growth of schooling, especially those related to the curriculum field. To the extent that this interpretive effort stimulates further inquiry into these matters, it will have accomplished its purposes.

Schools grew from an incidental position in the American experience to become a panacea for national crises and ills. The urgent question of today is whether schooling has the resources and the spirit to meet the demands of rising entitlements. Before the search for schooling solutions continues, perhaps it is important at this juncture to consider the possibility of forging a new, more realistic view of what schooling might become.

Noah Webster:
American Language
for Americans

In 1783, Noah Webster published a major document in America's intellectual and cultural independence. Born a quarter century before the Revolution began, Noah Webster was educated in colonial schools patterned after the English public school where he learned the English language with its spelling and grammar according to the gospel of Samuel Johnson. During the years after the Revolution when the young and aggressively independent United States was strugling to complete its political and economic independence from Britain, this American, with others, realized an expansion of the meaning of "freedom." Americans had commenced to develop a literature, to establish hair styles, manners of dress, and food items uniquely American. But Americans continued to accept the mandates of English scholars every time they wrote a sentence or engaged in conversation.

Webster's *Grammatical Institute of the English Language* (1783) offered the new nation a unity and common culture which it lacked. Known to later generations as the "Blue-Backed Speller," Webster's speller combined alphabet, primer, speller, and reader. The first book receiving a U.S. copyright, this speller apparently became a standard and almost universal medium of instruction. Further, its impact on the Americanization of English spoken in the U.S. was profound.

By 1828, the 70 year old Webster had completed his *An*

Noah Webster

American Dictionary of the English Language. With this dictionary, and its continuing editions, "Webster's" became the standard of American English. His insistence upon American spellings, definitions keyed to the American scene, and illustrative quotations from the Republic's founders achieved its goal.

Webster was an intellectual nationalist whose speller and dictionary helped immeasurably to consolidate American independence.

—*Karen Solid*

Lindley Murray:
Father of English Grammar in American Schools

I look, you look, he looks; we look, ye look, they look. Upon my soul, he's been studying Murray's Grammar!
—*Herman Melville*, Moby Dick

Soon after the American revolution, American grammarians began vying for status for the American language. Although still bound to Latin grammar and characterized by tedious memorization, parsing, and correcting, the new grammars that began pouring forth truly evidenced a break with the classical tradition and were an innovation for the American school curriculum.

Without doubt the most influential and widely used grammar text of the day was *English Grammar* by Lindley Murray. Originally published in England in 1795, the book passed through nearly fifty editions in its original form, and went through 150 other corrected or abridged editions, each selling thousands of copies. The wide use of the book and the extended period of its popularity established Murray's name as a household word and earned for him the sobriquet, "father of English grammar."

. . . the Compiler of the following work has no interest in it, but that which arises from the hope, that it will prove of some advantage to young persons, and relieve the labors of those who are employed in their education.[1]

Although Murray's book has been criticized by many for its obscurity, blunders, and deficient presentation of etymology, it was a work of great undertaking and made significant contributions to the teaching of the language. One of its chief accomplishments was to promote the systematic study of English in American institutions. Also, in addition to his attention

[1] Lindley Murray. *English Grammar*. Dublin, 1799.

to orthography, etymology, syntax, and prosody, all of which were deliberately presented through moral platitudes whenever possible, Murray did not ignore the nature of his students. He endeavored to create a book that would appeal to his readers; he later incorporated an appendix for advanced students; and he introduced such "extraneous" material as punctuation. In these specific areas and in others, Murray's work directly contributed to a movement to expand the curriculum in American schools.

Little is known about Murray except from that information contained in a series of letters that constitute his *Memoirs*.[2] He was

[2] Lindley Murray. *Memoirs of the Life and Writings of Lindley Murray.* New York, 1827.

born of Quaker parents in 1745 in Pennsylvania. He recalls early memories of going to good schools, playing hooky, having a favorite English teacher, doing a delightful writing assignment on decorated paper, and trying to satisfy his insatiable curiosity. As a young boy, he developed a love for reading and a desire for literary improvement, and these encouraged his entry into law. Failing health in later years, however, eventually resulted in his move to England where his afflictions allowed little activity but reading and writing. It was solicitations by English teachers dissatisfied with their texts that caused Murray to undertake his writing of his *English Grammar*.

—*Sandra Kuhlmann*

"The Advantage of the Public School"[1]

We have no place in America for dainty people—often called gilt-edged —who think that the army would be a good place if it were not for the rank and file. So it is better for a boy of ours to be pitched into a public school, to take pot-luck with all sorts and conditions of boys, and to learn, in the earliest life, that some of the best fellows in the world, not to say

[1] *The Faribault Republican* (Faribault, Minnesota), September 24, 1890. p. 1.

the brightest, never had a French nurse, and always black their own shoes, when they are blacked at all. In all such schools that I have known, the tone of honor is very high. And in such society one early learns the great lesson that all the people are wiser than any one of the people.

God hasn't much use for the man who does all his work with his mouth.

—*Timothy H. Morissey*

William Holmes McGuffey
and His Readers

Looking back upon the 1890's, when old values and styles were at their ragged edge and the trauma of social transformation rumbled under a fragile blanket of American tradition and stability, Henry Seidel Canby recalled that period in Amercan history as "the last time in living memory" when "everyone knew exactly what it meant to be an American."

William Holmes McGuffey (1800-1873) had known very well what being an American meant to his contemporaries. From the first publication of his famous "Readers" in 1836 until the waning of his profound influence upon American children and adults in the late nineteenth century, his collections of stories, poetry, and essays had stood as a solid and common source of idealism and ambition for Americans. More than one hundred and twenty million copies of the "McGuffey Readers," sold by the end of the 1800's, provided much more than a pedagogical guide to literacy. As Henry Steele Commager put it, perhaps the greatest contribution of the Readers rested with their provision of a "common body of allusion and of reference." While one might generally concede that our own children receive schooling superior to that provided a century ago, one might take pause to note that there is no such Reader for our age, no common source book of values or of knowledge; and, in taking pause, one might see the McGuffey Readers in a special light as a symbol of a vital center once common in the American experience.

McGuffey had been a rural school teacher before moving to collegiate instruction and administration. Over the years of his adult life he served as president, first of Cincinnati College, then of Ohio University; and was a professor of languages at Miami University, and of philosophy at Woodward College, before moving to his last position as professor of moral philosophy at the University of Virginia. His Readers, not surprisingly, were innocent of the compromises and condescensions of later readers. The vocabulary of the Readers was rich with unfamiliar words, as if taunting teacher and student alike to throw off their limitations and immaturity. Nor were students protected from vexing questions of adult life. They also learned that moral excellence was superior to intellectual attainment and that idealism should hold raw ambition in check. Where nationalism did show itself, its form was benign. Rather, it is the cosmopolitanism of the Readers that holds one's final attention.

As McGuffey put it, he had set out to combat "the crude notions and revolutionary principles of modern infidelity." The marks left in the heat of his combat, often salutary and occasionally dubious, were deep.

—*Charles Burgess*

Education for Girls: To Which Ends?

A reading of Minnesota newspapers in the 1890's indicates that the education of girls was frequently intended to develop the kind of person to which today's feminists object. Some examples follow:

Physical Culture for Girls [1]

How would I bring up a girl? I would begin when she was 2 years old and teach her to stand poised from the hips and slightly forward, chest up, abdomen contracted, toes turned out at an angle of 60 degrees, and neck erect, so that the collar-bone should be horizontal. You can teach a little girl to know whether she is standing properly or not by having her occasionally walk up against a door. She should touch it with hips, chin, chest and toes. . . . As she grew older she should not take above ten breaths a minute, but they should be full vigorous ones. Good breathing and good standing are almost enough of themselves to give good health and a good figure. . . . In her school days I would take pains to have her sit at her desk properly.

The Proper Education of Women [2]

A woman whose intellect is aggressive, who parades her knowledge before those of inferior intellect or education, is an object to be dreaded.

Mere learning in a woman is never attractive. It is on the contrary, offensive, unless coupled with feminine graces. School learning should sink into the character and deportment, and only exhibit itself as the perfume of a flower is exhibited—in a subtle, nameless and unobtrusive manner.

A woman's knowledge of grammar should not make her talk like an orator in daily life—it should simply make her conversation gracious and agreeable.

Mathematics should render her mind clear, and her judgments true; her geographical studies should teach her that the world is too small for falseness to find a hiding-place; and history should impress her that life is too short for unworthy ambitions.

The time between schoolroom and the altar should be not a mere harvest-time of pleasure, but a sowing-time for others, and of un-

[1] This quotation appeared in an interview with Eliza Putnam Heaton in: *The Faribault Republican* (Faribault, Minnesota), September 3, 1890. p. 1.

[2] This is a quotation from an interview with Ella Wheeler Wilcox in: *The Faribault Republican*, January 14, 1891. p. 1.

selfishness and benevolence which alone can make her a successful wife and mother.

Of course, there were some who dissented from these commonly accepted notions. For example, Helen E. Starrett asserted that:

Once you give full scope to the expression of woman's powers, in any and every form of activity that may correspond to those powers; relieve alike from fear of poverty and dependence, and from the tyranny of enforced inactivity; and womanhood will blossom in a beauty and strength and loveliness of character hitherto undreamed of.[3]

—*Timothy H. Morissey*

[3] *The Faribault Republican*, February 18, 1891. p. 4.

First day of school, September 1915, New York City. George Bain, photographer.

2

Building Curriculum:
Influences and Mechanisms

Francis P. Hunkins

WHAT WILL THE SCHOOLS TEACH? That question has dominated curriculum making from the beginning.

Yet however easily the question may be phrased, it has not been, probably cannot be, answered definitively. Responding requires that individuals confronted by the question have the philosophical and conceptual bases upon which to reply and also possess the techniques requisite for response. Moreover, that primary curriculum question subsumes two others. Traditionally the question of what schools will teach has been viewed, in a narrow sense, as matters of who will make curriculum and how curriculum will be constructed. A broader and more fruitful approach necessitates that these subordinate questions of who and how be placed in the context of influences and mechanisms of curriculum development. That is, the curriculum has been determined by a set of influences that include people, surely, but also pressures—both of tradition and politics. And it has been actualized by a set of mechanisms that collectively have both ratified existing practices and provided impetus for change.

This chapter treats historically and interpretatively some of these technical aspects of curriculum development. The chapter is not intended to provide an exhaustive history of curriculum making in the United States. Hopefully it will lay some foundation for individuals who wish

Left: Parents of rising generations in school studying agriculture, reading, writing, arithmetic in one of Mrs. Cora Wilson Stewart's moonlight schools, Rowan County, Kentucky, *ca.* 1916.

to build their own histories of the processes of curriculum development. It offers an invitation to readers to reflect on the curriculum field—past, present, and future—to take satisfaction in its achievements and to ascertain its shortcomings, in an effort to renew our commitment to the educational experiment.

Influences of Curriculum Development

Clearly, the number of forces that have influenced curriculum development in American schools has been large, and an extensive treatment is unfeasible in this survey. A few appear to offer interpretive interest. Tradition, understood not only in its more usual connotation as the conservative maintenance of the status quo but also in evolutionary, developmental terms, is one. Reformers and reform schemes are another. And teachers, perhaps the greatest and certainly the most immediate determiners of curriculum experiences in the classroom are yet another.

Tradition

Education, although considered very important by the colonials, was not a carefully conceived notion. Neither did it have carefully defined activities for determining what was to be included. Cremin has stated that the curriculum tradition in colonial schools was a rude one at best. The rural agragian settlements were not conducive to a precisely carried out educational effort. In our early years, education was viewed, if at all, as an opportunity to gain the basic tools of communication.[1]

The religious influence also was dominant in affecting the purpose of education and to a large degree what it included and excluded from the curriculum. In the Massachusetts Bay Colony, the Calvinist community held the belief that individuals were responsible for the salvation of their own souls. This required the ability to read and interpret the Bible. But one could not interpret the Bible in any way other than according to the Calvinist creed. Therefore, there was need for a somewhat structured educational experience. In New England, education and the resulting curriculum were conceived from the dual tasks of practicality and salvation.

Thus during colonial times, an educational precedent developed in New England that emphasized both practicality and religion. The early

[1] Lawrence A. Cremin. *The American Common School: An Historical Conception.* New York: Bureau of Publications, Teachers College, Columbia University, 1951.

schools during colonial times had curricula influenced by the Bible and any practical materials available. At first these materials were few, but as they became more numerous, the curriculum was affected to a greater degree. One can make a case that the technical principle of having the curriculum influenced, indeed determined, by the materials available was established in colonial schools. In the majority of schools, we still find that the curriculum is what the materials are.

The tradition established first in the New England area and later in New York created a solid foundation for public responsibility for education and gave impetus to the evolution of the common school. Much of the rise of the common school was facilitated by giants in the field of education. James G. Carter, one such giant, was a pioneer in New England education. In the early nineteenth century, he noted that the establishment of private education in New England was having a deleterious effect upon the curriculum offered in the public schools. Individuals were devoting their energies to the creation of quality private schools, thus neglecting the public schools. As Carter analyzed the situation, he discovered two major inadequacies in the public schools: poorly prepared instructors and limited quality school books. He realized that the quality of the curriculum as to what was included and what was stressed depended to a most significant degree on teachers and the material they employed. Carter felt that the most effective way of correcting the weaknesses of common school education was for the state to assert its authority over public education. To overcome the problem of poorly prepared teachers, he advocated the establishment of teacher training institutions that would have both a literary and scientific character. By this emphasis, Carter intended that such a character would filter into the curriculum of the common schools.[2]

Carter's efforts resulted in the establishment of the Massachusetts Board of Education in 1837. The previous year, the American Institute of Instruction had petitioned the Massachusetts General Court for the establishment and appointment of a superintendent of common schools. Such an individual, the Institute reasoned, might aid the common school and provide direction to the evolving school districts by monitoring the quality of their teachers and assessing the effectiveness of their instruction.

Creation of the position of superintendent was to have a significant effect on the school and its curriculum. It is of interest to note that not only was attention directed to teachers and their instruction, but also to determining the nature of the educational environment in which the cur-

---

[2] R. Freeman Butts and Lawrence A. Cremin. *A History of Education in American Culture.* New York: Holt, Rinehart and Winston, 1953. p. 205 f.

riculum would be experienced. This concern for the inclusion of particular types of learning environments has not received the attention it deserves.[3]

In 1837, an eight-member Board was appointed by the governor and the council. The Board had no direct authority, but it provided guidance to educators in the state through the publication of abstracts dealing with special school concerns. With the creation of the Board, most educators felt that Carter would be appointed superintendent. However, it was offered to Horace Mann. Mann remained in this position for twelve years, and carried out the Board's responsibilities via four communication channels: public meetings, county institutes for teachers, annual reports, and a biweekly publication entitled *The Common School Journal*. Mann's annual reports became especially significant documents in the evolution of American educational thought.[4]

Not everything that Mann advocated was greeted without resistance. Yet, as time went on, the state assumed an increasing role in ascertaining that instruction in the schools was both efficient and of high quality. It set the stage for influencing curricula. The seeds for the process of curriculum building were planted, even though the precise delineation of stages for curriculum decision making was still to be accomplished.

Largely as a result of Mann's efforts, the principle of public control became well established in Massachusetts. Those who controlled the educational process, both on state and local levels began to demand that public funds be withdrawn from those schools remaining under private direction. Thus the common school gained strength and included a broader curriculum and more students, while the private schools maintained their curriculum in a type of steady state, usually drawing from the classical model, reduced the number of pupils they served and aimed at serving a more select student population.

By the mid-1800's every state was involved in public support and control of education. The firm principle of state control in setting the guidelines for the curriculum and educational experience resulted in part from the legal precedents and enabling legislation that had occurred in previous years. Such state control resulted as the state contributed increasingly to the support of public education. The position of state superintendent facilitated this development.

---

[3] For additional comments on learning environments, see: Francis P. Hunkins and Patricia F. Spears. *Social Studies for the Evolving Individual*. Washington, D.C.: Association for Supervision and Curriculum Development, 1973.

[4] For a representative sampling of Mann's reports, see: Rena L. Vassar, editor. *Social History of American Education: Colonial Times to 1860*. Chicago: Rand McNally, 1965, Vol. I.

Even though the state had written itself into the dominant role regarding control of education and thus the curriculum, three positions were usually in evidence: (a) educational responsibility was given to the local community where decision making regarding inclusion and exclusion would be considered; (b) the state would control education through a delegation of powers to the local community wherever possible and feasible; and (c) the state assumed that the community would obtain financial support from the community.[5] This delegation of powers regarding educational decision making and support has evolved to the present time without too much alteration.

There were, of course, other reformers who contributed to the rise of the common school. Henry Barnard was active in Connecticut doing basically what Mann had done to make education more responsive to the needs of the time. In the South, Calvin Wiley of North Carolina and Charles Fenton Mercer of Virginia were active in advancing the common-school ideal. Caleb Mills of Indiana, Calvin Stowe, Samuel Lewis, and Samuel Galloway of Ohio, Ninian Edwards of Illinois, John D. Pierce and Isaac Drary of Michigan, Robert Breckinridge of Kentucky, and John Sweet of California all were actively involved in strengthening the common school.[6]

The American Lyceum, organized by Joshia Holbrook in 1826, was a most influential organization regarding the curriculum of the common school. This organization's major aim was the improvement of its members via obtaining useful information. But, the organization also was eager to advance the idea of popular education. The organization urged the introduction of uniformity in the school's curriculum as well as improvement in the materials and instructional methods. This significantly affected the issue of inclusion and exclusion of curriculum topics.

During the latter part of the nineteenth century, an individual emerged who was to contribute to the advancement of the technical aspect of curriculum development: Francis W. Parker. Dewey called him "the father of progressive education." Parker's ideas regarding curriculum were based on the unity of nature and the then recent findings of child study. Parker believed that instruction should be patterned on the child's natural way of learning. Children often learned in unstructured ways with no formal instruction. Following this idea Parker adopted the word method of teaching reading in which children learned to read the way in which they comprehended and gained facility in language. Conversation was cultivated as an art in the Quincy schools, which represented a significant innovation.

[5] Cremin, *American Common School*, pp. 142-50; 175-78.
[6] *Ibid.*, p. 49.

Parker also attended to the environment in which children would experience learning. Not all learning was to take place in the school; students in Quincy took field trips around the town to obtain information. Information was recorded via sketches and ideas were tested out using mud models of the Quincy landscape.[7]

Parker's efforts brought him fame and allowed him to go to Chicago in 1883 where he became the principal of the Cook County Normal School. At this institution, he developed his ideas on curriculum. He introduced into general discussion the theory of unification or concentration of subject matter, an example of the developing sophistication of the technical aspects of curriculum activity. Parker suggested that content be unified into central subjects. Such organization of subject matter would reflect a more valid representation of nature. As to what to include in these central subjects, Parker urged that we look to the child for suggestions. The child, he believed, experienced instinctively all subjects currently identified. Therefore, aspects of all the major subjects could be included in the curriculum but should not appear as separate subjects in the curriculum. This view appears as a predecessor to the concept of spiral curriculum.

Parker believed that all learning took place through the senses, and he divided learning into the categories of attention and expression. Under models of attention were observation, hearing, language, and reading. The study of central subjects would provide opportunities for learning the oral and written dimensions of language. Models of expression were physical, and Parker listed the following: gesture, voice, music making, modeling, painting, drawing, and writing. Both the modes of attention and expression were to be taught simultaneously.

Parker's theory of curriculum concentration or unification was based in part on Herbart's principles of correlation and concentration. But, whereas Parker indicated that the child was the pivotal point on which to formulate curriculum, Charles De Garmo, president of the Herbart Society, urged that the curriculum be organized around a central subject.

The idea of the primacy of content over the primacy of the child became a very real issue between the Herbartians and Parker. But, there was not total agreement among the Herbartians as to what content should serve as the central organizer. The Herbartians identified content subjects as distinguishable from formal subjects. Content subjects would be such as history, geography, or botany, while grammar and mathe-

[7] Daniel Tanner and Laurel Tanner. *Curriculum Development: Theory into Practice.* New York: Macmillan, 1975. pp. 197-201.

matics would be formal subjects. A technical guideline relating to the instructional component of curriculum was that students would learn the formal subjects and some of the content subjects by focusing on their relationships to the central subjects or topics of the curriculum. Arithmetic, reading, writing, and other formal or process subjects were to be related to history, science, and literature.[8]

De Garmo advocated that the principles that comprise the structure of a given subject were more important and more constant than the relationships that exist between one subject and another subject. In a sense, we have here an early expounding of the technical concept of structure of a discipline which would serve as a guiding technical principle in the selection and organization of content.

It was evident that educational thinking during these latter years of the nineteenth century was influenced by Darwin's evolutionary hypothesis of recapitulation. This belief implied that the child in his or her development must recapitulate the intellectual and moral development of mankind epoch by epoch. This idea became popular with the Herbartians as a principle for dealing with the technical aspect of content selection and sequence and material selection. What to include and what to exclude would be on the basis of the child's stage of development. A deficiency in this stance is that it ignores the contributions of the environment of the individual. Environments do differ and the environment of modern humanity is vastly different from the environment experienced by our early ancestors. A second danger in accepting this technical principle in total was that individuals do differ in their capacities for learning. Despite these limitations, the Herbartians adopted the theory as a major technical guideline for curriculum development and inclusion.

Superintendents also were frequently leaders in suggesting or retarding innovation for the schools in general and the curriculum in particular. One superintendent who played both roles was William Torrey Harris, superintendent of the St. Louis public schools. Harris was a spokesman for modern academic studies. He believed in both modern and classical studies for passing on the wisdom of the race. He did believe in the disciplinary value of certain subjects for training the will, but he was not an advocate of mental discipline. His view of education was that its function was to serve as a stabilizing force. One of his most creative views was that he considered a generation discon-

[8] Edward A. Krug. *The Shaping of the American High School.* New York: Harper and Row, 1964. pp. 99-111. See also: Mary Louise Seguel. *The Curriculum Field: Its Formative Years.* New York: Teachers College Press, 1966, for a discussion of Herbartian influence in curriculum thought.

tented with their lot a tribute to education, rather than a defect. He urged that the curriculum should stimulate in students a questioning view.

Harris's influence on education during the latter years of the nineteenth century was increased when, in 1889, he became Commissioner of Education. His belief in the practical dimension of schooling served to influence educational thinking during this time. Krug mentions that Harris's reputation as a giant in education was flawed only by his lack of enthusiasm for the increasing partiality of educators toward manual training in the school.[9] However, part of this lack of enthusiasm might have been due to the confusion of persons at that time regarding the meaning of manual training and vocational education.

Reform Proposals

With increasing knowledge about the nature of human development, there were individuals who began to question the basic organization of the schools' curricula. The ideas of flexible grading and promotion plans were suggested as means of meeting diversity among pupils. One approach which gained prominence was the Batavia Plan, inaugurated by Superintendent John Kennedy in the mid 1870's. This plan was designed to assist teachers in bringing slow achievers up to grade level in their subjects in order that they could be promoted with the rest of their class. A plan designed to meet the needs of gifted pupils was the Cambridge, Massachusetts Plan inaugurated in 1910. This plan had two parallel courses of study, one taking eight years and designed for the average child and a parallel course taking six years intended for the gifted child.

A more comprehensive approach that did attempt to meet the needs of a more inclusive student population began in late nineteenth-century Baltimore. The Baltimore Plan as conceived by Superintendent James H. Van Sickle provided, via a one-class school system, curricula that would meet the needs of individuals. The experiment's central idea was that all children were different in mental capacity and also in future possibilities. Children fell into three groups: the slow, the average, and the gifted. Educators, primarily teachers, were to create a course of study for each child tailored to his or her capacities and future possibilities. Here we had what some would call "personalized" education in the making.

The Baltimore Plan made provisions for students transferring from one group to another. In the first six years of schooling, the courses

---

[9] Krug, *Shaping of the American High School*, pp. 22-23.

prepared could vary in the amount of work done or expected, but the time dimension would remain the same. These were adjustments of scope primarily, with teachers making decisions to include "enrichment" topics for students classified as gifted. After the initial six years, which served somewhat as a sorting period to identify those students who would be included in the gifted category and conversely those who would be excluded from this category, the teachers were to provide the gifted students with opportunities to advance more rapidly, take extra studies, and enjoy educational advantages that would facilitate the development of their superior intellectual capacities.

This plan served as an example for educators wishing to establish differentiated classes and flexible grading. By 1890, such ideas were becoming rather commonplace. By 1910, special schools were being created in which individualized curricula were offered for special students in personalized learning environments.

The creation of plans to meet the changing perceptions of pupils' needs extended into the twentieth century. The Dalton Plan, introduced at Dalton, Massachusetts in 1919, used the regular curriculum but allowed pupils to follow their own paths through the program. Included in the curriculum were various "jobs," one for each month of the year. Each job was subdivided into 20 units. Pupils were given job cards, somewhat akin to today's pupil contracts. On each of these job cards, a pupil would record his or her work and measure his or her progress. At the end of each month, the teacher would ascertain with each pupil that all jobs for that particular month were completed. Critics of this program argued that the job cards restricted pupils to learning a highly structured curricular experience.

During the same year as the Dalton Plan, another plan for organizing the educational experience was developed in Winnetka, Illinois. Carleton Washburne conceived this plan to divide the curriculum into two main parts: (a) common knowledges or skills, such as reading, spelling, writing, counting, and language usage essential for all pupils; and (b) activities geared to self-expression. In the common curriculum division, students progressed at their own rate. But the variable was time, not content; once the essential content had been determined, all students had to experience it. However, there was great flexibility in the self-expression curriculum component. No fixed standards were adhered to, and an attempt was made to adapt to pupil ability.

One approach which gained national attention at the beginning of the twentieth century was the Gary Plan conceived by Superintendent Willard Wirt. Development of this plan occurred during the years 1908 through 1915. Wirt suggested a school run on a four-quarter plan, with each quarter consuming 12 weeks. Wirt attended to the school environment in addition to the curriculum. He created in his school plant a playground, a garden, a workshop, a social center, a library, and a traditional type school. Also innovative was the idea of housing elementary and high school under the same roof. This allowed for some elementary children being taught high school subjects as early as the fifth grade.

Wirt's plan envisioned maximum school use. Often he would have outdoor activities and shop work carried on at the same time as indoor classes. He even had his school in operation on Saturdays. In the evenings, his schools were opened as recreation centers and social-function places. Throughout the schools in Gary, play and vocational work were important features.[10] Optimal use of school plants was becoming popular at this time with the beginning of the efficiency movement. The Gary idea had features which make it look like the parent idea for such current and recent innovations as the Dual Progress Plan of George Stoddard, the school within a school organization, the continuous school year, and the community school concept. Many schools of the time modified the Gary Plan and created what became known as the platoon system.

These plans offered models for consideration by educators as to what to include and exclude in the curriculum as well as ways to organize the learning environment. Many of the central ideas of these plans supplied the foundation for the schools that were to be developed under the move to progressive education.

During the fifties and sixties, the schools entered a period in which the scholars assumed major responsibility for curriculum development. Along with the updating of content came an emphasis on having students experience subject matter in such ways as to develop their rational powers. Discovery was in. The emphasis on discovery was stimulated greatly by the publication of Jerome Bruner's book, *The Process of Education*.[11] Bruner explained the basic principles of discovery and also introduced to the general public and to the majority of educators the concept of structure. Neither discovery nor structure was a new idea. Parker had urged discovery and active involvement in learning. Dewey

[10] Ellwood P. Cubberley. *Public Education in the United States.* Boston: Houghton Mifflin, 1919. Revised edition, 1934. pp. 522-31. Although Cubberley's interpretations are somewhat outdated, his descriptive material, especially as related to these plans, is helpful. On the Gary Plan, see Ronald D. Cohen, "The Gary Schools and Progressive Education in the 1920's." Paper presented at the Annual Meeting of the American Educational Research Association, Washington, D.C. 1975.

[11] Jerome Bruner. *The Process of Education.* Cambridge, Massachusetts: Belknap Press, 1960.

had urged activity and processing of information. Yet, Bruner was accepted by the public and the profession, if not as the originator at least as the main advocate of discovery.

From the scholars and their work came numerous curriculum projects. In mathematics the University of Illinois Committee on School Mathematics (UICSM) created in 1951 the first mathematics curriculum project. Other mathematics projects created at the university level and introduced to the schools were the School Mathematics Program, the Madison Project of Syracuse University and Webster College, and the University of Maryland Mathematics Project.[12] Physics evolved a new program under the guidance of the Physical Science Study Committee and developed by Educational Services Incorporated. From the University of Illinois came the Elementary School Science Project. From the University of California came the Science Curriculum Improvement Study (SCIS) which is still one of the most popular of the science curriculum programs. The Biological Sciences Curriculum Study produced three sets of materials designed to differ in approach, but each organized around the same unifying concepts. Here an attempt was made to meet the diverse needs of students. In chemistry, the Chemical Bond Approach Project, originally directed from Earlham College in Richmond, Indiana, appeared on the educational scene. The American Chemical Society was instrumental in introducing the Chemical Education Material Study (CHEM STUDY).

Curriculum projects in the social sciences seemed to get a slow start. But, they made up for lost time and by the mid-1960's there was a legion of social science projects. Some of the early ones were the Minnesota Project, the Syracuse Project, the High School Geography Project, the Amherst Project, and the University of Georgia Project. All of the subject areas of the social sciences began to be represented either in separate subject approaches such as the Georgia Anthropology Project or in fused approaches such as the Greater Cleveland Social Science Program.

The scholars of the 1960's addressed their demands primarily to updating curriculum content, reorganizing curriculum elements, and introducing some innovative approaches to subject matter. In other words, they were concerned primarily with the development of materials rather than the procedures for creating curriculum or for introducing curriculum changes into schools. In their attention to specific content, the scholars

---

[12] John Goodlad, Renata Von Steophasius, and M. Frances Klein. *The Changing School Curriculum.* New York: The Fund for the Advancement of Education, 1966. pp. 11-15.

ignored for the most part the technical aspects of implementation and maintenance. Perhaps because of these oversights, many of the innovations of the fifties and sixties failed to achieve maximum or even optimal utilization.[13]

Teachers

When discussing significant persons affecting curriculum decision making relating to inclusion and exclusion, one cannot neglect the teachers and principals who worked in the schools. Surely it was the teachers who considered the ideas of the major figures in educational discourse and, when they shut their doors, became the crucial persons regarding what would be included or excluded from the curriculum.

During the period from 1860 to 1890, educators at all levels had a disciplinary conception of education. Subjects were included in the curriculum if they were thought able to contribute to the discipline of an individual's mental faculties. Yet educators also were coming to believe that school should assist in the development of the inborn capacities of children. School was to be a place where the potentials of children were developed to maximum fulfillment. This idea of school and thus the curricular experience was in large part influenced by the thinking of Pestalozzi.

Pestalozzi's ideas cast the teachers and principals not in the role of drill masters, but rather as stimulators of pupils' learning. Teachers were considered to have the crucial role in deciding upon the nature of the children's learning experiences.[14] Teachers selected the problems to which children would attend, and teachers provided the necessary guidance to assist children in studying the problems. During this time, teachers were coming to view the child and his or her needs and welfare as guidelines for curriculum inclusion rather than that of the subject matter which had been the case in the early part of the nineteenth century.

Mechanisms of Curriculum Development

Although subject to multiple influences, the curriculum acquires concrete form and substance through a set of mechanisms which arbitrate tradition and change for a given historical era. Conventional dis-

---

13 *Ibid.*

14 For an early definitive statement on Pestalozzi, see: Hermann Krüsi. *Pestalozzi: His Life, Work, and Influence.* New York: American Book Company, 1875.

course has tended to concentrate on conscious deliberation among curriculum workers as the prime avenue of curricular change. Significant though these reflective procedures may be, curriculum modification has also resulted from the more implicit and frequently more continuous processes of accretion and changing social sensibilities. The following sections contain a selective review of these mechanisms, both systematic and incidental, which have served to fashion curriculum in American schools.

Action by Committees

Beginning in the latter part of the nineteenth century, several national committees were established to deliberate on the content and direction of American education. These committees not only influenced the curricular offerings of schools but also created a pattern for curriculum development practices at the state and local levels. The curriculum committee became a means of deciding the content and structure of the educational program and, perhaps even more important, a method of including professional and lay participation in curriculum construction. In many ways the reports of these committees as well as the composition of committee membership defined the nature and thrust of schooling at a given point in American educational history.

The first wave of national committees resulted from the efforts of Charles W. Eliot, president of Harvard. Eliot, in 1888, read a paper entitled "Can School Programs Be Shortened and Enriched?" at the NEA meeting in Washington, D.C. As a result of this speech, three committees were created by the National Educational Association: the Committee of Ten on Secondary School Studies, the Committee of Fifteen on Elementary Education, and the Committee on College Entrance Requirements. It is of some interest to note that there was no attention directed to pupil abilities, social needs, student interests, student capacities, or special training for students.[15] In one sense, the committees were hindered by a myopic vision of the subject-centered or disciplinary emphasis of the curriculum.

Eliot as chairman of the Committee of Ten delved into his task believing the French and German schools superior to those in the United States. Thus he tended to view what to include and exclude in the curriculum utilizing a rather limited model. He did, however, believe in the elective principle, for he felt that mental discipline was best

[15] Tanner and Tanner, *Curriculum Development*, pp. 172-74.

developed when people worked in depth on a few subjects in which they possessed both interest and capability.[16]

The Committee of Ten focused largely on determining what needed to be included in secondary education to allow entrance into college. Of course not all were to attend college, but the members of the committee believed that the education which would prepare one most favorably for entrance into college would also prepare one for successful participation in life. The Committee selected nine subjects on which recommendations were made: Latin; Greek; English; other modern language; mathematics; physics, astronomy, and chemistry; natural history (biology, including botany, zoology, and physiology); history, civil government, and political economy; and geography (physical geography, geology, and meteorology. The Committee's inclusion of these subjects and the exclusion of others set the pattern for the modern secondary school curriculum. Many readers will recognize their current secondary curriculum divisions. The Committee's efforts were a significant factor in making the status quo a very permanent feature of the secondary school curriculum.

What the Committee of Ten did for secondary school curricula, the Committee of Fifteen, chaired by Superintendent William H. Maxwell of Brooklyn, did for the elementary school curricula. The Committee members organized themselves into three subcommittees; one dealing with the training of teachers, one centering on the organization of city school systems, and one focusing on studies relating to elementary education. Attention was on what to include, whom to include, and in what educational environment the curriculum and the clients would interact.

Maxwell, early in the Committee's deliberations, used the term "coordination of studies" but then changed to the term "correlation of studies." Correlation was becoming a popular term, and it referred to the relationships among studies and to those arrangements requisite for bringing out and developing these relationships. One problem was that the "correlation" was a term used by both the Committee of Ten and the Herbartians. To the Herbartians, correlation meant the relationship of some of the subjects of study to the central subjects or centers of concentration which were to serve as organizers. However, there was no agreement as to what subjects should be the curriculum organizers.

The Committee's report was presented on February 20, 1895 to a session of the Department of Superintendents at Cleveland. The report covered not only correlation but presented a plan for an eight-year elementary school period with a program of studies including reading,

---

[16] Krug, *Shaping of the American High School*, p. 19.

writing, spelling, English grammar, arithmetic, United States history, general history, geography, vocal music, natural science, physical culture, and manual training or sewing plus cookery. Drawing some influence from the Committee of Ten, the elementary report suggested Latin in the eighth year of schooling and algebra and geometry in the seventh and eighth years.[17]

To many the report presented nothing new. Nicholas Murray Butler dismissed the entire report as nothing more than a defense of the status quo, for the report did not advocate the inclusion of any subject matter or experiences that were not then treated in some fashion. As with the Committee of Ten's report, this report had the respectability of being the "best" thinking of the "best" minds in the nation. The questions of what to include in the curriculum, what to exclude from the curriculum, and whom to consult about the nature of the curriculum were answered: Curriculum should be designed by Committee proclamation. These two committees did much to establish a frame of reference with regard to curriculum decision making.

During the first two decades of the twentieth century, increasing attention by educators and lay public was being given to the efficiency of the educational effort. This interest led in 1911 to the creation of the NEA Committee on the Economy of Time. The goal of the Committee was to eliminate waste in the curriculum and the total educational effort. The Committee also dealt with two emerging issues of substantial consequence. First, new research was being published that called into question the idea of mental discipline. Therefore, this concept could no longer serve as a central principle for content selection. Second, research was revealing that the period of time spent on particular subjects had little relationship to the results. Hence there was a need to reconsider the allocation of time in schools.

The Committee's work was done in phases with the first directed at determining what was being taught in the schools. The Committee found that there was no overall basis to support the median time spent on a particular subject. What was done became the guide for what should be done. Tanner has called this process curriculum development by common denominator.[18] The Committee's second phase was directed to specific content of the curriculum. The Committee employed the principle of social utility to determine appropriateness of curriculum content. In essence, the Committee determined that what children ought to be learning in their curriculum was what people outside of school

[17] *Ibid.*, pp. 97-100.
[18] Tanner and Tanner, *Curriculum Development*, pp. 285-86.

knew and did. History content was selected by what the history books, the encyclopedias, the newspapers, and the current magazines were talking about. One possible shortcoming is that such an approach determines curriculum inclusion by using "today" as the basis for "tomorrow." Such thinking, unless it takes into consideration trends, usually recommends the creation of a curriculum that perpetuates the status quo.

By the end of the second decade of the twentieth century, it was evident that some of the suggestions of the Committee of Ten and the Committee of Fifteen had not served educators as well as originally thought. Studies were revealing that the citizen's dollar for education was not being used in a way that optimized learning for the greatest number of pupils. Few children leaving elementary school proceeded to secondary school, and of those attending the secondary school, only one third opted to stay until graduation. What was included in the curriculum, as determined by the "scholars" in the disciplines, was causing many students to decide to exclude themselves from the formal school experience. The needs of a democratic society were not being met by the narrow interpretation that only "classical" education was necessary for meeting the needs of the twentieth-century citizen. Also, new educational theory was being formulated that required educators to reconceptualize their views of the curriculum and the total educational experience.

A spokesman for an expanded view of the purpose of education was Abraham Flexner. In 1916 he wrote *A Modern College and a Modern School* in which he indicated that the purpose of education was to prepare individuals to function effectively on their own. Such functioning required an understanding of the physical and the social world, an understanding which necessitated opportunities to encounter content dealing with contemporary industry, politics, and science.[19] This program was in direct contrast with what Eliot and his committee had recommended.

Tradition by itself was an inadequate guide as to what to include or exclude, Flexner asserted. In his school the curriculum was organized around four basic fields: science, industry, aesthetics, and civics, with science as the central organizer. In Flexner's schools, teachers had an active role in the issue of control of the curriculum. They were responsible for developing and testing educational materials and were charged with reconstructing the curriculum to reflect the emphases advocated by Flexner.

Flexner's school, which opened in 1917, was later called the Lincoln School of Teachers College. It represented a joint effort of the General Education Board, which had been created by John D. Rockefeller in

19 *Ibid.*, pp. 221-22.

1902, and Teachers College. In the school traditional education still had a place, and the introduction of new subjects into the curriculum was made only after careful analysis of the need and use of the subject. New ideas were often tested in a laboratory setting in the school. Perhaps the central point of the school was that educators were involved dramatically in the curriculum arena.

Times were changing and the ideas relating to the purpose of the schools' curriculum were being reanalyzed. In 1913, the National Education Association appointed the Commission on the Reorganization of Secondary Education. Educators now realized the need for new principles to guide educators in creating curricula that would meet the needs of educating a populace for full participation in democracy. Again, we have curriculum development being practiced by a committee. After five years of work, the Commission issued its report under the title of the *Cardinal Principles of Secondary Education.*

In the report it was stated that "secondary education should be determined by the needs of the society to be served, the character of the individuals to be educated, and the knowledge of educational theory and practice available." [20] With this document the Commission made known the bases for curriculum development: the society, the nature of the student population, and educational theory. This report had a profound effect and still maintains dominant influence on the nature of the secondary school and its curriculum. Certainly the three major sources of the curriculum as outlined by the Commission became the defining elements of curriculum discourse in the twentieth century.

The crux of the Commission's report names seven principal objectives or "Cardinal Principles": (a) health, (b) command of fundamental processes (reading, writing, arithmetic, and oral and written expression), (c) worthy home membership, (d) vocation, (e) citizenship, (f) worthy use of leisure time, and (g) ethical character. The comprehensive high school was deemed as the most appropriate vehicle for achieving these goals. What was to be included and excluded in the curriculum was to be determined in large part by these principles.

The Commission's work represents a clear example of how the direction of curriculum emphasis has been affected by the work of committees. Even today, the major thrusts of curriculum are influenced in a similar manner. However, how much current thinking regarding the nature of curriculum actually appears in the classroom depends upon the decisions and judgments of the classroom teacher. It was then and

---

[20] Commission on the Reorganization of Secondary Education. *Cardinal Principles of Secondary Education.* Washington, D.C.: U.S. Government Printing Office, 1918. p. 7.

still is a truism that the classroom teacher is the crucial person in the control of the actual curriculum.

Educational commissions continued to be dominant influences of the curriculum well into the twentieth century. In 1935, the NEA created the Educational Policies Commission to confront the crisis created by the Great Depression. From their deliberations resulted a report stressing four comprehensive aims of education: (a) self-realization, (b) human relationships, (c) economic efficiency, and (d) civic responsibility. The first aim stressed the inquiring mind, reading, writing, calculating, speech, health, creation, aesthetics, and character. The second aim addressed itself to respect for humanity, friendship, cooperation, courtesy, and home membership. The third aim centered on vocation and consumer economics, and the fourth aim was concerned with social justice, social understanding and action, critical judgment, tolerance, and democratic citizenship.[21]

The National Education Association still is active in providing national direction for the American school. The NEA's Center for the Study of Instruction gathered educators together in December of 1969 to address the question of the nature of schools for the coming decade. "It was little short of astonishing that within four hours after the Schools For The 70's Seminar began, each of the six discussion groups concluded independently that the major goal for educational reform in the coming decade was that of making the schools humane institutions—the same conclusion resulting from a three-year study conducted by Charles E. Silberman and financed by the Carnegie Corporation."[22] The Seminar participants concluded that the development of humaneness, the development of each student as a totally effective human being, was a crucial and integral goal of the curriculum. This emphasis should be included and developed in such a way that it is the essence of the curricular experience. The Commission members urged that the curriculum lessen the emphasis on the retention of facts and increase the emphasis on the processes of inquiry, comparison, interpretation, and synthesis. The stress was to include in the curriculum situations which would facilitate "learning how to learn" and the creating of a desire to continue the learning process. Additionally, the curriculum of the present and future school should consider the development of students' emotions, attitudes, ideals, ambitions, and values. Students should be

[21] Educational Policies Commission. *The Purposes of Education in American Democracy.* Washington, D.C.: National Educational Association, 1938.

[22] NEA Center for the Study of Instruction (A special project of the National Education Association). *Schools for the 70's and Beyond: A Call to Action.* Washington, D.C.: the Center, 1971. p. 17.

allowed to use these areas as valid foci for investigation. Such accentuation would assist individuals in developing a sense of respect for self and others, the crucial dimension of humanism.

When reviewing the past three quarters of a century, one can see that change has taken place, however gradual it may have been. But, change is still necessary, for time is not a static phenomenon. However, one thing that has remained rather constant is the influence of national "blue ribbon" committees in playing a role of determining the major directions of the curriculum in American schools.

Significant Groups and the Curriculum— Demands and Mechanisms for Involvement and Input

Throughout our history individuals have organized themselves into groups or have been recognized as group members by others for myriad reasons. This organization and/or recognition of a group as a significant

Field trip to Chesapeake and Ohio Canal, Washington, D.C., *ca.* 1900. F. B. Johnston, photographer.

element to be involved in the educational experiment has taken different stances at particular periods in our nation's development. Demands for involvement and input have really been in response to the basic questions of who shall experience education and what is the nature of that experience.

Public schools are public institutions and certain segments of the public have, during various times, demanded involvement, and in some instances, control of the direction of the school and its curriculum. Currently, schools are involved dramatically in the issue of control; schools are engaged in responding to political power plays by specific groups. Much of the current politicalization of the school has resulted from activities of the 60's. During those years there arose a call from many citizens for involvement, for community participation. Federal school aid legislation of this period also encouraged citizens to participate in their schools' decision making as to the nature of curriculum and the functions it was to serve. In many instances advisory commissions were required, and schools were directed to consult with community groups.

The movement which began in the 60's has continued to gain momentum in this decade. Educators are confronted today by demands from a multitude of interest groups, all wishing to supply input into educational decision making. These interest groups run the gamut from quasi political groups such as the Daughters of the American Revolution, Veterans of Foreign Wars, and the John Birch Society to Students for Democratic Action and other New Left organizations. In between are groups representing various minorities that wish to have the curriculum include more content dealing with their role in the development of our nation, as well as special kinds of education to meet their unique needs. Many of these groups can be considered crisis groups, for crisis, either real or perceived, has spawned them. Many of them have used protest as a means to focus their concerns and pressure educators for concrete action. Unlike the pattern in the recent past, most groups today are proceeding through more usual legal and social channels in their attempts at providing input. One should also include in interest groups the school boards, superintendents, administrative personnel, teachers and students. Connected with these groups are various professional organizations, such as the NEA and the ASCD, which provide considerable weight behind demands for involvement in curriculum decision making. Too there are still indirect and direct attempts to influence the curriculum-making process and the resultant curriculum by business organizations that may have interest in education from the standpoint of receiving graduates able to be assimilated effectively into their businesses. Educational publishers and foundations are also very influential groups in controlling the nature of the curriculum, especially from the standpoint of what will be included or excluded.

At the present time in our nation's history, the demands by special minority groups for involvement in curriculum decision making for the purpose of making education more meaningful for their children are at an apex of activity. For this reason, some attention is given here to how the schools have dealt with blacks, Chicanos, Indians, and women in the past, and also to how education currently is dealing with these groups.

Blacks and the Curricular Experience

Throughout colonial and early national periods there were whites who believed that blacks should receive some type of education. They should, it was felt, be included in some type of formal or semiformal curriculum. During the demands for freedom in the period leading to the American Revolution, individuals like Patrick Henry and James Otis at least felt that slaves were entitled to some freedoms. Many of these people did free their slaves. Those who were freed required some degree of education in order to function in the free society. Missions and churches often took the responsibility for educating them.

Yet even before the increase in the number of freed people, some individuals in the colonies advocated education for blacks. Usually these people fell into three classes: masters of slaves who desired to improve their investments in slaves by making them more efficient; sympathetic persons who felt compelled to assist the oppressed blacks; and missionaries, who believed it their duty to bring the Christian religion, via education, to the blacks.[23]

The gradual freeing of the slaves and the educating of the resulting freed people might have happened during the early period of our nation's history had it not been for two things. The first was the worldwide industrial movement. Industrialization revolutionized the textile industry with the invention of spinning and weaving machines. The introduction of this technology resulted in an increased demand for cotton which in return required vast acreage devoted to cotton. Thus the plantation system of the South was given a great impetus and the demand for slaves became firmly established. Southern planters felt it unwise to educate one destined to live the life of a slave. Many planters considered it more profitable to work a slave to death than to educate a slave to perform more efficiently. Thus there occurred a reversal in thinking

[23] C. G. Woodson. *The Education of the Negro Prior to 1861.* New York: Arno Press and the New York Times, 1968. p. 2.

from a view of a profitable slave as one who was educated and efficient, to one who was strong, uneducated, and easily expendable.

The second force which caused a reversal in thinking about educating blacks was that many freed blacks who had received education were now circulating information among the slaves as to the injustices perpetuated by the ruling whites. Additionally, black refugees from Haiti who resettled in Baltimore, Norfolk, Charleston, and New Orleans originated stories of how they had righted their wrongs. Stories of insurrection were common. Slaveholders lived in fear of servile insurrection. In response to these two forces, Southerners created a reactionary posture to education of any sort for blacks. By the time of the American Revolution, the majority of whites in the South had concluded that education was inappropriate for people destined for servitude and that education made them unfit for this condition.[24] The slaveholders considered education to be a powerful vehicle for improving a person's stance and also for changing society. White Southerners did not wish to share this power.

Legislation appeared in the South to exclude blacks from any type of educational experience. They were forbidden to associate freely for fear of having education passed on. Schools that had been established by the churches were closed. Several states made it a crime for blacks to teach their own children. Thus, while reformers attempted to bring more whites into the common-school experience, blacks were being excluded systematically from experiencing any education. This systematic maintenance of ignorance created a tradition which would be most difficult to overcome in the years after the Civil War.

But the reactionary movement of systematically excluding blacks from the school experience was not confined to the South. Many white communities in the North felt that the large numbers of freed and escaped slaves in their communities would be detrimental to their home environment. Anti-abolition riots occurred in the North. Free blacks were prevented from opening schools in some places and often teachers of blacks were driven from the community.

The restrictive legislation did not eliminate completely the education of blacks. Southern whites saw that it was impossible to enforce the law completely, as children of slave owners sometimes taught slaves to read and write and missionaries still tried to teach slaves the ways of Christianity. Many whites ignored the breaking of these laws as long as there were no slave insurrections. This was, after all, the main fear that had led to the drastic change of attitude toward educating blacks. By the middle of the nineteenth century, southern whites were more

[24] *Ibid.*, pp. 2-9.

disposed to educating their blacks in some of the basics of reading and religion.[25] After the Civil War vast numbers of freedmen required education to work effectively.

With the realization that the blacks now required education many philanthropists came to their aid. Most of these reformers felt that blacks needed practical education, and they attempted to provide such training by creating schools called "manual labor schools" where both classical and vocational courses would be offered. These schools were not successful and educators finally advocated actual vocational training for the blacks.

Those who recommended including blacks in the formal education experience usually recommended separate systems. Separate school systems for the blacks had been developed before the Civil War in many northern communities. Often the blacks had played significant roles in establishing these schools. Part of the impetus was because education of blacks, especially at the levels of secondary and higher education, was prohibited by the refusal of academies and colleges to admit persons of African blood. In most northern states, separate schools for the blacks were not eliminated until after the Civil War. After the war, it was the liberated blacks who built in the southern states their first effective system of free public education.

Part of the educational reform for blacks was connected to reform for the total educational system in the South. After the Civil War, the region was in need of money and ideas for rebuilding. In 1867, George Peabody established a trust fund that totaled approximately $3½ million. The purpose of the fund was to promote education in the southern states. This fund can be considered the first of the great educational foundations. The significant feature of the fund was its liberal and elastic conditions. Trustees were free to use it in any manner they deemed important for the improvement of education in the South. Monies from the fund were used to assist in the establishment of school systems in larger towns and cities. Assistance was supplied until local authorities could assume control. Thus the tradition of local control in the curriculum decision-making process was maintained. Monies also were given to support the schools until legislatures could assume responsibility for public education. The fund also established normal schools for black teachers. Another fund, the John F. Slater Fund, established in 1882, was especially created to benefit black students. It provided for the training of teachers and for industrial education for blacks.

These two funds contributed greatly to reducing the hostility held by many whites to the idea of educating blacks. Yet much of the credit

[25] *Ibid.*, pp. 11-12.

Sharecropper mother teaching children, Transylvania, Louisiana, 1939.

for the reduction in hostility must be given to the blacks themselves and to black educators who provided needed direction in the striving for including blacks in the educational experiment of this country.

One educator who made a monumental contribution to the blacks was General Samuel Chapin Armstrong. In 1866, he had been appointed superintendent of education for the colored people of Virginia under the direction of the Freedmen's Bureau. Until his death in 1893, Armstrong was a giant in influencing the policy of education for blacks and for American Indians, who were included under his jurisdiction in 1878. In 1868, Armstrong founded a new type of institute, known as Hampton Normal and Agricultural Institute. The main objective of this institution was the training of teachers and industrial leaders for both blacks and American Indians. Emphasis centered on character building, the missionary spirit, agricultural instruction, vocational courses, and the homemaking arts.

This institute was the archetype for several others throughout the country. The one that achieved the greatest national attention was that founded by a Hampton graduate, Booker T. Washington. Washington founded the Tuskegee Institute in Tuskegee, Alabama, in 1880. The curriculum at Tuskegee emphasized teacher training and included in its curriculum industrial courses and hospital and nurse training courses. It created an extension division which influenced the emphasis of black education throughout the South.

Booker T. Washington's influence spread well beyond Tuskegee Institute. Until his death in 1915, Washington was the most widely known black leader in the United States. His views on black education and on the role of the black man in society were most influential. Washington's views that blacks should prove they could be good workers before they asked for social equality largely determined the curriculum in black schools as well as the goals of black education. Washington felt that once blacks had proven their worth, the whites would grant them equal rights.[26] Time has proven Washington's basic thesis incorrect. Washington did not comprehend the importance of technical changes occurring during the period of his influence. His curriculum included emphases on jobs that were rapidly disappearing. In some cases, the expansion of the curriculum for the blacks was hindered by Washington's views of education and his powerful influence on the thinking of the black populace.[27]

An influential black who was a severe critic of Washington's views was William Edward Burghardt DuBois. DuBois felt that blacks should not wait to be accepted after proving themselves. He held that blacks should strive for equality and that the school curriculum should cater to their minds as well as their hands. DuBois challenged black intellectuals to organize for the purpose of promoting the rights of blacks in the United States. In 1905, thirty men met at Niagara Falls, Canada to consider DuBois' challenge. A result of the meeting was a list of demands which called for the termination of all forms of discrimination against blacks in the schools and in the general society. DuBois' efforts to create a viable Niagara Movement were not successful, due largely to Washington's opposition to the central thesis of the movement. With Washington against the movement, blacks as well as whites failed to support the idea advanced. However, the Niagara Movement was not in vain, for out of this initial movement was born the National Association for the Advancement of Colored People in 1910. This organization became a significant factor in influencing what would be included and excluded in the experience of blacks.

Since before Emancipation, blacks have demanded quality education and inclusion in the development, maintenance, and experiencing of common-school education. On May 17, 1954, the United States Supreme Court issued a decision of historic significance in relation to the case of *Brown* v. *the Board of Education of Topeka*. This ruling not only supported the demand for equal schools and a cessation of excluding blacks from white schools, it also upheld the drive to end racial segregation in all aspects of American life. Currently, blacks are still striving in many situations to have the full interpretation of the law enforced. Blacks and whites must analyze their current behaviors and outline what needs to be done in order to have the common school and its curriculum available to all persons.

[26] James A. Banks and Cherry A. Banks. *March Toward Freedom*, 2nd Edition. Belmont, California: Lear Siegler, Inc./Fearon Publishers, 1974. p. 83.
[27] *Ibid.*, p. 85.

Chicanos and the Curricular Experience

The successes of black Americans in achieving more of their rights triggered demands by other large minority groups previously excluded from participating in the American promise. According to Ramiréz and Castañeda [28] the Mexican American experience in public education is a statement of neglect, of exclusion from experiencing the curriculum of the common school and a prevention of incorporating in the common curriculum contributions of their culture. This neglect has prevented the Mexican American adult population from effective participation in modern American society. Ramiréz and Castañeda indicate that Mexican Americans share with the American Indian a position of dubious honor, the common experience of conquest and annexation. The Treaty of Guadalupe Hidalgo in 1848 annexed large parts of what was then Mexico and made the citizens of that region "new" citizens of the United States. However, the cultural ties and cultural ways of Mexico were not eliminated. Thus these people and their children have steadfastly maintained their culture. American schools have done much to attempt to assimilate Chicano children into the dominant Anglo culture. In this attempt they have consciously and unconsciously tried to eliminate the Mexican and Spanish cultures. Schools, in striving to implement the melting pot theory, often punished Mexican Americans for engaging in any activities of their cultures. Many schools enacted disciplinary actions for any Mexican American child caught speaking Spanish in the schools. Teachers without knowledge of the Mexican American culture and without facility in speaking Spanish were brought in to teach these children. The major components of the Spanish-American culture were excluded from the curricular experience.

The educational process has been none too successful for Mexican Americans partly because of the above reasons. Heath [29] has maintained that public school teachers have approached the education of Mexican Americans from the belief that the learners should be decultured. This process of deculturation takes place in what is included in the curriculum as well as the tests and other means which are employed to measure success.

Recently, there has been some recognition of the need for the Mexican American to experience aspects of his own culture in the common school. Part of this was evident when Title VII of the Elementary

[28] Manuel Ramiréz III and Alfredo Castañeda. *Cultural Democracy, Bicognitive Development, and Education.* New York: Academic Press, 1974. p. 1.

[29] Louis G. Heath. *Red, Brown, and Black Demands for Better Education.* Philadelphia: The Westminster Press, 1972. p. 57.

and Secondary Act of 1965 encouraged the teaching of Spanish in the schools. Grants were offered for the development of bilingual and multicultural education programs.

Part of the difficulty experienced by Mexican Americans and other minority groups stems from the schools having only one major model of the common school and one major model of the educated person. Until recently, American educators have attempted to be creative in a box. Our model of the school and its purposes has caused us to be ignorant of or to dismiss as unimportant factors from other cultures and other models of educated and successful persons. This myopia is being corrected as we seek for diversity within our unity.

There is a danger of oversimplification in our attempts to meet the needs of the Mexican Americans. Indeed the use of the term Mexican American is an oversimplification. In fact, many do not regard Mexican American as an acceptable term. There are Spanish-speaking groups in the United States who wish to be called Latin Americans, Chicanos, Hispanos, Spanish-Speaking, and La Raza.[30] These groups are diverse and any attempt to make them alike under the appellation of Mexican American or Chicano will fall short of the goal of creating curricula to meet their needs. Educators need to remain cognizant of this fact in dealing with all cultural or ethnic groups, including whites and women, served by the educational institution.

American Indians and the Curricular Experience

The educational experience of the Native Americans has been somewhat unique in that Indians are the only major minority that has a special treaty relationship with the United States government. However, they did, as previously noted, share some common distinctions with the Mexican Americans, that of being a conquered people and being included by the process of annexation. However, with the American Indian, the process of annexation and the creation of reservations have kept American Indians excluded from the mainstream of American "Anglo" life.

Heath has maintained that contemporary Indian education is neither Indian nor education.[31] It is a conscious attempt to acculturate, to integrate the Indian into the white culture at the expense of his own culture. Again, the model of the melting pot theory has, until recently, required that Indian children make a choice, inclusion in the white culture and exclusion from the Indian culture or vice versa. Now,

[30] Ramiréz and Castañeda, *op. cit.*, p. 13.

[31] Heath, *op. cit.*, pp. 28-30.

Training laundresses at U.S. Indian School, Carlisle, Pennsylvania, 1903.
F. B. Johnston, photographer.

attempts are being made to include the crucial aspects of both cultures
without excluding or eliminating one culture.

Indians currently are making demands that Indian schools be under
the control and influence of Indians. They are demanding that the
Bureau of Indian Affairs adjust its posture which previously ignored
that there was an Indian way or ways of life with particular demands
and requirements that should be met. Indians are demanding that Indian
teachers be trained and employed in Indian schools to provide effective
exemplars. Heath maintains that only a small portion of the teachers
in the Bureau's schools are Indian and while the others may be dedicated
white teachers, often they lack sufficient understanding of tribal ways
and ethnic emphasis to relate effectively to their Indian pupils.

Some of the problems relating to blending the best from several
cultural worlds are being met by Indians themselves. Some Indians are
running their own schools. Heath states that perhaps the most important Indian-administered educational institution is the Navajos' Rough
Rock Demonstration School. Another example includes the Mesquakies'
control of their own school near Tama, Iowa.

"Red Power" has not just appeared; Indian leaders organized for
political activity in 1944. The result of their efforts was the establishment of the National Congress of American Indians. This organization
has local groups around the nation which address themselves to the
many needs of Indians, including education.

Today, many Indians believe that there should be an institution
of higher education that deals solely with Indian needs. At such an
institution, Indians could be trained for authentic tribal leadership.
Indian teachers could be educated for work in Indian-run schools. In
one sense, Indians making these demands are asking for the means to

effectively exclude themselves from the major culture group. The problem of balance of not just two cultures, but the balance of many still confronts educators.

Women and Schooling

We find that, from its outset in New England, education was valued by the Puritans and that education was considered important. However, the high value which the Puritans placed on literacy for women was for a different purpose from that espoused for men. Educating women was to enable them to study the scriptures under the appropriate guidance of men. Education was not to create independent thinkers among women. In fact, the Puritans established prohibitions against women publishing books.[32]

The colonials' view of the female mind and how it could be educated was influenced by English and French thinking of the eighteenth century. Biological determinism as to role was dominant in colonial thought. Benjamin Franklin did reject the view of females as being lesser creatures than males by asserting that women also were rational beings capable of seeking and achieving happiness. But Franklin still was a product of his times, and he was influenced by biological determinism and thought that women's education should develop in them those qualities which would ensure their happiness and effective functioning within the institution of marriage. Franklin believed that marriage and reproduction were woman's natural destiny. And having such a destiny should influence that which was to be included in the curriculum for them. Women were to use their rational powers in the role of wife and mother.

This view was reinforced after the Declaration of Independence. Benjamin Rush, a Philadelphia physician, in discussing women addressed the patriotic duties of the women of the new republic. Women were to be effective members of this new republic and therefore required knowledge of domestic economy to carry out their prime responsibility of household management. The young new nation would have no servant class; therefore women would have to be competent in matters of the household. Conway notes that Rush was not bothered by the implicit assignment of women to an unofficial servant class.[33]

Rush pointed out that the American woman was indeed different from her European sister. He indicated that on American women rested

---

[32] Jill K. Conway. "Perspectives on History of Women's Education in the United States." *History of Education Quarterly.* Spring 1975, pp. 1-12.

[33] *Ibid.,* p. 3.

a responsibility not shared by other women in the world. The children of American women would be free to participate actively in the nation's government; therefore, it was their responsibility to help prepare their sons for responsible citizenship.[34]

The early pressures of the new nation facilitated a division of labor for the sexes. Males were thought responsible for political and economic matters while women were responsible for the administration of the home. In the early days of the nation, women also became the guardians of the moral standards of the nation and of the high vision of citizenship. This role of women was uniquely American and in a sense still is common in today's society. It also has implications for what women will experience in today's curriculum.

Rudolph indicated that the colonial view of woman was that she was intellectually inferior, incapable of great thought. Her place was in the home, where man assigned her a number of useful functions. Of course, on the frontier, women served many roles that in the eastern communities were reserved for men. As people settled the western regions of the new nation sex roles became less stereotyped.

Most people in the eighteenth and early nineteenth centuries considered women inferior to men intellectually, or at least different. At first, these differences demanded that if women were included in formal education then the education, the curriculum, should be such as to meet their unique needs requisite for successful functioning in the home.

This idea of a compensatory value of the female intellect was not modified to any great extent even when women were allowed entrance into college. In 1837, Oberlin College in Ohio enrolled four female freshmen. Thus was inaugurated the era of higher education for women. Women were offered the regular courses and also a special "ladies' course," the completion of which was recognized by the awarding of a diploma. A dominant aim of educating women at the collegiate level was to assist them to become effective helpmates to their husbands in settling the West. Many of these colleges were designed to train ministers for the West, and therefore coeducation was viewed by many as a way of allowing women to be helpful to their husbands.

Oberlin College gave evidence of this compensatory view by indicating that the presence of women was thought to contribute to the emotional and mental balance of the male students. This beneficial effect thus ensured the men spending their time most productively in pursuit of their studies.[35]

[34] Frederick Rudolph. *The American College and University.* New York: Alfred A. Knopf, 1962. p. 309.

[35] Conway, *op. cit.,* p. 6.

In 1839, The Georgia Female College at Macon opened. This college was the first college for women only and initiated a bold experiment in the inclusion of women in higher education. This move, along with the introduction of women students in land-grant colleges and state universities advanced the case for the inclusion of wcmen in higher education. However, the opening of doors to women was not done overnight. In 1855, the University of Iowa admitted women, followed in 1863 by the University of Wisconsin, then by Indiana, Missouri, Michigan, and California.[36]

The widespread skepticism about higher education for women declined as a result of the successful demonstration of coeducation at Cornell. After the Civil War era the number of women attending colleges grew. Many women's institutions founded after the war were duplicates of their male counterparts. The curriculum for these schools was determined in part by the curriculum of the elite male schools. The schools wished to avoid taking a stance that could be viewed as compensatory.

The struggle to extend the curriculum of higher education to women was met with resistance. Many Americans, bound by tradition in their views, criticized females who attended college, and stated that such education would create a generation of Amazons lacking in maternal feelings.[37]

Some women educators believed that the college was a natural outgrowth of the move to provide for intelligent domestic engagement. This view was, in a sense, an extension of Franklin's and Rush's ideas of the previous century. For others in the women's movement, the inclusion of women in college was a chance for women to emancipate themselves from what many considered the stagnation of the domestic scene. This duality of purpose was the concern of educational reformers relating to women.

One college which viewed higher education as an opportunity for emancipation of women from the home and the development of their full potential was Bryn Mawr. Bryn Mawr was modeled on the classical and literary curriculum of male elite schools.[38] Under the presidency of Martha Carey Thomas, an institution was created in which the graduate became a member of an intellectual aristocracy. Thomas viewed progress not as consisting of a group performing complementary, unchanging functions whose value would be judged by the products;

---

[36] Rudolph, *op. cit.*, pp. 314-15.

[37] Roberta Wein. "Women's Colleges and Domesticity 1875-1918." *History of Education Quarterly.* Spring 1975, p. 32.

[38] Conway, *op. cit.*, p. 8.

rather, she saw the reality as fluid and dynamic. In such a reality, individuals, men and women, would vie for positions. Reality would be an arena in which there would be a struggle for superiority, not a settling for complementary functions. This approach required that only the most qualified of women would be included in the collegiate experience. Bryn Mawr fostered an elitism which often found expression in a contempt for male institutions.

Not all institutions adopted this posture. Many considered it necessary to balance the domestic with the intellectual components. Wellesley College saw value in both the intellectual and the domestic realms and approached these traditions with more caution. The president of Wellesley, Alice Freeman Palmer, did not share Martha Thomas' views on collegiate education for women, at least not entirely. Of course, Wellesley, like many of the other early women's institutions, did establish a curriculum that was similar to that in the male colleges because of the necessity to prove that women could engage in the study of serious content and comprehend such courses. For its beginning in 1875, Wellesley College had great respect for sanctified womanhood and motherhood. Yet, its leaders also believed in education for life, not education for some specific position. Education should be a freeing experience, not geared to the assuming of a particular role or the overthrowing of a particular role.

Some Ideas on Group Involvement

Today few people would urge that only educators be allowed a voice in curriculum decision making or any of the other myriad decisions that relate to running American schools. However, for those who would respond "all" to the question of whom to involve, we have the problem of coordinating each involvement. Macdonald suggests that if curriculum development is to have responsibility, it must involve in curriculum decision making those persons affected by education.[39] Macdonald interprets responsibility to mean "respond-ability." His thesis is that without input from all affected persons, the curriculum cannot respond to their needs. Macdonald's curriculum development model involves scholar experts, teachers, teacher organizations, students, parents, and professional educators. The prime role of the curriculum specialist is to coordinate the input of these persons all of whom would have equal responsibility for determining the schools' curricula.

Eisner also addresses himself to the question of control by indicat-

[39] James Macdonald. "Responsible Curriculum Development." *Confronting Curriculum Reform.* Boston: Little, Brown, and Company, Inc., 1971. pp. 120-34.

ing that we have the dilemma of choosing between two goods, community control and student-initiated curriculum making and large-scale curriculum development created by governmental or national curriculum concerns.[40]

Throughout our history, education and its curriculum have been influenced by a multitude of persons and situations. We have had curriculum development or at least curriculum influence by commercial materials, by government edict, by common masses participation, by professional association activities, and by pressure groups too numerous to list. Today, we are still being influenced by many such persons, situations, and organizations.

It is the role of professional educators, especially those involved in curriculum decision making, to study the issue of control and to facilitate and monitor the input coming from the legion of sources and then to process such input so that nothing is excluded from the curriculum which is determined necessary by a significant segment of the client population that the schools are created to serve.

The question is not whom do we include in the curriculum decision making process. We need to assume that anyone affected by education should be involved in some aspect of control. The educator's responsibility is to define what is meant by control, by involvement, and then to create viable means for persons to exert some control or share control with professional educators in the management of the American educational experiment. The experiment is grand in scope and in its goals. Control should facilitate the advancement of the experiment, rather than stifle it.

Materials as a Mechanism of Curriculum Determination

Since the materials available had such a profound effect on the curriculum in early schools and in reality determined what the curriculum would be, some attention to these early books is warranted. Perhaps the book that had the greatest influence on the curriculum of the early school was the *New England Primer*. This book was in active use for over one hundred years. Sections of the *Primer* contained such items as "The Dutiful Child's Promises," the Lord's Prayer, the Creed, the Ten Commandments, and a catechism. This book was sold in nearly every New England bookshop and was present in almost every New England home. Imitations of the *Primer* appeared throughout the colonies; the

[40] Elliot Eisner. "Persistent Dilemmas in Curriculum Decision-Making." *Confronting Curriculum Reform.* Boston: Little, Brown, and Company, Inc., 1971. pp. 162-73.

New York Primer and the *American Primer* were published. Even Benjamin Franklin published a close imitation called the *Columbian Primer*.

Schools did not supply books during these early days, but curriculum development consisted of saying only that such books were necessary. Parents were expected to supply their children with the required material. In the latter half of the 1700's, the *Primer* was supplemented by Thomas Dilworth's *A New Guide to the English Tongue* originally published in England in 1740. This text provided a more secular emphasis to the curriculum. Still the process of curriculum development was nothing more than making a selection of a particular textbook. Dilworth's book, even though it was more secular in treatment of content, did contain much of the same content as the *Primer*. Dilworth's book contained the alphabet, a table of words, a short grammar of the English tongue, and a "useful collection of sentences, Prose and verse, divine, moral and historical."

If the process of curriculum development was nothing more than selection of a book, the instructional method employed was even more primitive. Teaching of reading from these materials was largely by rote and imitation. It is doubtful that children derived much meaning from approaching the material in this manner.

After the American Revolution, additional materials began to appear, and American publishing began to be a factor in American life. In 1783, Noah Webster had published the "bluebacked" *American Spelling Book*. This book significantly influenced the curriculum of spelling and reading. The book followed a format developed by Dilworth, but the content was American. The book contained easy standardized pronunciation, substituted moral reading lessons for the English prayers, and American historical and geographical names for similar English names in Dilworth's book. This "bluebacked speller" was to become one of the best selling books in the history of books. By 1880, it was estimated that its sales had exceeded 80 million.

The publication of Webster's spelling book was only the beginning of a long line of spellers and readers. One, entitled *An American Selection, or Third Part* was an example of the first school reader in a modern sense. Other reading textbooks that achieved success in influencing the nature of the curriculum and also the method of instruction were Caleb Bingham's *American Preceptor*, published in 1794 and the *Columbian Orator* published in 1806. The Preceptor was graded and it soon largely replaced a reader by Webster entitled *Reader's Assistant*. At least educators were now having to decide from which materials to "make the curriculum."

In the area of mathematics, Dilworth in 1743 published a book entitled *The School Master's Assistant*. This book remained dominant until the appearance in 1788 of an American textbook, written by Nicholas Pike, *New And Complete System of Arithmetic*. In 1796, Pike's book was given competition with the publication of Erastus Root's book, *An Introduction to Arithmetic for Use of Common Schools*.

There is no doubt that the curriculum was influenced by the materials available. In fact, the materials were the curriculum. And, the curriculum that was being experienced in New England schools was similar to the curriculum in those schools in the South and Middle States. The materials, even though under different titles, were quite similar and thus they had a commonizing effect upon the curriculum in the schools throughout our young nation.

During the first three decades of the nineteenth century, the number of books increased dramatically. But still, the schools had not delineated any precise procedure for the selection of materials. However, those persons selecting books must have taken into account some of the demands of the public as to what were the major purposes of the school. Even with the increase in textbooks, for well into the nineteenth century, the curriculum offered and the textbooks used represented an attempt at having schools deal with the minimum. Later, schools were urged by such individuals as Horace Mann to expand their curriculum, enlarge their course of studies as desired by the public and needed by the students. These attempts at expansion and altering of the direction of the curriculum were not done via careful enactment of curriculum procedures, but rather were reactions to attempts made by particular reformers. The change in the curriculum, from earliest times, seemed to come from outside the school.

During the early years of the 1800's, the common school was just becoming established. During this time there were published in Cincinnati two books that marked the beginning of one of the most remarkable series of graded readers ever to be produced. These were William H. McGuffey's First and Second Readers. In the following year, McGuffey published the Third and Fourth of the series. In 1841, the Fifth was published. For the next 60 years, these readers became the most widely used reading books outside of New England.

These books were instrumental in establishing the graded school with its particular class organization. Thus we have an example in which the organization of the educational experience was not carefully thought out by educators, but rather evolved from the use of particular types of materials available on the commercial market.

As new materials were printed, the curriculum of the common

school expanded. In 1784, the Reverend Jedediah Morse published his *American Universal Geography*. In 1795 appeared a small descriptive school geography by Nathaniel Dwight entitled, *A Short but Comprehensive System of Geography of The World*. In 1821 appeared William C. Woodgridge's *Rudiments of Geography*. This book was descriptive but did contain a number of illustrations and did have an Atlas.

The area of history in the curriculum was stimulated by the appearance in 1821 of B. Davenport's *A History of the United States*. In the next year appeared a book with the same title written by Samuel Goodrich. Noah Webster got into the history field with the publication of his *History of the United States* published in 1836.[41]

Without a doubt, these early materials did much to determine the curriculum of the evolving American common school. Also, it should be noted that since many of the early books were European in origin, the ideas of Europe, especially Great Britain, played a significant role in determining much of the content of the school's curriculum. Not only did we import the type of school organization such as the grammar and infant school, we imported the curriculum that was to occur in such schools.

The Accretion Process, an Emergent Mechanism

With the demand for a more practical education in the late nineteenth century new subjects had to be added to the "standard" curriculum. To respond to the needs, some technical procedure needed to be inaugurated. The technical procedure that did evolve, curriculum development by accretion, was not very sophisticated or technical, but it is still in use today to some degree. This process, basically that of adding new subjects to the curriculum as a result of public demand while retaining old subjects, became firmly established by 1875. This process was not carefully described. What was included in the curriculum depended in part upon the force of the public demand, from which social quarter the demand originated, and the philosophical orientation of the advocate as well as that of the educator. By the latter part of the

---

[41] On textbooks and other print material in early American educational history, see: John A. Neitz. *Old Textbooks*. Pittsburgh: University of Pittsburgh Press, 1961; Charles H. Carpenter. *History of American Schoolbooks*. Philadelphia: University of Pennsylvania Press, 1963; Ruth M. Elson. *Guardians of Tradition: American Schoolbooks of the Nineteenth Century*. Lincoln: University of Nebraska Press, 1964; Erwin C. Shoemaker. *Noah Webster: Pioneer of Learning*. New York: AMS Press, 1966; and John A. Neitz. *The Evolution of American Secondary School Textbooks*. Rutland, Vermont: C. E. Tuttle, 1966.

nineteenth century, however, the school's curriculum had grown to include courses in algebra, geometry, geography, astronomy, surveying, rhetoric, natural and moral history, physiology, botany, zoology, physics, and chemistry, in addition to the "basic curriculum" of reading, spelling, penmanship, arithmetic, grammar, literature, manners, morals, and the history of the United States. Almost yearly, the curriculum became more crowded with the addition of new subjects.

The process of continually adding subjects to the curriculum without deleting any placed demands upon teachers which were at times unrealistic. Many teachers lacked competence to teach the new subjects. Also, sufficient materials were often unavailable for teachers to employ in teaching the new subjects. Thus teachers, feeling threatened by the new subjects or overwhelmed by the implied new responsibilities, tended to resist the new subjects. Curriculum development by the "technical" process of accretion also caused the curriculum to be created in isolated pieces. Curriculum development was not guided by the concept of unification in which subjects could be fused into subjects such as general science, social studies or language arts. Rather, what happened was the adding of bits to other "bits" of the curriculum. The resulting curriculum tended to be disjointed and lacked relevance to the real world.

The process of accretion did stimulate some discussion within the education profession. From 1880 through 1910, there were two opposing camps regarding the addition of new subjects to the curriculum. One camp, representing the old point of view, urged the maintenance of the status quo in education. New subjects should be removed from the curriculum. School curriculum should represent standardization, uniformity, and a formal "lecture" method of teaching. An opposing camp felt that the school curriculum should be responsive to the needs of the populace, that it should be flexible, more individualized in organization and treatment, and based on the normal activities of the child. Individuals who urged this view included Francis Parker, Charles Eliot, James M. Greenwood, and John Dewey. Educators such as these men did not ignore the need for eliminating some subjects from the curriculum. These educators recommended that little-used information or information not useful for modern life should be excluded from the curriculum. The technical process relating to subject selection was beginning to be guided by the principle of "usefulness" to modern life.

Dewey offered a suggestion for dealing with a crowded curriculum. He urged the abandonment of old subject classifications and the introduction of the technical concept of the project. But Dewey did feel that the curriculum needed expansion as well as adjustment. The reasons given for the expansion of the curriculum were tied to the growth of the new knowledge in a rapidly changing society. Since the society and the knowledge base were in a state of progressive flux, the curriculum and the resulting technical processes should be dynamic in nature.

One of the first persons to conceptualize curriculum change as a continuing process was William Russell. He wrote in his *American Journal of Education* [42] that "No system of education, however perfect at the period of its establishment, can fully accord with the progressive improvement of society. If the pursuits of life change, in the course of ages, so ought education to change to meet the demands of the public." Russell's statement is profound, for it states that the curriculum must be always in a dynamic stage. Reality is evolutionary, and therefore the curriculum should be evolutionary. One really can never arrive at the "perfect" curriculum.

Curriculum Development: Evolution of the Mechanisms

In the second decade of the twentieth century, certain individuals, the most prominent being Franklin Bobbitt and W. W. Charters, came to believe that the methods of scientific thought and technology could best serve education. They emphasized that most curricular decision making was not very orderly or scientific and launched efforts to rectify this situation.

In his book, *The Curriculum*, Bobbitt suggested that there were two antagonistic schools of thought regarding education.[43] One school considered the subjective results of schooling: enriched mind, quickened appreciation, refined sensibility, discipline, and culture. People possessing this view emphasized the ability to live rather than the practical ability to produce. The opposing view held that education was concerned primarily with efficient practical action in a practical world. The educated person is one who can perform efficiently the labors of his calling. Such a person is one who can function in all aspects of society: work, leisure, raising of children, and social relations with his fellow man. Bobbitt favored this latter view, but realized that the subjective dimensions of schooling could not be ignored.

Bobbitt was against curriculum being developed by guess and personal opinion. If educators continued to create their curriculum in such ways, then education would be neither efficient nor relevant. To correct the lack of precision in the technical aspects of deciding what

[42] William Russell. *American Journal of Education.* 2: 67-88; February 1927.
[43] Franklin Bobbitt. *The Curriculum.* Boston: Houghton Mifflin, 1918.

to include and exclude in the curriculum, Bobbitt espoused a central theory for curriculum development. He indicated that human life, regardless of its myriad variations, did consist of basic common specific activities. Educators needed to identify these and to create an educational experience that prepared an individual to assume these specific activities.

A main task of the curriculum worker was to generate procedures to observe the real world and identify the particulars which comprised the activities of various individuals. Such analysis would reveal the abilities, attitudes, habits, appreciations, and forms of knowledge requisite for special tasks which would then become the objectives of the curriculum. The curriculum, Bobbitt reasoned, would consist of a series of experiences which students would require in order to attain the identified objectives. This was the central theory of Bobbitt, and one which, with some modification, underlies the needs analysis, goals analysis, and behavioral objectives movements of the current time.

In his book *How To Make a Curriculum* [44] Bobbitt likened the railroad engineer to the curriculum engineer. He stated that the engineer who planned construction of a railroad from Omaha to Los Angeles commenced his work by obtaining an overview of all the region that lay between the two points. As a first step he examines the lay of the land identifying all the factors that will need to be taken into consideration. "To plan the route that a growing man must travel from infancy to the goals of his growth, his culture, and his special abilities, is an immeasurably more complicated task than the simple one of planning a thin steel line across the continent." The first task of Bobbitt's method was, therefore, analysis of human nature and human affairs. Only after the first step of analysis is accomplished will one engage in the generation of means. But before means can be suggested one must ascertain the total range of an individual's habits, skills, abilities, forms of thought, valuation, emotions, and other aspects necessary for effective performance of particular vocational labors.

Throughout most of his writing, Bobbitt indicated that only as we came to reach consensus as to the major areas of schooling would we be able to identify the aims and objectives of schooling. And only then, with the establishment of objectives, would educators be able to recommend what training should be provided in the inclusion of specific aspects of the curriculum. The educator's guide for what to include and emphasize in the curriculum could only result from a delineation of the

[44] Franklin Bobbitt. *How To Make a Curriculum*. Boston: Houghton Mifflin Company, copyright © 1924.

errors and shortcomings of human performance in each of the areas of human activity.

With the publication in 1922 of his book *Curriculum Making in Los Angeles* he outlined in extensive detail how teachers in that school district employed the method of curriculum development, primarily the analytic survey, to generate objectives for the various subject fields of the curriculum.[45] Discussion in this book centers on how various departments within the school system worked cooperatively in applying scientific curriculum making. This publication records long lists of objectives which most likely served as exemplars for teachers in other parts of the country. Bobbitt indicated that the initiative for the curriculum work originated with the school superintendent. From the central office, responsibilities were delegated to other administrators. The general direction of the Los Angeles project rested with two assistant superintendents. The Department of Educational Research in the school district coordinated the creation of committees composed of high school teachers. One committee was formed for each high school department, and each subject in the high school had a subject-matter leader. Some faulted Bobbitt for gearing education to the status quo. Critics also attacked the employment of an industrial model to explain educational activities. But Bobbitt retorted that the problem of determining activities was not to ascertain what was usually done, but to identify what ought to be done. Activity analysis was not to isolate the average performance, but to gain perceptions necessary for formulating a model of ideal or optimal performance. Such analysis required not only scrutiny of the current scene to determine what should be included in the curriculum, but also the formulation of a model of the educated man. Such a model would be drawn from a philosophical orientation as well as some futuristic perceptions of society and education.

Along with Bobbitt, W. W. Charters was a major figure in the scientism movement. But, whereas Bobbitt believed that the curriculum should include those things which would correct the errors that evolved through the unstructured experiencing of reality, Charters believed that curriculum development was a process of identifying valuable ideas. According to Charters, since ideals or valuable ideas were the key organizers of the curriculum, the determination of such ideals was the key technical task of the curriculum worker.[46] Ideals are fluid and, Charters argued, could not be scientifically evaluated. Therefore, the task was to determine either via individual decision or faculty group

[45] Franklin Bobbitt. *Curriculum Making in Los Angeles.* Chicago: University of Chicago Press, 1922.

[46] W. W. Charters. *Curriculum Construction.* New York: Macmillan, 1923.

decision, those ideals considered most valuable to the society and therefore necessary for inclusion in the curriculum.

Educators could isolate ideals via three methods. The first was a
listing of activities that people did and then determining which ideals
were most efficient in accomplishing the identified duties. The second
means was by faculty consensus of ideals, with the faculty then selecting
activities which would assist one in achieving the ideals identified. The
final and third method was individual character analysis. Here a list of
ideals would be submitted to teachers, and they would be asked to think
of one pupil and determine which of the ideals needed to be stressed
with him or her. This method was somewhat similar to Bobbitt's analyzing the errors in students' behaviors and thinking.

A technical contribution of Charters relating to curriculum activity
was the processes of functional and structural analysis. By functional
analysis, he meant determining the logical relations between a function
and the parts of a structure developed to carry out the function. In
contrast, structural analysis referred to separating the structure into
parts without an explicit indication of their function. Functional analysis
could only occur after organizing the structure into parts and identifying
the relationships of each part to the achievement of the function. Thus
the function became the standard by which a decision was made as to
the value of any part. Translated into educational terms, the curriculum
worker first had to establish overall objectives, then items of the curriculum had to be selected, and finally each item selected had to be evaluated
in terms of the objectives. Such evaluation had to be performed con-
stantly. The functions became the control elements for determining
what should be included in or excluded from the curriculum.

In 1950 Tyler published the syllabus for his general curriculum
course taught at the University of Chicago.[47] This document combined
the scientism of Bobbitt and Charters with certain features of the progressive movement in American education. In essence Tyler outlined a
procedure by which curriculum workers could analyze curricular sources,
select basic objectives, generate educational experiences, and evaluate
learning outcomes. Tyler also identified three major sources of the curriculum: studies of society, studies of learners, and the subject matter
of the world. Given the synthetic nature of the "Tyler Rationale," the
syllabus had a profound impact on discourse within the curriculum field.

Hilda Taba's contribution to curriculum thinking was also substantial. She stressed the importance of the order in which curriculum
decisions were made and the criteria employed in arriving at conclu-

[47] Ralph W. Tyler. *Basic Principles of Curriculum and Instruction.* Chicago:
University of Chicago Press, 1950.

sions.[48] In her framework the order of the decision making contained seven steps: (a) diagnosis of needs, (b) formulation of objectives, (c) selection of content, (d) organization of content, (e) selection of learning experiences, (f) organization of learning experiences, and (g) determination of what to evaluate and of the ways and means of doing it. This sequence was comparable to that advanced by Tyler and also reflected the thinking of Bobbitt and Charters. In addition her view was compatible with Dewey's ideas as to the function of education.

Systems Models and Theory in Curriculum

One can criticize scientism in education as simplistic, but one cannot fault these early thinkers for attempting to make precise what up to the early 1920's had been a vague field of decision making. Many of the ideas of this era were sound, and, with minor modification, can assist educators in identifying means for the creation of meaningful curricula.

The main criticism of Bobbitt and Charters and others of the scientism movement was that they viewed change from an atomistic framework rather than an organistic framework.[49] Today, those concerned with curriculum are debating the value of employing systems theory and concepts in the technical aspects of curricular activity. There are some who maintain that the use of systems thinking leads to a dehumanized educational experience. Supporters of the use of the systems approach argue that it enables educators to create curricula that will embody humanism.

Benathy points out that the systems view is a way of thinking, a point of view.[50] It provides one with an approach to the technical which allows both a macroview of curricular activity as well as a microview of curriculum's component parts. Folowing such an approach, one gathers information from various systems to provide oneself with input for his thinking. Next, one transforms this input into generalizations about systems. Third, one generates an output of systems concepts and principles and systems models constructed from these concepts and

[48] Hilda Taba. *Curriculum Development Theory and Practice.* New York: Harcourt, Brace and World, 1962.

[49] For an early criticism of scientism, see: William L. Patty. *A Study of Mechanisms in Education.* New York: Bureau of Publications, Teachers College, Columbia University, 1938.

[50] Bela H. Benathy. *Developing a Systems View of Education.* Belmont, California: Fearon, 1973. See also: Roger A. Kaufman. *Educational System Planning.* Englewood Cliffs, N.J.: Prentice-Hall, 1972; and David S. Bushnell and Donald Rappaport, editors. *Planned Change in Education: A Systems Approach.* New York: Harcourt, Brace, Jovanovich, 1971.

principles. Finally, one engages in observation of the output to determine if the model constructed agrees with the reality observed. This final stage is called feedback. By engaging in feedback, one can make any adjustments required.

The use of systems allows one to generate models which can help in describing, studying, and manipulating reality. Models are frames of reference, and they can be of different types. Benathy denotes three basic types: a systems environment or systems-context model; a spatial-structural model; and a process model. The first model examines systems from the context of their environment; the second model focuses on what the system looks like, basically how it is organized. The third model is concerned with examining and explaining the behavior of the system over time; it is concerned with process.

All models have the same basic components: input processing, transformation processing, output processing and feedback and adjustment processing. However, for a model to be most useful, it should represent a reality that changes over time. Thus the model reveals at a particular time a system in the process of adjustment.

Once one comprehends the basic components of the system, it is possible to identify the technical aspects of decision making that occur at various junctures in the system. For example, in curriculum development, deciding upon what to include in the curriculum relates primarily to the input functioning of the system. Input in turn can be broken down into the operations of interaction, identification, and activation. Thus, these three operations become the transformation processes applied to the overall input, and the results of the activation of these processes is an output which then provides input for the overall system.

Feedback and adjustment are crucial aspects in systems functioning. With regard to curriculum development, this stage of activity allows the model to adjust to the changing demands of the time. According to Benathy, feedback and adjustment involve collecting evidences of the adequacy of the output and systems operations; analyzing and interpreting these evidences; constructing a model of adjustment; and introducing adjustment in the system.

Using the systems model, one can easily identify Taba's steps of curricular decision making. The diagnosis of needs and the formulation of objectives are primarily input operations. The selection and organization of content and learning experiences are aspects of the transformation stage, while the determining of what to evaluate relates to both the output stages and the feedback and adjustment stages.

Any curriculum development activity involves input from various sources and participation by a number of professional and lay groups.

At a very minimum significant curriculum development requires the joint efforts of students, teachers, administrators, counselors, and citizens. The systems approach to curriculum planning provides an excellent means for defining the nature and scope of input from various sources and locating the role of these sources in the total development process. In addition, the systems model offers a procedure for coordinating the actions of separate groups within an overall planning enterprise.

In addition to providing for the coordination of multiple roles in curriculum development, a systematic approach to planning also establishes a comprehensive framework necessary to overcome some of the impediments to meaningful and permanent educational change. In the domain of educational innovation, Sarason contends that the more things change the more they remain the same. In his analysis of schooling, Sarason found that those innovations which were most widely accepted were precisely those which represented the least amount of change from the status quo.[51] Part of this failure to achieve significant educational change is the result of what Lindbloom and Braybrooke have called "disjointed incrementalism."[52] As outlined by Wirt and Kirst, this incrementalism process involves: (a) acceptance of the broad outlines of existing situations with minimal expectation for change; (b) focusing on only a few policy alternatives while eliminating radical options; (c) consideration of a limited number of consequences of any given policy change; (d) adjustment of objectives to fit policy and vice versa; (e) willingness to reformulate the problem as new data arise; and (f) serial analysis and piecemeal alteration rather than a comprehensive attack.[53] Such an approach to planning obviously fails to account for the magnitude and complexity of educational change.

Currently this nation is involved in striving for humanism in the schools and in society at large. If one defines humanism as an attempt to provide opportunities for individuals to optimize their own potentials and to make effective their dealings with their fellow human beings, then one can argue that being precise in curriculum deliberations will assist in achieving the goal of humanistic education.

Weinstein and Fantini have presented an eight-stage model for developing a curriculum for affect.[54] The first step is that of identifying

---

[51] Seymour B. Sarason. *The Culture of the School and the Problem of Change.* Boston: Allyn and Bacon, Inc., 1971. p. 220.

[52] Charles Lindbloom and David Braybrooke. *A Strategy of Decision.* New York: Free Press, 1963.

[53] Frederick M. Wirt and Michael W. Kirst. *The Political Web of American Schools.* Boston: Little, Brown, and Company, Inc., 1972. p. 206.

[54] Gerald Weinstein and Mario D. Fantini, editors. *Toward Humanistic Education: A Curriculum for Affect.* New York: Praeger, 1970.

the learner group. The second is identifying the shared concerns of this group. In a humanistic curriculum, one attends to three major concerns of students: concern about self-image; concern about disconnectedness, about being isolated from the rest of their peers; and concern about control over their own lives.

The third step involves diagnosis of underlying factors affecting students' needs and perceptions. The fourth step requires curriculum workers to identify key organizing ideas to serve as central foci around which the curriculum will be constructed. In sum, the basic input, transformation, and output stages of systems analysis and design are reflected in a number of contemporary models of educational planning and decision making. The extent to which these stages permeate planning proposals suggests that the systems framework simply makes explicit a rational approach to problem solving which cannot be ignored in curriculum development. The achievement of a humanistic curriculum depends not on the planning strategy used but rather on one's philosophical orientation and perception of the needs and interests of students at a particular time. To maintain that the systems approach will dehumanize education is, in this writer's belief, to admit ignorance of the fundamental nature and demands of systems and curriculum planning.

Conclusion

The American educational experiment, begun modestly over three hundred years ago, has changed dramatically. From the simple schoolhouse where the technical, if at all recognized, meant copying what had been done before in England or what was suggested in the available books, to the complicated school systems of today, curriculum decision making has undergone many changes. But the technical is still in a state of evolution. There are still advocates and critics. And this is necessary, for change which meets no challenge often is not of great value. Advocates of change not only in the substance of curriculum but in the technical means by which curriculum can be created, implemented, maintained, and evaluated have to think more fully of their positions if resistance is encountered.

Yet a problem confronting education today is that critics are suggesting the "tearing down" of the educational system without any careful attention to the generation of a new system or to the ways in which a new system would be produced. This is understandable, for people find it easier to tear down the old than to build the new. Many of the critics urging us to destroy first the current system, and then to establish a Phoenix from its ashes would have us deal in emotionalism and then flounder for lack of technical expertise.

The domain of the technical since the beginning of the second decade of this century has really been expanding in both methodology and complexity. Such expansion has created a need for teachers competent in the realm of curriculum as well as systems. Most teachers have been educated to "teach" in the narrow sense. Most of their courses have been and continue to be in the area of "methods." Few teachers, especially at the undergraduate level, receive courses in curriculum development, curriculum systems, curriculum theory, sociology of the schools, political theory relating to the schools, organizational theory, decision theory, and planning theory. Teachers need to broaden their competencies to function effectively in the technical realm. Administrators and supervisors also require competence in the realm of the technical.

Educators must consider curriculum from a standpoint of ecological interaction. The total milieu in which education functions must be clearly perceived when technical decisions are enacted. It is this writer's belief that educators need a macroview of the school system as well as a microview of the classroom.

Throughout our history, many cultural, ethnic, and racial groups have contributed to the development of the American school. The school and its curriculum have been very successful in meeting some of the major demands and needs of American society. However, the charge given to education is not done. The task of providing curricula which will allow all students to develop optimally is still paramount.

The technical deals with inclusion and exclusion of content, of experiences, of educational environments, and of people. What to include in the school curriculum; who will experience these curricula; who will be involved in creating these curricula and in evaluating their successes: the technical will always have to deal with these questions. In the future, different groups will generate different demands. And to be responsive, the school will have to activate technical procedures.

The field of curriculum, and the subfield of the technical is dynamic. Today, educators are urging that curriculum workers assume leadership in managing the technical aspects of curricular activity. Those who possess technical expertise will become the key actors in the curriculum arena.

The American educational experiment has been conceived and carried forward by people working with the best knowledge and perceptions available at their time. Some critics have faulted educators and the school for being less than perfect and omniscient. However, this writer believes that critics must realize that they are dealing with human educators. Critics need to be cognizant that the record of American formal education is better than that in most countries.

This writer urges all to take a realistic stance when considering the American school and the technical concerns of curriculum building. The curriculum of the American school has a noble goal, the education of all to their fullest potential. We need to realize that we have not achieved this goal in all instances or for all students. Yet, we need to understand that total and complete achievement of the goal is not a static one which will be arrived at and completed once and for all at a future specified time. The concept of fullest potential will change as educators achieve greater understanding of human beings in the cognitive, affective, and psychomotor domains.

The American experiment in the past two hundred years has achieved many successes envied by the world. Yet the experiment has some serious shortcomings. The challenges are evident to those who attend to the current scene and who possess the means by which to interpret the current scene as well as to forecast and create futures. The technical in all of its ramifications will allow the American educational experiment to continue. The future belongs to those who have the means to develop educational plans and the resources by which to accomplish such plans.

BICENTENNIAL VIGNETTES

"Philosophy Can Bake No Bread"

Who is largely responsible for establishing the high school as a legitimate sector of public education? Who is responsible for the first American public school kindergarten? Who is largely responsible for the introduction of art, music, and manual training into the public school curriculum? Who is recognized as the most influen-

William Torrey Harris

tial American educator between Mann and Dewey? The answer, in all cases, is William Torrey Harris —student of phrenology and spiritualism, teacher, philosopher, writer, editor.

Harris was possessed of prodigious energy. He served as St. Louis public school superintendent for twelve years and as U.S. Commissioner of Education for seventeen years (1889-1906). He published over five hundred titles, both articles and books. He was recognized as the foremost American authority on G. W. F. Hegel, his real preoccupation being German literature and philosophy. He founded and edited the *Journal of Speculative Philosophy* which was recognized as the only substantive American philosophical journal of its day. His work as an editor was prolific.

Harris saw education as the process through which society becomes "ethical." He saw university education as more "practical" than high school training, since, "Ethics is certainly the most practical of all branches of human learning."

Harris is not well remembered, probably due to the fact that he ushered out an era of American education rather than ushered one in, as many of his contemporaries thought he had done.

—*Charles Russell*

Susan Blow
Founds the Public Kindergarten

The first public school kindergarten in the United States was started in 1873 in St. Louis, Missouri, by Susan Blow under the superintendency of William Torrey Harris. From this beginning, public sponsorship of schooling in kindergartens, earlier called preschools, has expanded throughout the nation.

Development of this first public kindergarten reveals several important points about society, individuals, and schools in the years between the Civil War and the new century. Kindergartens in the U.S. prior to Miss Blow's classes were privately run and received funding from tuition or charity organizations. Costs of these early preschool programs were prohibitive for attendance by any but children from wealthy families or those attending on a charitable basis. Miss Blow and Mr. Harris began the public school kindergartens with the avowed intent of reaching the deprived children in St. Louis. Both Blow and Harris believed that the formative years (ages 3-7 years) were important to child development. They saw the children of the slums growing up in the streets with what they termed as "vice and iniquity" as their environments. They wanted to provide kindergarten as a redemptive center for these children by providing exposure and experience to the societal norms of "virtue and culture." This same idea was later extended to include the children of the wealthier families.

Superintendent Harris was very effective in persuading the school board and public opinion to accept the idea of a public kindergarten. He proved to be an able advocate in resulting court battles concerning the legitimacy and legality of public kindergarten. Harris selected Susan Blow to implement the idea of kindergarten about which he felt so strongly.

Susan Blow was a young lady from a wealthy St. Louis industrial family. She had been educated in private schools that her father funded for the benefit of his daughter and had traveled extensively in Europe. She had been in New York studying with a Dutch teacher about the techniques of Froebel when Harris called upon her to ask if she would implement the public school kindergarten in St. Louis. She agreed and educational history was made.

The basic teaching approach chosen by Miss Blow included the gaming techniques and the "gifts," developed by Froebel and widely used in Europe at that time. Important to remember is that the major purpose of the school was moral discipline for societal reasons. Thus, the kindergarten games were used as pedagogical tools. Verse games were used to sing the praises of the "wholesome life." Skill games were used as tools to develop and build skills needed in further schooling, societal participation, and a valuable life. The games were not intended to be "play and frolic" games but purposeful games, with the overriding goal of school being an antidote to the "evil" learned on the streets.

The St. Louis program grew from 68 pupils, Miss Blow, and three unpaid assistants in 1873 to 166 paid teachers, 60 unpaid assistants, and 7,828 children in 1878, when Susan Blow resigned from the program to pursue other ventures. The system for which Susan Blow was responsible quickly became a model for other systems in the U.S. The teachers she trained and worked with in the St. Louis system went on to found and operate programs in Baltimore and other cities throughout the nation.

Notable changes were made in some of these programs, particularly in the light of teachings by Patty Smith Hill, of Teachers College, Columbia University. She was influential in changing the traditional Froebelian approach toward a program more in line with the philosophy of John Dewey, the psychology of G. Stanley Hall of the Child Study Movement, and the teachings of William Heard Kilpatrick.

—*Eric C. Lundgren*

Dewey's School:
No Playground but a Structured Laboratory

The year was 1896 and the place was the University of Chicago. The event: the founding of the Laboratory School. Instituted to test, through practical application, the philosophical and psychological ideas of John Dewey, it has been characterized, since its demise in 1904, as a freewheeling, child-ruled, educational playground. Facts insist that the Dewey School was none of these. As befits the term "laboratory," the school was a place of purposeful activity guided by directive ideas and leading hypotheses. Dewey had carefully thought out what was to be taught, how, and by whom. For him, as well as others concerned with its development, the school was a highly structured experimental laboratory.

Dewey noted that (pp. 39-40):

The primary business of school is to train children in cooperative and mutually helpful living, to foster in them the consciousness of interdependence, and to help them practically in making the adjustments that will carry this spirit into overt deeds. . . .

These individual tendencies and activities are only organized and exercised through their use in an actual process of co-operative living: the best results follow when such a process reproduces on the child's plane the typical doings and occupations of the larger, maturer society into which he is finally to go forth; and it is only through such productive and creative use that valuable knowledge is secured and clinched.[1]

A major focus for Dewey's Laboratory School, then, was occupations. Being reproductions of or running parallel to work carried on in life, whether past or present, these occupations furnished things for the child to do. The school became a form of community life. Since the development of civilization occurred through cooperative endeavors, Dewey felt that the school itself, in order to prepare its students for future social life, must become a small scale cooperative society. Skills such as reading and writing were to grow out of needs generated by the occupations studied, as were discipline, knowledge, and understanding.

Occupations chosen for study depended upon the child's stage of

[1] All references from Katherine Camp Mayhew and Anna Camp Edwards. *The Dewey School.* New York: D. Appleton-Century Co., 1936.

growth. Dewey believed that certain stages were characteristic of child growth. Never sharply defined, these stages often overlapped and merged with each other, but nonetheless affected what the child could learn. Thus, young children began with occupations of the home, gradually moving toward occupations outside the home —farming, mining, the larger social industries. By age eleven pupils were examining occupations in tenth-century England, analyzing the feudal system, investigating tools used, seeds available, and trades practiced. Emphasis was placed on man's continual refinement and specialization of occupations and the social problems these refinements and specializations engendered.

Dewey's concern with the "whole child" as well as the needs of society led him to create a school which "could become a cooperative community while developing in individuals their own capacities and satisfying their own needs" (p. xvi). That many of Dewey's ideas and the school itself still seem fresh diminishes the time between a school which ushered in the Progressive Era and a school of today.

—*Marilyn Maxson*

Bobbitt's Principle

The curriculum may . . . be defined in two ways: 1) it is the entire range of experiences, both undirected and directed, concerned in unfolding the abilities of the individuals; or 2) it is the series of consciously directed training experiences that the schools use for completing and perfecting the unfoldment.[1]

When synthesizing this principle, Bobbitt stated that the education profession usually understood curriculum as in the latter definition. But both interpretations are necessary. Implicit in this principle is the need to ascertain just what experiences learners have had in order to plot a curriculum for "the completing and perfecting of the unfoldment." From this principle, Bobbitt introduced a novel way of conceiving of and performing curricular activity. Before Bobbitt, the starting point for curriculum consideration was the subject matter; the discipline provided the substance of the curriculum. Bobbitt argued that the more productive entry point into curricular activity was the analysis of life activities themselves, the process of activity analysis.

[1] Franklin Bobbitt. *The Curriculum*. Cambridge, Massachusetts: The Riverside Press, 1918. p. 43.

Bobbitt's principle was not without its critics. Indeed, W. W. Charters took Bobbitt to task by indicating that errors perceived as the results of activity analysis did not suggest specific content, but rather denoted areas requiring emphasis in the curriculum.

Reactions continue to this present day with some educators

Pestalozzian object lesson, Washington, D.C. F. C. Johnston, photographer.

urging activity analysis for determining content, and others countering that the disciplines are the source of content. One can argue the validity of the principle and lose sight of Bobbitt's contribution.

Bobbitt provided educators with the seminal idea that curriculum was more than a listing of facts and principles. Curriculum was a process, a process by which meaningful learning experiences could be perceived, conceived, and implemented. Curriculum was a dynamic activity enabling educators to process continually reality in order to meet both current and future student needs.

Presently, curriculum workers are concerned with analyzing the entire range of learner experiences, both directed and undirected. But educators need to query themselves

as to the preciseness of means for engaging in curricular activity. Do we possess vehicles for analyzing total reality so as to provide, if not content, at least emphases in curricula? Do we have and do we activate procedures by which to proceed from our perceptions of goals to educational realities? Are we progressing in ways of studying our procedures such that we will advance the realm of curriculum knowledge? Where are we in our quest for a central theory or theories relating to curriculum?

Bobbitt's principle contributed to a new direction in curriculum dialogue over a half century ago. Such dialogue remains necessary, especially now as the principle has increased visibility and quite specific criticism.
                                                                    —*Francis P. Hunkins*

Purposes of Education for the Nation

The purpose of democracy is so to organize society that each member may develop his personality primarily through activities designed for the well-being of his fellow members and of society as a whole. . . .

Education in a democracy, both within and without the school, should develop in each individual the knowledge, interests, ideals, habits, and powers whereby he will find his place and use that place to shape both himself and society toward ever nobler ends.[1]

Prior to 1918, little systematic attention was given to stating purposes of education throughout the vastness of America. Individuals,

[1] *Cardinal Principles of Secondary Education.* Washington, D.C.: U.S. Bureau of Education Bulletin, No. 35, 1918.

to be sure, asserted statements of purpose and, occasionally, groups issued or assented to common statements. Too, the educational enterprise was not systematized and nationally ascribed purposes were matters more implicit than

One-room school, Crossville, Tennessee, 1935.

explicit. Nevertheless, in the early twentieth century, secondary education, specifically, was generally assumed to exist to prepare students for college entrance. The report of the Commission on the Reorganization of Secondary Education was entitled *Cardinal Principles of Secondary Education*, and it examined the broad spectrum of education and its underlying purposes.

The committee report listed seven specific objectives, termed Cardinal Principles, and included health; command of fundamental processes; worthy home membership; vocation; citizenship; worthy use of leisure time; and ethical character. The committee also recommended in the report that schools should be organized with six elementary grades, a three-year junior high school, and a three-year high school.

The Cardinal Principles were clearly ideas whose time had come. Difficult it is to judge if they were only reflections of contemporary educational thought or were truly innovative thoughts by the committee members. Likely, the final results were tempered by both factors. In any case the impact was immediate, changing school organization, if not educational purposes, almost overnight.

Other commissions in later years offered both more and fewer goals and objectives for education. Most of these, however, seem intimately related to the Cardinal Principles. Perhaps the best example is *The Central Purpose of American Education*.[2] It proposed that the development of rational powers was the central purpose of education. Then, it proceeded to relate this purpose to the Cardinal Principles, objective by objective.

The significance of the Cardinal Principles merits continued reexamination. Regardless of the gap between their rhetoric and the reality of schooling, many have referred to this statement as the Declaration of Independence by the high school from college domination.

—*Larry L. Krause*

[2] Educational Policies Commission. *The Central Purpose of American Education.* Washington, D.C.: National Education Association, 1961.

3

Schooling and Control: Some Interpretations of the Changing Social Function of Curriculum

Gerald A. Ponder

A culture is not a flow, nor even a confluence; the form of its existence is struggle, or at least debate—it is nothing if not a dialectic.

—Lionel Trilling[1]

It is the ideal of democracy that the individual and society may find fulfillment each in the other. . . . Consequently, education in a democracy, both within and without the school, should develop in each individual the knowledge, interests, ideals, habits, and powers whereby he will find his place and use that place to shape both himself and society toward ever nobler ends.

—The Commission on the Reorganization of Secondary Education[2]

THE HISTORY OF A CULTURE is filled with paradox, tension, and conflict. That culture's institutions reflect those tensions—the dialectic, as Trilling would have it. And they respond to them. For the history of American schooling, one of the most important of these tensions has been that

Left: Principal helping in shop class, Gee's Bend, Alabama, 1939.

---

[1] Lionel Trilling. *The Liberal Imagination: Essays on Literature and Society.* New York: Viking Press, 1950. p. 384.

[2] Commission on the Reorganization of Secondary Education. *Cardinal Principles of Secondary Education.* Department of the Interior, Bureau of Education Bulletin, 1918, No. 35. Washington: Government Printing Office, 1918. p. 9.

between the forces and demands of diversity and those of conformity. From the first colonies, American society has been a diverse amalgam. Distinctly different religious and social groups settled here. Diverse life-ways developed as a result of the interaction between the modes of living imported by the settlers and the demands of the new land. Economies developed differently, as New Englanders became merchants and manu-facturers while Southerners became planters. Loyalties were directed toward locales and regions, and American society was dispersed among a multitude of pockets. We were a country of island communities, so weakly linked and so deeply divided on fundamental issues that the new nation erupted in civil warfare less than a century after it was born. Diversity in many forms has always characterized this society.

Yet the rhetoric of unity—and even of conformity—has been pres-ent from the beginning, too. The slogans of democracy, the demands of the social compact, the long-held myth of a melting pot culture, all attest to a conscious desire for a national identity, for a "glue" that would meld the diverse elements of American society into a solid entity. This society is no different from any other in that respect. All organized societies tend to solidify themslves by trying to produce some degree of sameness among their members. And they all go about it in much the same way—through their educating institutions, whether those institutions educate in an informal way, as families often do, or in more formal ways, as schools intend to do.

From its beginnings, the American common school has been asked to serve the social function of minimizing tensions caused by social diversity. The program of the school has been called on to act, really, as a mechanism for control. But the approach to control has not been static. Society has changed in the last two centuries; so has schooling and the rhetoric about schooling. This essay explores some of those changes by focusing on the relationship between the school curriculum and the concept of control. The purpose of this chapter is to suggest some very tentative interpretations of the functions of schooling that seem reasonable in the light of recent scholarship or that may prove interesting to future investigators. The context in which the interpreta-tions of the changing social functions of the curriculum have been placed is a larger historical framework than that provided by a review of the development of theoretical curriculum positions. This is intentional. It emphasizes my belief that curriculum history cannot be separated from the larger history of schooling and of society. Recounting such events as the Twenty-Sixth Yearbook and the Eight-Year Study is useful and necessary. But analyzing such events to the exclusion of corresponding social and institutional development may provide illusory interpretations of the past by elevating rhetoric to the status of reality.

American Schooling: A Brief Historiography

A review of some prior directions in the history of schooling may provide a better framework for the interpretations contained in this essay. In order to simplify the review, only three major interpretive traditions will be described. The descriptions for these traditions were chosen to provide deliberate contrast, and they are not intended to characterize the histories in any kind of analytical depth.[3]

Until about two decades ago the dominant thrust in educational history was clear. It presented a somewhat romanticized view of the successful rise of the American public school. Led by Cubberley's *Public Education in the United States*,[4] this interpretive tradition viewed the common school as the product and cornerstone of democratic government, the provider of social and economic opportunity, and the greatest hope for the future of society. These historians focused on the educational ideals of the past, couched their analyses in moralistic overtones, and hoped to strengthen the commitment of prospective teachers to the public school system. Moreover, their interpretations were "narrowly institutional," neglected to account for social developments outside the school system, and tended to equate schooling with education.[5]

The social and cultural upheavals that characterized the 1960's coincided with the rise of revisionism in social and educational history. The power of the mass media, a growing recognition of the web of biases and inequities in society, and a generalized loss of faith in the unlimited efficacy of American institutions combined with a growing dissatisfaction with earlier interpretations of the past to generate new historical questions, methods, and approaches. The result has been a wide range of new perspectives. One group of revisionists looked again at the history of schools and held them accountable for their "mistakes" as well as their successes. These histories, from Kliebard's reviews of the Bobbitt-Tyler tradition and Callahan's investigation of the efficiency movement in school administration to the later "new left" works such

[3] Other reviews examine the historiography of education more extensively. For one, see: Douglas Sloan, "Historiography and the History of Education." Chapter 8 in *Review of Research in Education 1*, Fred W. Kerlinger, editor. Itasca, Illinois: F. E. Peacock Publishers, Inc., 1973. pp. 239-70.

[4] Ellwood P. Cubberley. *Public Education in the United States*. Boston: Houghton Mifflin, 1919.

[5] Lawrence A. Cremin. *The Wonderful World of Ellwood Patterson Cubberley: An Essay on the Historiography of American Education*. New York: Teachers College Press, 1965.

as Greer's, are dissimilar in many respects.[6] But they bear some simi-
larities in tone. An implicit feeling in these studies is that American
schooling has had a great deal of control over its development, that it
has made some unfortunate (or outrageous, depending on the historian)
choices regarding future directions, and that the choices of the past are
largely responsible for the predicaments of the present. This is not to
imply that the schools were different from other social institutions in
this respect. Indeed, the schools may have been guilty of reflecting social
values only too well; they may only have disagreed too little.

The third interpretive tradition to gain currency in recent years is
also revisionist in nature. It, too, has done much to "demythologize"
the history of public schooling, but it differs somewhat in tone from the
"new left" and from Kliebard and Callahan. This group of histories,
led most notably by Robert Wiebe's study of the Gilded Age and Progressivism and by David Tyack's chronicle of the development of urban
school systems, seems more analytical than evaluative in tone and
more evolutionary in point of view.[7] The impression of change running
through these works is one of limited choice. The feeling given is that
the directions taken by social institutions during the watersheds of
American history were the ones that "won out" over competing directions because they seemed to fit the then-current conditions best. They
seemed to produce at least the best illusion of control over an apparent
chaos of competing pressures and demands. And, once taken, the directions themselves produced a system of pressures and vested interests
that maintained the surviving direction. So, for example, the language
of science and efficiency and the methods of bureaucracy and centralization became the response to urbanization and industrialization that
seemed to produce order in a society in transition from agrarianism to
urbanism. Moreover, the organizational patterns and special interests
produced by this response took on a life of their own that served to
perpetuate the system and help determine the nature of schooling and
other social institutions that have characterized the recent history of
this nation.

---

[6] Herbert Kliebard. "Bureaucracy and Curriculum Theory." In: *Freedom,
Bureaucracy, and Schooling*. Vernon F. Haubrich, editor. Washington, D.C.: Association for Supervision and Curriculum Development, 1971. pp. 74-94; "The Tyler
Rationale." *School Review* 78: 259-72; February 1970; Raymond Callahan. *Education and the Cult of Efficiency: A Study of the Forces That Have Shaped the Administration of the Public Schools*. Chicago: University of Chicago Press, 1962; and
Colin Greer. *The Great School Legend*. New York: Viking Press, 1972.

[7] Robert H. Wiebe. *The Search for Order: 1877-1920*. New York: Hill and
Wang, 1967; David B. Tyack. *The One Best System: A History of American Urban
Education*. Cambridge, Massachusetts: Harvard University Press, 1974.

It is this analytical, evolutionary viewpoint that currently seems most promising for increasing our understanding of the history of curriculum and schooling, and it is from this frame of reference that I had hoped to write. However, this essay contains both analytical and evaluative comments; it analyzes, praises, and criticizes, all within a short narrative space. This is probably unavoidable and may be more a function of interpretive reading rather than writing. This public caution is not intended to dilute my comments. Instead, it has been inserted to underscore the need to minimize presentism and to reduce the tendency to find heroes and villains to the exclusion of understanding the context in which they lived.

Bureaucracy, scientism, and efficiency have not always been characteristic of American schooling, of course. But pressures to respond in some way to diversity have been. The responses have varied, but they have been rooted always in social conditions and they have reflected the views of those exerting power. The variance can be explained largely by changes in society and changes in the membership of power groups. That assertion hardly offers any new interpretive grist. It has been made by historians and sociologists for some time now. Much of the remainder of this essay is also reassertion, a reassertion of the ways in which schooling has been used to exert—and dispense—control. These reassertions may prove useful, though, in looking at ways in which the curriculum has sought to produce conformity and the effects it has had on diversity.

Conformity by Coercion: Social Control

Analysts and critics of American public schooling recently have increased their allegations that schools teach more than skills and subject matter, that they also inculcate middle-class values, reward acquiescence, socialize students toward political conservatism, and, by a systematic process of sorting and selection, maintain traditional class structures. They have, in short, rediscovered that part of the "hidden curriculum" that attempts to produce conformity among young people.[8] Despite the recency of these allegations, there is little new in the relationship between schooling and conformity. Social control—the production of some

---

[8] See, for example: Norman Overly, editor. *The Unstudied Curriculum: Its Impact on Children.* Washington: Association for Supervision and Curriculum Development, 1970. George S. Counts advanced many of these same charges in: *The Selective Character of American Secondary Education.* Chicago: University of Chicago Press, 1922.

degree of conformity—has long been one of the primary functions of schooling. Only the rhetoric justifying that function has changed.[9]

The earliest settlers in America were imitators first and innovators only later. The forms of education they used were copies of those in England, and, as such, they had remained largely unchanged for generations. The primary agency for education and socialization in colonial America was the family.[10] It bore the responsibility not only for "elementary socialization," as Bailyn described it, but also for training in the rudimentary skills of a vocation, "good Christian cultivation," and "proper deportment."[11] But the family was not the only educative agency in the colonies. The community, with its intricate network of intermarriages, kinship ties, and shared traditions was another. And the church was still another. Both the family and the community were informal agencies of education, instructing their children in the ways of work and modes of living of that area easily and naturally, as it was often difficult to tell where the affairs of the family left off and the affairs of the community began.

Of the three, the church was the most formal and explicit in its educational function. It supported schools, informed the community of accepted standards of behavior, and—significantly—instructed the community's children "in the system of thought and imagery which underlay the culture's values and aims."[12] It also began a tradition which has continued until the present—assigning the responsibility for social control to the most formal agency of education.

This process by which the church-as-educator acquired the function of social control can be seen most clearly in Puritan New England. In the words of John Winthrop, "wee must Consider that wee shall be as a Citty vpon a Hill, the eies of all people are vppon vs . . ."[13] The Puritans were people with an extraordinary sense of destiny, determined not to fail in their mission in the New World. Yet conditions in the settlements threw their traditional system of cultural transmission based

---

[9] Elizabeth Vallance. "Hiding the Hidden Curriculum: An Interpretation of the Language of Justification in Nineteenth-Century Educational Reform." *Curriculum Theory Network* 4(1): 5; 1973/74.

[10] Bernard Bailyn. *Education in the Forming of American Society: Needs and Opportunities for Study.* Chapel Hill: University of North Carolina Press, 1960. p. 15.

[11] *Ibid.*, p. 16.

[12] *Ibid.*, p. 17.

[13] John Winthrop. "A Model of Christian Charity." *The Winthrop Papers.* Boston: Massachusetts Historical Society, 1931, p. 295. Reprinted in: David Tyack, editor. *Turning Points in American Educational History.* Waltham, Massachusetts: Blaisdell Publishing Company, 1967. Copyright © John Wiley & Sons, Inc. Reprinted with permission.

on the hierarchical, patrilineal, extended family into disarray. Respect for, and obedience to parents were eroded as children adapted more readily to the demands of the frontier than did their elders. This was a serious threat to the Puritan conception of order since parents bore the greatest obligation to inculcate proper beliefs and practices in their inherently sinful children. When, near the middle of the seventeenth century, Puritan leaders became highly concerned at the "great neglect in many parents and masters in training up their children in learning, and labor," their response was to pass a series of laws they hoped would buttress the authority of the family. Although these laws compelled only literacy and job training and did *not* make *schooling* compulsory, they signalled a change in the approach toward social control. As Tyack put it, "Now certain tasks of socialization which had been done unconsciously in a more static social order needed to be explicitly defined. A new consciousness about education emerged." [14]

This same kind of consciousness about inducing conformity— establishing and maintaining social control—carried over into the establishment of the first common schools in the nineteenth century. Faced with extraordinary religious and ethnic diversity in most areas of the new nation, schoolmen had to develop a common basis for instruction. This was done in two ways: by making English the language of the schools and by widespread adoption of the moral principles found in the catechism and the *New England Primer*.[15]

Throughout the nineteenth century, social control—the intentional inculcation of conformity to certain norms and habits—was viewed as one of the primary benefits of public education and, as such, was specifically included in the rhetoric justifying schooling. However, the *purpose* ascribed to social control changed. Instead of calling for schools to help *create* a national character, the rhetoric of common school reform asked the schools to preserve and extend the spirit of national unity.

It seems clear that the mid-nineteenth century marked the beginnings of urban education in America.[16] In the 1830's, an influx of immigrants posed the first great threat of conflict and diversity, and the nation's leaders became concerned that the hodgepodge collection of schools, some public, some religious, some run by charities, was too weak to meet new demands. This threat of cultural diversity was felt

[14] Tyack, *Turning Points*, p. 4.

[15] R. Freeman Butts and Lawrence A. Cremin. *A History of Education in American Culture*. New York: Holt, Rinehart, and Winston, Inc., 1953. p. 74.

[16] See, for example: Vallance, "Hiding the Hidden Curriculum"; Tyack, *Turning Points* and *The One Best System*; and Michael Katz, *Class, Bureaucracy, and Schools: The Illusion of Educational Change in America*. New York: Praeger, 1971.

most keenly in the urbanized manufacturing areas of the northeast, where the greatest number of immigrants settled. It was here, also, that the common school movement had its beginning and received its greatest impetus.

The problem was clear to reformers advocating the establishment of common schools: it was to preserve the basically "Anglo-American" national character. To do this, a consciously guided process of assimilation was to be directed toward new immigrants through the aegis of the common school. As Calvin Stowe expressed it in 1836, "It is altogether essential to our national strength and peace that the foreigners should cease to be Europeans and become Americans." The vehicle for Americanization was to be the schoolhouse: "The school-house is that crucible [of social amalgamation], and the schoolmaster is the only alchemist who can bring free gold out of the crude and discordant materials."[17]

Structurally, the period following the Civil War was marked by extension and centralization. The common school was transplanted into rural areas and western frontiers in forms much like those it had assumed in New England. In these areas the schools were controlled by local communities and justified largely as agents for moral conservation.[18] But in the cities, the developmental pattern was different. The extension of the common school into urban areas resulted in a clash between the function of Americanization and the principle of community control. Even as more and more immigrants made their way to this country, resulting in intensified demands for the schools to act as assimilators, control of the schools lay in the hands of ward politicians, special interest groups, and the very ethnic groups the schools were to Americanize. Such complexity seemed to be an intolerable threat to order, and educational reformers switched their oratory toward demands to centralize the organizational structure while leaving the school program with its large measures of moralism and Americanism intact. By the late 1800's, virtually every city in the United States had begun to move toward centralization.[19]

The movement toward centralization was accompanied by an increasing focus on uniformity and efficiency. The pursuit of efficiency was hardly a new phenomenon in American education by the late nine-

[17] *Transactions of the Fifth Annual Meeting of the Western Literary Institute and College of Professional Teachers.* Cincinnati: Executive Committee, 1836, pp. 65-66, 68-71, 75, 81-82. Reprinted in: Tyack, *Turning Points*, pp. 148-51.

[18] Vallance, "Hiding the Hidden Curriculum," p. 12.

[19] See: Katz, *Class, Bureaucracy and Schools;* and Tyack, *The One Best System* for extensive accounts of centralization.

teenth century. As early as 1815, several eastern cities had witnessed the rise of monitorial instruction as practiced by the Lancastrian system. Named for its developer, Joseph Lancaster, the major appeal of this system was its economy and efficiency. Large numbers (as many as a thousand) of pupils were placed in one room with one teacher. But one teacher was all that was needed, since pupil monitors did all the teaching while the teacher acted mainly as an "inspector."[20] The Lancastrian system functioned because its program was organized in great detail, and teachers were not allowed to waver from the specified plans of selecting the brightest students, teaching them the lesson, and then having them teach what they had just learned to the rest of the pupils.

While the Lancastrian schools indicate the long-standing appeal of the idea of efficiency, that doctrine asserted its greatest influence in the late nineteenth and early twentieth centuries. The efficiency movement in these decades developed as an artifact of an increasingly urbanized, industrialized, and centralized society, and it was led by persons in search of ways to control and order the new threats posed by a society in transition. Throughout the nineteenth century, school reformers had sought to systematize the apparent chaos they saw. Creating and then conserving an American character meant unifying the people, and to unify the people, "public education must itself be unified and efficient."[21] Unification and efficiency meant standardization—of textbooks, the curriculum, teacher training, and the grading of classes.

At least in rhetoric, if not in fact, a great deal of standardization in the school program had been accomplished by the last quarter of the nineteenth century, as indicated by the "Statement of the Theory of Education in the United States of America as Approved by Many Leading Educators."[22] The school program described in this statement emphasized homogeneity, efficiency, and obedience to authority. It stated that, since the "peculiarities" of American society weaken the family's hold over its children, a system of public education was necessary to develop the discipline and morals required by the "modern industrial community." Further, education had to coincide with the "commercial

[20] Daniel Tanner and Laurel Tanner. *Curriculum Development: Theory Into Practice.* New York: Macmillan Publishing Co., Inc., 1975. pp. 159-60.

[21] Tyack, *Turning Points*, p. 314.

[22] Duane Doty and William T. Harris. "A Statement of the Theory of Education in the United States of America as Approved by Many Leading Educators." Washington, D.C.: Government Printing Office, 1874. Reprinted in: Tyack, *Turning Points*, pp. 324-28. This statement was signed by seventy-seven college presidents and city and state superintendents of schools. When this statement was written, Doty was superintendent of the Detroit Schools and Harris was superintendent of the St. Louis Schools.

tone" of this industrial community by placing "great stress" on "military precision . . . punctuality, regularity, attention, and silence as habits necessary through life for successful combination with one's fellow men in an industrial and commercial civilization."[23]

The name most synonymous with the application of the efficiency-oriented principles of scientific management to the curriculum is that of Franklin Bobbitt, the "man who gave shape and direction to the curriculum field."[24] Like other educators of the early 1900's Bobbitt espoused many of the principles of scientific management set forth by Frederick W. Taylor, adapting them first to school management and then to curriculum design.[25] When applied to curriculum design, the principles of scientific management translated into an analogy in which individual children became the raw material that the schools, like factories, were to fashion into finished products according to the specifications of society. Further, these specifications were to be derived from an analysis of the kinds of knowledge, skills, attitudes, and habits needed in adult life. These intended outcomes would be controlled for quality by developing "definite qualitative and quantitative standards . . . for the product," just as the railroad industry knew that each rail "must be thirty feet in length and weigh eighty pounds to the yard."[26]

But these intended outcomes would not be the only things controlled by principles of business efficiency. The subjects themselves, the heart of the school curriculum, were to be analyzed by the procedures of cost accounting. Again using the model of standardization found in railroad administration, Bobbitt pointed out that railroad companies knew that repair costs for locomotives should average six cents per mile and the "lubricating oils should cost about . . . twenty-five cents (per hundred miles) for freight locomotives."[27]

Here, in Bobbitt's insistent comparisons of railroads and school programs, was the drive for control through the production of conformity extended to its limit. Moreover, the efficiency model and the principles of scientific curriculum making became embedded in cur-

[23] Tyack, *Turning Points*, p. 326.

[24] Herbert M. Kliebard, "Bureaucracy and Curriculum Theory," p. 79.

[25] See: Raymond E. Callahan's *Education and the Cult of Efficiency* for an exhaustive study of the adoption of business methods by school administrators.

[26] Franklin Bobbitt. "Some General Principles of Management Applied to the Problems of City-School Systems." Twelfth Yearbook of the National Society for the Study of Education, Part I. Chicago: University of Chicago Press, 1913. p. 11.

[27] Franklin Bobbitt. "High-School Costs." *The School Review* 23(8): 505; October 1915.

riculum theory through Bobbitt's landmark work, *The Curriculum*,[28] to the extent that they form, in Kliebard's words, "the central metaphor on which modern curriculum theory rests."[29] That metaphor has been strengthened, over time, by the Tyler rationale[30] in the 1950's, and by the current emphasis on specifying learner outcomes in behavioral terms.

The response of many modern educators to bureaucratic standardization and "particularization" of curriculum components has been one of regret. Efficiency and standardization seem dehumanizing. But the reformers, such as Bobbitt, who advocated these procedures hardly considered themselves villains in the piece. Indeed, the principles of scientific management and the efficiency models they proposed seemed to be the answer to their search for order and control in the rapidly changing, urbanized, industrialized society which robbed individuals of recognition and their sense of personal efficacy. Wiebe has explained the triumph of scientific management by writing that "the ideas that filtered through [all of the responses to social change] and eventually took the fort were the bureaucratic ones peculiarly suited to the fluidity and impersonality of an urban-industrial world."[31] And cultural analyst Leo Marx has described the powerful fascination of the locomotive and the railroad for nineteenth century American reformers, including the representative figure of Franklin Bobbitt, by writing: "In the popular culture of the period, the railroad was a favorite emblem of progress—not merely technological progress, but the overall progress of the race."[32] The demands of diversity had remained; the rhetoric and forms of control had changed. They had become symbols of progress.

Diversity by Denial: Institutional Selectivity

One of the most constant demands on the school curriculum has been to function as a mechanism for assimilation, as one means for melding diverse cultures into a unified society. Certainly that argument comprises a large portion of the rhetoric of social control and school reform in the nineteenth century. Those same demands are present, if not always as prominent, in more recent calls for equality of educational opportunity. But assimilationism, of course, is not the only social pres-

---

[28] Franklin Bobbitt. *The Curriculum*. Boston: Houghton Mifflin Company, 1918.

[29] Kliebard, "Bureaucracy and Curriculum Theory," p. 80.

[30] Ralph W. Tyler. *Basic Principles of Curriculum and Instruction*. Chicago: The University of Chicago Press, 1949.

[31] Robert H. Wiebe, *The Search for Order: 1877-1920*, p. 145.

[32] Leo Marx, *The Machine in the Garden*, p. 27.

Shop class, Ashwood Plantation, South Carolina, 1939.

sure on the school program. The curriculum, especially since the advent of an increasingly complex, technological, and impersonal system of production, has also functioned to select, to sort, to approve some for entry into the social and economic mainstream while rejecting others. Moreover, this process of selection has systematically—though not always intentionally—favored certain groups while denying others.

To report that the school curriculum has been characterized more by the function of selection than by assimilation or democratization is to acknowledge the obvious, just as it is an acknowledgement of the obvious to recognize that the school program has exercised its sorting powers more vigorously toward minority groups. But such acknowledgements do underscore the strong conflict between those two functions. The curriculum has failed to become a strong mechanism for assimilation precisely because of its power as a selector. It has helped maintain cultural diversity in this country because it has helped to deny access to mainstream society.

There are, of course, many factors which contribute to the selective character of American schooling, and an extensive listing would be unfeasible in this brief space and redundant of much other work. A few of these factors, however, offer interpretive interest and seem to apply in some way to the relationship between the school curriculum and most of the minority groups in this country, whether those groups are defined by race, sex, or religion. In most cases, there appears to have been some form of an initial denial of access to the school. There has been a concurrent development of an inferiority theory, usually synthesized in some way with meritocratic theory. At roughly the same time, some form of Social Darwinism has emerged to rationalize the minority group's lower status.[33] And the phenomena of bureaucratization and institutionalization have resulted in a consequent tendency to intensify the system's inflexibility. What follows is not intended as proof of these suggestions, but as examples of them. Because the history of the education of blacks in America is currently both more extensive and more available than that of Mexican Americans, American Indians, women, or Catholics, for example, the instances have been drawn from black history. It can, of course, be argued that black history is an exception in the larger history of American minorities. While that argument clearly has validity, I believe the exceptional qualities are ones of degree more than of kind. While the tactics used to deny educational opportunity to blacks have usually been more severe than those directed toward other minority groups, all groups have felt the effects of inferiority theories, Social Darwinism, and the machinations of bureaucracy and institutionalization.

Schooling is a social institution, and the relationship between any minority group and the school curriculum reflects that group's relationship with the larger society. As with most of the history of black Americans, their experience with the selective power of the curriculum is rooted in slavery. Slavery was, for this country, the "price of union," the cost of birth. Its characteristics of autocracy, absolutism, and human degradation flew in the face of the principles of freedom and equality on which the founding fathers based their declarations of independence from England. The existence of so antidemocratic an institution as slavery in the midst of a new republic required extensive rationalization. Such rationalization was hardly new, as slavery had always posed a considerable problem in the moral and religious philosophies of the

---

[33] Some explanation is necessary to distinguish between the connotations of the terms "inferiority theory" and "Social Darwinism." In my usage, inferiority theory refers to a set of justifications for the continuation of a condition or status, such as slavery, that has been *imposed*. Social Darwinism, instead, seeks to explain a set of conditions by rationalizing that those conditions exist because of some process of natural selection. In this view, for example, people live in poverty because of some defect in their character such as lack of willingness to work. That is, they have power over their lives and their fate is self-imposed, rather than controlled externally by some power elite.

western world.[34] But in other areas such as Africa and South America, the power of slaveowners was checked somewhat by legal and ecclesiastical tradition. In this country there were no safeguards on the lives of slaves. The powers of the master were absolute. Consequently, new arguments to justify slavery were developed. Alexis de Tocqueville wrote that "the only means by which the ancients maintained slavery were fetters and death; the Americans . . . have discovered more intellectual securities for the duration of their power." [35]

The "intellectual securities" de Tocqueville described were rooted in inferiority theory. Slavery was acceptable—even beneficial—according to the rationale, because the Negro race was inherently inferior. As a whole, Negroes were neither as intelligent, industrious, nor as "civilized" as whites, and consequently actually benefited from slavery as the paternalistic master provided for their needs and their welfare.[36] There were, of course, safeguards designed to ensure the continued validity of the theory of inferiority. A prohibition against schooling was one safeguard.

The Civil War ended the legal prohibition against black schooling. But the procedures for denial only became rooted in more subtle forms of the inferiority theory. They grew in large measure from a series of developments in the history of American schooling that effectively institutionalized the selective nature of the curriculum.

The first set of developments derived from the nature of society and schooling in the post civil war South. After the war, former slaves of both sexes and all ages "flocked to study the alphabet and spelling book and Bible in old plantation sheds or at town streetcorners." [37] The first generation of freed slaves trusted that schooling would lead them up the ladder of economic and social opportunity. But for school learning to contribute to upward mobility the mobility must be real. And as time passed, it was not American society but slavery itself that was reconstructed into a rigid system of caste and servitude by the "Jim Crow" laws. The hallmark of these laws was segregation, and great care was taken to ensure that blacks would be separate from whites in all things, including schooling. Public education, especially in the South, had not begun in any large-scale fashion until Reconstruction, and it was con-

---

[34] David B. Davis. *The Problems of Slavery in Western Culture.* Ithaca, New York: Cornell University Press, 1966.

[35] Alexis de Tocqueville. *Democracy in America.* New York: Vintage Books, 1945. p. 102. Reprinted by permission of Alfred A. Knopf, Inc. *Democracy in America* was originally published in 1835.

[36] There were many pro-slavery arguments in the pre-Civil War literature, and most of them included some form of this deficiency argument. See, for example: George Fitzhugh. *Cannibals All!* Richmond, Virginia, 1857.

[37] Tyack, *Turning Points,* p. 264.

fronted from its inception with serious financial problems. The southern states all had agricultural economies and rural populations. They
were relatively poor states, even in good times, and the Civil War had
devastated many of them. Further, nearly all of the Reconstructionist
state legislatures compounded the high cost of providing schools for a
rural population by establishing two school systems—one for whites and
one for blacks. After 1877, when the conservatives regained control of
the state legislatures, expenditures for education dropped sharply and
apportionment of funds saw black schools sometimes receive less than
one per cent of the total. Given the combination of the harsh end of the
hope of mobility and drastic reductions in the financial support for
black schools, it is hardly surprising that school attendance among the
recently emancipated slaves soon dropped sharply.

The resumption of many of the ways of slavery coincided with
other developments in American history that have helped to mold the
relationship between black students and the school program. One of
these was the increasing influence of industrialization and technology
and their attendant demands for higher levels of knowledge and skill.
As Patricia Graham has suggested, "Between 1865 and 1918 a watershed
was passed in America; literacy became an economic necessity." [38] The
schools began an ascendancy into their place in industrial society as
purveyors of certification. While the economic mainstream was raising
its requirements for access, blacks were being denied, more subtly than
before, opportunities to participate in the program of the schools.

At the same time, the schools' propensity toward selectivity was
buttressed by a reaffirmation and extension of inferiority theory in the
form of Social Darwinism. Social Darwinism, the application of the
Darwinian principle of natural selection to socioeconomic circumstances,
accepted as fact the principle of equality of opportunity. In a fluid,
mobile society such as the United States, the argument ran, opportunities for social and economic gain were essentially equalized. Consequently, those who advanced their status were necessarily the most
skilled, the most astute, the most meritorious. In short, they deserved
whatever riches they amassed. Conversely, the people on the bottom
rungs of the ladder, those working in menial jobs and those living in
poverty also "deserved" their station. Although the arguments of Social
Darwinism were developed by economists and social theorists to explain
the vast differences in wealth in American society and to justify the
relative conditions of the laborers and industrialists, the application of a
similar theory of "haves" and "have-nots" to education was not long in

[38] Patricia A. Graham. *Community and Class in American Education, 1865-
1918.* New York: John Wiley and Sons, Inc., 1974. p. 5.

coming. It was to be rooted in science, one of the religions of progressive America.

The Gilded Age saw a boom in technology; the Progressive Era witnessed the deification of science. In education, the scientific movement produced a rush to measure, an "orgy of quantification," as Harold Rugg later recalled.[39] Nearly everything related to schools was measured and compared. This was especially true of the "raw material" of the school program, the native intelligence of students. The beginnings of group intelligence testing, with Binet's work and the Army's Alpha and Beta tests during World War I, the application of the tests to children and adolescents in a school setting, and the subsequent controversies surrounding the uses of intelligence tests are well known and often told.[40] Only a few points need mentioning to underscore the role of the measurement movement in the development of the selective function of the school curriculum, especially with respect to black students.

From their beginnings, intelligence tests were intended to serve the cause of efficiency. They would allow, it was thought, the sorting of individuals into jobs and roles according to their innate abilities. As E. L. Thorndike explained, "dull normals" could never graduate from a reputable law school because environmental differences such as family life and schooling accounted for less than a fifth of the variation in intelligence among individuals. Leadership roles would be entrusted to the more intelligent while more menial tasks would be assigned to "the lower percentiles." Testing would provide a shortcut for the process of natural selection inherent in the views of Social Darwinians by selecting early in life. For the schools, this meant channeling students into programs geared toward preparing them for their pre-selected stations in life. Those who scored high on intelligence tests were to be placed in a college preparatory course while those with low intelligence scores would be given commercial or technical courses where there was more emphasis on manual arts.

Test construction is, of course, a culture-bound activity. The items developed for the test reflect the values and perceptions of the testmaker

---

[39] Harold Rugg. *American Life and the School Curriculum: Next Steps Toward Schools of Living.* Boston: Ginn and Co., 1936. p. 38.

[40] Despite an occasional tendency toward blunt, somewhat heavy-handed interpretive statements, Edgar B. Gumbert and Joel H. Spring provide a concise, pointed account of intelligence testing and its effects from Binet to the present in: *The Superschool and the Superstate: American Education in the Twentieth Century, 1918-1970.* New York: John Wiley and Sons, Inc., 1974. Moreover, their bibliographic essay (pp. 186-88) provides a descriptive summary of many of the major publications related to intelligence testing and the nature-nurture controversy so closely associated with it.

and the population on which the test is validated. Not surprisingly then, IQ scores from the beginning paralleled lines of social class and race, with low-income blacks repeatedly scoring at the bottom of the scale. This finding meshed with long-held beliefs in the innate inferiority of the Negro race, imbuing such beliefs with an air of scientific respectability and reinforcing the apparent explanatory power of Social Darwinism. More than that, though, the theory and procedures of systematic selectivity matched the demands and biases of a still young, but potentially powerful school bureaucracy.

Like Social Darwinism, the bureaucratization of schools was largely a product of the second half of the nineteenth century.[41] It was a product of urbanization, certainly. But more than that, the development of bureaucratic organizations represented a large-scale attempt to control the complexity and diversity of early industrial society. Bureaucratic organization made systems of schools and, in so doing, profoundly affected the programs of the schools. Committee organization became the way to develop curriculum.[42] The curriculum increased its uniformity, became even more impersonal, and solidified its rigidity. In short, the school program became institutionalized. And in the process of bureaucratization and organization, the values of whiteness, maleness, and middle-classness became the institutionalized characteristics of the school curriculum. Reason, logic, and rationalism were prized, emotionalism was devalued. The scientific method became the exemplar while intuition was more tolerated than extolled. Relationships and events became explainable in terms of cause and effect; time became the most used dimension and the future became its most prized element.[43] Subtle selectivity, the "hidden curriculum," had become part of the system by the 1920's.

Conformity by Consensus:
"The Best Is the Best Everywhere"

The rhetoric of educational reform in the nineteenth and early twentieth centuries demanded that the school program consciously and

[41] David B. Tyack carefully describes the historical development of bureaucratic urban school systems and the spread of bureaucratic values during the late nineteenth century in: *The One Best System.* See especially pages 39-59.

[42] The Twenty-Sixth Yearbook of the National Society for the Study of Education, *The Foundations and Technique of Curriculum Construction.* Bloomington, Illinois: Public School Publishing Co., 1926, is in one sense a monument to this approach.

[43] Haubrich, editor, *Freedom, Bureaucracy, and Schooling.* See especially

intentionally produce conformity among pupils. In the mid-nineteenth century, the common school curriculum was to help impose higher status values on lower status citizens.[44] During the later years of that century and the early years of this one, the schools were again asked to help assimilate and "Americanize" large numbers of students. The strongest cries for schooling to function as an agency of social control arose in response to an influx of immigrants: first the Irish, with their staunch support of Catholicism, and then the Italians and Slavs, bringing not only new ways but a new language to American shores.[45]

The rhetoric of reform in these years asked the schools to aid in the overt imposition of habits and values to produce conformity as an explicit means of social control. But the history of American culture is also replete with examples that support the contentions of anthropologists that all societies are characterized by strong tendencies to produce conformity among their members. In this view, conformity is an expression of cohesiveness, strength, and progress. It is a necessary part of the search for the "one best system" manned by true believers. Here conformity is a good. It is also more tacit than explicit, more hidden than open, less intentional imposition than the development of consensus.

The uncoerced, but nonetheless systematic development of consensus almost as a byproduct of schooling seems to be largely a phenomenon of this century. It is manifested in the regimentation, regularities, and value systems that form the "hidden curriculum," to be sure. But consensus has also been an easily seen, if little expressed, part of the rhetoric of the curriculum. It appears in the Progressives' emphasis on problem solving, in Dewey's conception of the social nature of education, in the focus on inquiry so prevalent during the 1960's, and in our current concern with values clarification and moral education.

Consensus has long been an integral part of the American way of life. And it has long produced marked differences of opinion regarding its relative virtues and liabilities. As early as 1835, for example, Alexis de Tocqueville warned his American audience of the dangers inherent in what he called the "tyranny of the majority." "I know of no country," he said, "in which there is so little independence of mind and real freedom of discussion as in America. . . . freedom of opinion does not

---

Chapter 1 (pp. 3-28), "Freedom and Bureaucracy in the Schools," by Donald Arnstine, and Chapter 16 (pp. 269-80), "Does the Common School Have a Chance?" by Vernon F. Haubrich.

[44] Robert H. Wiebe. "The Social Functions of Public Education." *American Quarterly* 21: 147-64; Summer 1969.

[45] See: Michael Katz. *The Irony of Early School Reform*. Cambridge, Massachusetts: Harvard University Press, 1968, for an account of the effects of the Irish immigration on society and schools in Massachusetts.

exist [there]." [46] Tocqueville further noted, with some disdain, that Americans appeared to take pride in sameness and even to sing its praises, a phenomenon that historian Daniel Boorstin later described as "Boosterism." [47]

To the boosters—the evangelists and promoters of dozens of causes from patent medicines to new "cities"—consensus was a much-sought goal. The multiplication of similarity and sameness was an affirmation that a thing was right and that it represented progress. The spread of schools even to the tiniest villages and hamlets on the frontier, for example, is probably less attributable to their effectiveness in producing an educated citizenry than to their status as symbols of civilization and progress. Every town wanted one, and every town wanted theirs to be the best around. But the programs in these schools looked much the same, no matter whether the schools were in farming villages, mining camps, or river towns. As John Philbrick, Superintendent of Schools in Boston, said in the language of the boosters, "the best is the best everywhere." [48]

If the multiplication of American schools in the nineteenth century was striking, the mushrooming number of colleges during those years was almost ludicrous. Probably the principal cause of "the excessive multiplication and dwarfish dimensions" of the colleges that sprouted in the West was denominationalism. Each religious sect was determined to have its own institution of higher learning. But although these boosters were religious leaders rather than business or school leaders, their results looked the same—more schools than could be filled. This particular result of boosterism caused Columbia University's President, Frederick A. P. Barnard, to marvel in 1880 that England, with its 23 million citizens, managed well with only four degree-granting institutions, while Ohio, with a population of only three million, had licensed thirty-seven.[49]

While the examples of de Tocqueville's concern over the tyranny of the majority and the boosterism that characterized so much of nineteenth-century expansionism indicate the longevity of consensus as a factor in American culture, it has been only in this century that the conscious use of the properties of group agreement—consensus—has

[46] de Tocqueville, *Democracy in America*, pp. 273-75.

[47] Daniel Boorstin. *The Americans: The National Experience*. New York: Random House, Inc., 1965. pp. 113-68.

[48] John D. Philbrick. *City School Systems in the United States, 1885*. Reprint. U.S. Department of the Interior, Bureau of Education. Circulars of Information, No. 1. Washington, D.C.: Government Printing Office. p. 19.

[49] Boorstin, *The Americans: The National Experience*, p. 155.

been recommended to the schools in a programmatic sense. Those recommendations arose, as have so many others in this century, from the rhetoric of Progressivism. And they came after a stunning social crisis graphically illustrated that man apparently no longer had control of the social forces that affected his life.

John Dewey had hinted at the possibilities inherent in the use of developing consensus as a consequence of schooling at least as early as 1916, in *Democracy and Education*.[50] There he wrote that schools are, in fact, a vital agency for socialization. Each new generation acquires many of its traits there, thus allowing society to continue its existence. That recognition represented no real departure in the rhetoric of schooling. But Dewey went on to suggest that schooling could be used to *influence* the direction of social change. If a conception of the "good" society could be developed, its features could be discussed and experienced by groups of students—groups who would, without coercion, come to accept and support the most valid features of that "good" society.

While the impact of this notion on the school curriculum was hardly immediate, Dewey's assertion was a harbinger of a shift in thought regarding the control function of schooling. While the rhetoric

[50] John Dewey. *Democracy and Education.* New York: The Macmillan Co., 1916. pp. 12-28, 117-29.

School in church, Gee's Bend, Alabama, 1937.

of the nineteenth century said that a major function of schooling was to control the members of society, the rhetoric of the twentieth century was to become increasingly insistent that schooling could be used to help control society. The belief that social problems were amenable to solution by the school program has, until recently, been one of the most persistent assumptions of this century. Moreover, the means by which such problems were to be solved was frequently that of "problem-solving" in groups—the development of consensus.

Dewey's analyses of the process of education made much of the interaction between children and the society in which they grew up. But while Dewey's analyses carefully integrated both the child and the society into an interdependent relationship, the progressive movement in education split itself into "child-centered" and "society-centered" factions.[51] The child-centered progressives, "hard working and sincere evangelists of a better childhood" as Rugg and Shumaker [52] described them, dominated progressive education until the early 1930's. They viewed the mission of schooling in large measure as that of providing "natural" environments and a variety of materials to permit the free expression of the felt needs and interests of children. The society-centered progressives, on the other hand, based their views of the purposes of schooling on social analysis. "The question is not," as Boyd Bode wrote in 1927, "whether social vision affects educational practices, but whether in the long run anything *else* affects them." [53]

The debate between these two factions of progressivism constituted a very large share of the rhetoric about the purposes of schooling from the 1920's through the 1940's. In 1932, a new sense of urgency and intensity was added to that debate by George S. Counts' challenge to the schools to reconstruct a social order torn by the ravages of the Great Depression.[54] Child-centered progressivism's view of the school program, Counts asserted, clearly had many virtues. But it lacked any social orientation, "unless it be that of anarchy or extreme individualism." [55] This,

[51] See: Lawrence A. Cremin. *The Transformation of the School.* New York: Random House, Inc., 1961; and Patricia A. Graham. *Progressive Education: From Arcady to Academe.* New York: Teachers College Press, 1967, for extensive analyses of progressive education, including the conflict between the child-centered progressives and the society-centered progressives.

[52] Harold Rugg and Ann Shumaker. *The Child-Centered School: An Appraisal of the New Education.* Yonkers, New York: World Book Co., 1929.

[53] Boyd H. Bode. *Modern Educational Theories.* New York: The Macmillan Co., 1927. p. iv.

[54] George S. Counts. *Dare the Schools Build a New Social Order?* New York: The John Day Co., 1933.

[55] George S. Counts. "Dare Progressive Education BE Progressive?" *Progres-*

he believed, was unacceptable in view of the "culture lag" that existed between the urbanized, industrialized, technological reality of the twentieth century and the outmoded but still extant pastoral, individualistic, laissez-faire value system of the nineteenth century. His answer was for educators to define the directions society needed to take and to develop a system of values appropriate to those directions. The schools would then be used to transfer those values to students.

Public reaction and the history of education have labeled Counts and the other social reconstructionists as radicals. And indeed, their rhetoric about social problems and their proposed solutions *was* radical— at least in the Thirties.[56] But their outline of the purposes and forms of the curriculum was not. As developed in various sources, the school program to be used to reconstruct the social order was to consist largely of the study of acute social problems.[57] These problems were to be studied through collective use of the scientific mode of inquiry, with the expectation that the group would achieve consensus not only about the nature of the problem but also about its potential solution. As Broudy recently characterized the reconstructionist view of the purpose of schooling, the school program was to help institute "a social order that would be based on consensus. . . . What the muckrakers had turned up about the evils of American society would be 'found out' by the pupils themselves, and thus pressure for liberal legislation would be created rationally and naturally in and by the schools."[58]

The view that consensus about social problems should be a legitimate outcome of schooling was extended even further by the social reconstructionism of the Forties. The leading reconstructionists of the Thirties viewed the process of collective inquiry and decision making as a way to learn about society's problems and proposed solutions. But the

---

sive Education 9(4): 257; April 1932. This article, the text of Counts' address to the Progressive Education Association, later appeared in slightly revised form in *Dare the Schools Build a New Social Order?*

[56] For a lengthy investigation of social reconstructionism see: C. A. Bowers. *The Progressive Educator and the Depression: The Radical Years.* New York: Random House, 1969.

[57] See, for example: William H. Kilpatrick, editor. *The Educational Frontier.* New York: The Century Co., 1933, especially Chapter V, pp. 160-92, "The School: Its Task and Administration," by Gordon Hullfish; Harold O. Rugg. *American Life and the School Curriculum: Next Steps Toward Schools for Living.* Boston: Ginn and Co., 1936; and Theodore Brameld. *Design for America.* New York: Harper and Brothers, 1945.

[58] Harry S. Broudy. "Democratic Values and Educational Goals." In: R. M. McClure, editor. *The Curriculum: Retrospect and Prospect.* 70th Yearbook of the National Society for the Study of Education. Chicago: University of Chicago Press, 1971. pp. 132-33. Copyright © NSSE.

authors of *The Improvement of Practical Intelligence*,[59] R. Bruce Raup, Kenneth Benne, George Axtelle, and B. O. Smith, saw their method of cooperative problem solving—achieving consensus—as an end in itself. They sought to pave the way for more adequate social planning by practicing students in the method of "practical judgment," a process in which students publicly identified their ideals and goals and then developed plans for achieving them. The key factor in this procedure was the process of "democratic deliberation," so named because its aim was to develop dedication and devotion to common ends and causes. This required individuals to "grow" into the method of practical judgment by progressively subordinating their own desires to those of the group until they became identical. Truth and right were to be defined by consensus.[60]

While they were less concerned with the mechanics of developing a "group mind" than with the practical problems of daily living, the life-adjustment educators of the 1940's and early 1950's also utilized the development of consensus as a problem-solving mechanism. The primary goal of life-adjustment education, according to the creed adopted by the Commission on Life-Adjustment Education for Youth, was to equip "all American youth to live democratically."[61] In order to reach this goal, the school curriculum was to help young people adjust themselves to the demands of an industrialized democracy by examining both present and future problems. It would be concerned with dating as well as voting, with communications with parents as well as with future employers. It was to instill a belief in the dignity of work. And it was to teach students to think of government as an instrument which people used collectively to do things for the common good. Further, the government was not the only instrument that could promote the common good. The "group" also would be available for "collective deliberation" of problems brought to it by individuals. The subtle but powerful force of consensus, it seemed, could not only control the direction of society, it could aid individuals to adjust to the new directions.

Whether the intent of the reconstructionists was to use the curricu-

[59] R. Bruce Raup; Kenneth D. Benne; George E. Axtelle; and B. Othanel Smith. *The Improvement of Practical Intelligence*. New York: Collier Books, 1949.

[60] See: Bowers, *The Progressive Educator and the Depression*, pp. 204-10; and G. A. Ponder. "Conflict, Collectivism, and Consensus: A Historical Analysis of Social Reconstructionist Curriculum Theories." Unpublished doctoral dissertation, The University of Texas at Austin, 1974. pp. 128-36, 193-202, for more complete analyses of *The Improvement of Practical Intelligence*.

[61] U.S. Department of Health, Education, and Welfare, Office of Education. *Life Adjustment Education for Every Youth*. Washington, D.C.: Government Printing Office, 1947. p. 4.

lum for social engineering or for solving everyday personal problems, the means was to be collective deliberation and the development of consensus. But this was not, at least in the reconstructionist view, a consensus of mediocrity. Instead, there ran throughout these proposals a firm belief in the rationality of man. The group would agree on the most viable solution because it would also be the most reasonable. Not so different, it seems, from our current fascination with the clarification of values and the focus on the structures of the disciplines during the last decade. The same faith in reason is there, if less explicitly. Public discussion of value positions, it is assumed, will lead to the adoption of the most rational set of beliefs. Nor will the procedures of "inquiry" or "discovery" lead students to "wrong" conclusions about the nature of knowledge. Each discipline's organizing concepts and generalizations are there because they are the most true. The curriculum is based largely on a consensus developed by specialists.

Diversity by Design: Shifting the Locus of Control

The tension between diversity in American society and the constant demand for some degree of conformity has, in some way, defined the social function of the school curriculum since its inception. In the past, that function has been one of exerting some form of centralized control over diversity. The school program was to impose American ways on immigrants, for example, or it was to contribute to social reconstruction by developing a newer, more enlightened social and economic consensus, or it was to control access to the mainstream by processes of selection. But some changes are apparent in the recent history of schooling. Even while the most strident critics of the public schools condemn them for perpetuating a caste system of social class, inculcating docility and acquiescence and destroying freedom, schooling appears to have begun to respond to social and cultural diversity in different ways. There are indications that alternatives for students are being opened, rather than restricted, that "the system" is at least tolerating diversity, rather than trying to repress it. The social function of the curriculum appears to be moving from controlling diversity to promoting it by placing more and more control over schooling in the hands of the individuals and groups most affected by it.

If decentralization, dispersion of control, and the multiplication of options are indeed becoming characteristics of the curriculum, they are so, again, because they increasingly reflect the nature of society. Historian Samuel P. Hays has described mid-twentieth century America as an "organizational society," indicating some characteristics in the development of such a society that may also be helpful in exploring the current status of the public school curriculum.[62] Hays suggests that the formative period of modern America, the years from the late nineteenth century through the depression of the 1930's, was filled with the rhetoric and images of science and technology, efficiency and system, and "businesslike alternatives." This language, these symbols were expressions of new and pervasive cultural values. But more than that, they gave rise to new forms of social organization; in Hays' words, "they transformed the manner in which American society was put together."[63] One of these transformations was the development of "technical systems"—systems through which some people organized and controlled the lives of others by using the comparatively new processes of reason, science, and technology. Another transformation was the growth of patterns of functional organization—relationships among people with common interests, whether they worked in the same kinds of jobs, consumed the same kinds of goods or services, or specialized in some branch of one of the emerging professions. Whatever the function around which organization developed, the spirit was the same. Functional organizations promoted collective action designed to exert control over the surrounding environment.[64]

These facets of organizational society help to explain parallel events in the history of American education. They help offer explanations for the beginnings of the curriculum as a field of specialization near the end of World War I; for the efficiency movement led by school administrators; and for the extraordinary faith in the powers of science, reason, and schooling exhibited by the social reconstructionists in the 1930's and by the rest of society in subsequent years. Technical systems and functional organizations also help to explain more current examples of curriculum change, especially when they are combined with the third of Hays' dimensions of organizational society, "the shaping of linkages between smaller and larger contexts of life."[65]

As this century has passed, technological developments in the areas

[62] Samuel P. Hays. "The New Organizational Society." In: Jerry Israel, editor. *Building the Organizational Society*. New York: The Free Press, 1972.

[63] *Ibid.*, p. 1.

[64] For a more extensive discussion of these facets of organizational society, especially as they apply to professionalization in education and curriculum making, see the essay in this volume by Walter Doyle, "Education for All: The Triumph of Professionalism."

[65] Hays, "The New Organizational Society," p. 9. Hays' description of the development of these linkages and the consequent results is closely related to similar explanations in Wiebe's *The Search for Order*.

of communication and transportation have inexorably led to a closer integration of the social order. First the railroad and the telegraph, then the automobile, telephone, and radio, and more recently the high speeds associated with jet aircraft, freeway systems, and television have greatly modified the experience and values of the American people, drawing them always closer together, making them less isolated and more alike. These changes, however, were not everywhere the same. They began in the cities, the "larger, more cosmopolitan centers," and they were pushed relentlessly into ever smaller, more isolated areas. The process of organization, of shaping linkages between the larger and the smaller, took two forms. There was first "penetration," in which the cosmopolitan values of secularism, variety, and technology were carried from larger areas to smaller ones by the new modes of communication and transportation. Then there was "involvement," a process whereby the inhabitants of more isolated areas became first attracted to the wider world and later heavily involved with it. Society became more organized—and more homogenized. Rural areas resisted the invasion of cosmopolitanism, lost their children to it, and finally accommodated it. Ethnic neighborhoods in the cities retained some of their flavor, but became much more involved with city-wide politics, business, and entertainment. Smaller school districts consolidated into larger ones and the scope of administrative agencies widened. A new organizational society arose out of an older, more isolated, less interdependent social order.

The informal linkages of cosmopolitanism and the more formal organizational forms of technical systems and functional associations have resulted in many changes in society and its institutions. To quote Hays:

> The new organizational society increased enormously the range of options as to what one could think, be, and do. Variety and choice replaced a limited number of vocational alternatives, of leisure-time activities; of manners of personal behavior, of what views one could legimately hold....[66]

It also produced further advances in technology, and it greatly increased the number of people involved in the exercise of political power. These changes are reflected in recent curricular concerns with individualization, cultural pluralism, and content segmentation.

Individualized education has a considerable history. Its theory base began at least as far back as the eighteenth century, with Pestalozzi, and it survived the Darwinian and Spencerian scientism of competition and natural selection in the last century. There were working examples of individualized schooling in the early years of this century—Helen

[66] *Ibid.*, p. 14.

Parkhurst's in Dalton, Massachusetts, and Carleton Washburne's in Winnetka, Illinois, to name but two.[67] But individualized education has never before received the attention and support typical of the past decade. That attention has resulted, in part, from the promise of equality, implicit in programs designed to account for individual differences and so appealing to an increasingly democratized system of schooling. With that appeal, however, the more recent systems of individualized education also have demonstrated a greater maturity that has resulted from technological advance and the rise of technical systems.

This dual advance in the technology and technical systems of individualized education is largely a product of the past ten years.[68] With the support of large research and development centers, individualized education changed from its nearly exclusive reliance on programmed instruction and its inability to accommodate more than varying rates of progress through an instructional sequence to more complex, sophisticated systems using a variety of instructional modes and environmental management techniques. In the process, a more extensive technical language marked by acronyms—IGE, IGM, IPI—and a new umbrella term, "personalized instruction" were created to type the new generation of programs and separate them from the old. And newer, more demanding administrative structures were developed to manage the people involved with the programs.[69] Technical systems developed during the evolution of the organizational society have begun to make individualized instructional programs available to larger numbers of students and to total school systems.

The history of the concept of cultural pluralism is still too brief to allow definitive statements. The concept itself has only recently achieved some measure of public awareness. Cultural pluralism is only now struggling to become an institutionalized goal of education, it is a policy in only a few places, and a reality nowhere. The number of ethnic studies courses in the school curriculum at any level may be

[67] See: Helen Parkhurst. "The Dalton Plan"; and Carleton Washburne. "Burke's Individualized System as Developed at Winnetka." Both in: *Adapting the Schools to Individual Differences.* Twenty-Fourth Yearbook of the National Society for the Study of Education, Part II. Bloomington, Illinois: Public School Publishing Company, 1925.

[68] Maurice Eash. "Introduction." In: Harriet Talmadge, editor. *Systems of Individualized Education.* Berkeley, California: McCutchan Publishing Corporation, 1975. p. 1.

[69] Herbert J. Klausmeier. "IGE: An Alternative Form of Schooling." In: Talmadge, editor, *Systems of Individualized Education.* The acronym IGE stands for "Individually Guided Education"; IGM stands for "Individually Guided Motivation"; and IPI for "Individually Prescribed Instruction."

decreasing rather than increasing or even stabilizing and plans for making the schools into vehicles for cultural pluralism are, at this point, little more than rhetoric. Yet the viability and future of cultural pluralism do not negate its current impact on the social institution of schooling and the social function of the curriculum. In 1974, for example, the National Society for the Study of Education devoted one volume of its "Contemporary Educational Issues" series to an exploration of cultural pluralism.[70] At nearly the same time, the Association for Supervision and Curriculum Development accepted cultural pluralism as one of its goals for education. Publishing houses have scrambled to produce materials oriented toward different ethnic groups, and many urban school systems have begun to examine their curricula for previously unacknowledged institutional racial biases. Such responses, even if they are largely superficial and rhetorical, suggest expectations that are clearly different from those of even a half century ago.

The shift in curricular rhetoric from exclusionary social control to cultural pluralism resulted largely from the exercise of political power and the exertion of pressure. Such events are consonant with Hays' conception of an evolving organizational society and are predictable from the phenomena of functional organization and cosmopolitanism. Moreover, if the explanation holds, cultural pluralism should continue to be a force pressing for even greater diversity and option in the curriculum. Ironically, perhaps, such pressures for diversity will occur at the same time that American society is becoming more homogeneous.

Another noticeable example of the organizational society's production of diversity in the curriculum is that of content segmentation. By content segmentation, I refer to an apparently increasing tendency to package the content of schooling in smaller, more discrete pieces, often with the expressed intention of providing more variety and choice for students. Continuous progress systems are one kind of segmentation, with a year's worth of mathematics, for example, broken into smaller chunks for individual consumption. Even better examples of diversity by design can be seen in schools where the elective system has been expanded almost geometrically—middle school theory, especially, typifies this approach by proposing the use of a large number of short exploratory courses or sequences. Minicourses, developed partly in response to pressures for year-round schooling, provide still more examples of segmentation and expanding options. And the recent push for career education, with its attendant elevation of the status of vocationalism, offers yet another instance of expanding options within the system of American

[70] Edgar G. Epps, editor. *Cultural Pluralism.* Berkeley, California: McCutchan Publishing Corporation, 1974.

schooling. Although many of these apparent changes will undoubtedly be reduced to the status of gimmickry and faddism, their existence does provide some evidence of increased option, sophistication, and cosmopolitanism.

Conclusion

The interpretations of the changing social function of the curriculum contained in this essay are, at this point, largely suggestions in need of further study. Certainly they could have been labeled differently with no loss of validity. And the impression of change may be more illusory than real. Any suggestion that rhetoric about schooling describes events in classrooms is highly debatable. It is quite possible, in fact, that curriculum implementation at the classroom level is remarkably stable over time, that the planned experiences students have in schoolrooms, the activities they engage in and the materials they interact with result almost entirely from idiosyncratic choices made by individual teachers. This is a history as yet unavailable, as Geraldine Clifford indicated in a recent position paper.[71] It is a history that must be gleaned from diaries, letters, autobiographies, and plan books. When—if—that history is written, perhaps it will be as Clifford suggests, a "people-centered institutional history" of schooling that will be neither a celebration nor a condemnation but an analysis of the unevenness in the performance of educational institutions, of the ambivalence in the social function of the curriculum, of the benevolence as well as the baseness in the people who develop the purposes and forms of public education.

[71] Geraldine Jonçich Clifford. "Saints, Sinners, and People: A Position Paper on the Historiography of American Education." *History of Education Quarterly* 15: 257-72; Fall 1975.

BICENTENNIAL VIGNETTES

Collings' Experimental School in Rural Missouri, 1917

In 1917, barely two years after William Heard Kilpatrick began to develop his project method of learning, one of his students, Ellsworth Collings, established an experimental project method school in rural McDonald County, Missouri. Collings believed that a school could operate effectively with the curriculum selected directly from the real life purposes of boys and girls. He saw the curriculum as a series of guided experiences so related that what is learned in one experience serves to elevate and enrich subsequent experiences and he identified the learnings to be encouraged as those needed to carry on better the enterprise under way.

During a four-year experimental and assessment period from 1917 to 1921, forty-one pupils guided by a teacher and an assistant teacher under Collings' supervision demonstrated that a school organized around these ideas could operate effectively. Collings' account of the experiment[1] served as his doctoral thesis at Teachers

[1] Ellsworth Collings. *An Experiment with a Project Curriculum.* New York: Macmillan, 1923.

College, Columbia University, and for years was recognized as an authoritative study. Now, half a century later, it is seldom cited and seems little known.

Pupils in Collings' school worked in three multiage groups and engaged in four categories of activities: excursions, construction, storytelling, and play. Play activities included games, social events, and dramatizations. Storytelling involved primarily the retelling of stories and picture stories. Construction or hand projects were varied. Some were as simple as making cocoa and soup for the school cafeteria. Others involved building such things as ironing boards, fly-traps and storage cabinets, or growing gardens. Excursion projects also varied greatly. A simple excursion was a visit to Mrs. Murphy's sunflowers with follow-up study of the cultivation and uses of sunflowers. A more elaborate excursion project involved the study of the possible causes of typhoid in a home where members of the family regularly had the disease and concluded with recommendations to the homeowner of ways to correct the situation. Frequently, the reports of major excursion projects were made at community meetings held in the evenings and open to all.

Comparisons were made between the Collings school and two closely matched control schools. Even though in the experimental school, traditional subject matter was learned subordinately only as it was needed, academic achievement measured by standard achievement tests was higher than in the control schools, although the differences, except for geography, were small. In all other comparisons, however, great differences favored the experimental school. These differences were manifest in pupils' attitude toward school (e.g., attendance, tardiness), children's conduct outside the school (e.g., reading habits, practice of certain health habits), parents' attitudes toward school (e.g., voting record on school issues, using the school as a resource), parents' conduct in the home and community (e.g., testing seeds before planting, incidence of contagious diseases), and introduction of home conveniences (e.g., screened doors and windows, use of ironing board).

Kilpatrick, in his introduction to Collings' book, called this school a pioneering effort with respect to the guiding aims of the school, to the means of attaining those aims, and the type of data advanced to substantiate success. Collings' school and his research do not deserve obscurity; they seem to merit renewed attention.

—*Earl Kenyon*

Washburne's Winnetka Plan: Less a Plan than Ideas

In a little suburb 20 miles outside Chicago, a group of prosperous businessmen gathered to discuss the possibilities of establishing a private school for their children. Sometime during the course of that meeting, Edwin Fletcher rose to ask, "Why don't we make the public schools of our village so good that we will be proud to send our children to them and will need no private school?" (p. 4).[1] Although

[1] All references from: Carleton W. Washburne and Sidney P. Marland, Jr.

Fletcher was voted out of order by the chairman, the idea nonetheless caught fire. Others joined Fletcher with the result that another meeting was called, this time with mothers present. The conclusion reached at this second meeting was to have historic significance not only for the schools in the village of Winnetka, but also for other

Winnetka: The History and Significance of an Educational Experiment. Englewood Cliffs, New Jersey: Prentice-Hall, Inc., 1963.

schools later influenced by the innovations taking place in the Winnetka school system.

These two meetings of concerned parents in Winnetka occurred in 1911 or 1912. Few significant changes were made in the school system, however, until 1918. At that time, the school board decided to seek a new superintendent. Board members, taken with Fredric Burk's work at San Francisco State Normal School, sought his advice. By May 1919, they had chosen Carleton Washburne, a man who had worked under Burk for five years, to be the new superintendent.

Washburne brought to Winnetka ideas on the use of self-instructional materials, intelligence and achievement testing, and diagnostic testing. These and other ideas he introduced to the schools along with his abundant enthusiasm, energy, and a willingness to experiment. Yet, Washburne's success in helping fashion a school to which parents "would be proud to send their children" may be ascribed, in large measure, to the amount of productive time spent by the staff, including Washburne himself, in cooperative planning.

Throughout Washburne's 24 years as Winnetka superintendent, staff members met frequently to plan research, write and revise self-instructional materials, and develop diagnostic testing among many other tasks. These meetings offered a key to the emergence of the Winnetka school system and its philosophy—a philosophy in which each child was stimulated and helped "to develop his own personal and social potentialities in accordance with his individual design of growth" (p. 22).

An essential part of the Winnetka program, besides self-instruction and correction, diagnostic testing, and individual rates of progress, were the group projects. At the junior high level these projects became economic enterprises. One of the earliest was the "Skokie Livestock Corporation." Briefly, several of the pupils decided to raise rabbits. Since there seemed to be a great demand for baby rabbits around Easter time, they expected to make a profit. First, however, they needed money to buy and feed rabbits, and lumber for their shelter. Further, they decided that those who did the work of feeding and cleaning the shelter should be paid. These conditions required capital. To gain the necessary money, the pupils, with the help of the arithmetic teacher, formed a corporation and sold stocks. Gradually, the entire school became involved. When "unrest" developed among the laborers, the social studies teacher introduced the topic of labor unions, and a union was formed. The corporation continued for many years with some successes, failures, elaborations, and variations. It serves mainly as an example of the many and diverse projects carried on at the school, some short lived, others surviving for many years.

The "Skokie Livestock Corporation" is more than just representative of the economic enterprises, however. The enthusiasm, interest, ingenuity, and cooperation were and are continuing characteristics of the Winnetka school system itself. Often misnamed "The Winnetka Plan" by interested universities, colleges, school superintendents, teachers, and boards of education, Winnetka, in the words of Carleton Washburne, "is and was a spirit, a condition, an attitude of teaching, but never a fixed plan" (p. 169). Winnetka never tried to set a pattern for all the nation's schools. It worked to provide the best possible education it could for each child in that district—a goal any school can hope to achieve.

—*Marilyn Maxson*

Rugg's Textbooks: Bootstrap Curriculum Development and Bookburning in America

In August 1922, Harold Ordway Rugg began shipping the first of his social study pamphlets. Feeling the need for new and better social studies material Rugg envisioned materials that both cut across discipline areas to deal with man and society, and stimulated discussion of controversial issues. Unable to finance the venture and finding no foundation funds Rugg wrote to three hundred school personnel in public and private schools asking them if they would buy, sight unseen, a social study pamphlet series for grades seven through nine. The

Nursery school for workers' children, Orange, Texas, 1949. Boy at left is the son of the first woman riveter hired in the shipyard; his father is in the army.

response was overwhelming. Advance orders came in by the thousands. With a tight schedule to follow Rugg wrote while his brother Earl did the research and an assistant revised and read proof. By April 1923 the last contracted-for pamphlets had been shipped. Rugg had emerged as a curriculum writer.

Rugg's entrance to the world of curriculum making was dramatic. Three hundred and seventy-five school systems throughout thirty-eight states used about three thousand copies of Rugg's series experimentally. Through commercial publication, the series was later expanded to 14 volumes including grades three through six. Rugg's career could have rested on this accomplishment alone had not the advent of the depression and Rugg's concern with the plight of his fellow man plunged him into adult education. Among other things, Rugg proposed that teachers be trained to lead adult discussion groups throughout the country, exploring economic and social problems. The idea created a stir but received no financial support. In the interim Rugg wrote two study guides later incorporated into his controversial book, *The Great Technology* (1933). The book's theme—the redesigning of the school, curriculum, and society by artist-teachers. Rugg envisioned a school-centered society where school and society continually worked together to improve each other.

Rugg was no less an innovator than Dewey, Kilpatrick, or Counts, but, as Progressive Education began to wane, Rugg was the one who drew the most stinging criticism and attack. His books were banned, and in Bradner, Ohio, they were burned. As early as 1927 Rugg's social study pamphlets were criticized as being subversive. By 1940 a major movement was under way to oust his books from the schools. Pressure groups, power, money, and the mass media were mounted against him. In defense Rugg asked, "Have you read the books in question?" Invariably the answer was, "I haven't read the books but I have heard they are bad" (p. 104).[1] The defense made little impact.

The controversy over Rugg's books ended abruptly as the United States mobilized for war. Rugg and his books were forgotten. The pendulum started its swing back toward more traditional views, Americans responding to Rugg's life work with, at best, a difference of viewpoints. Among other issues were the beliefs of too many people that children would not, or should not, respond to the realities of poverty, crime, and injustice. Once called a communist, Rugg's retirement in 1951 from Teachers College went little noticed. Un-

[1] Franklin Parker. "The Case of Harold Rugg." *Paedagogica Historica* 2: 95-122; 1962.

daunted, he continued writing until his death in 1960—perhaps in the belief that understanding comes only through facing the issues squarely and discussing them.

—*Marilyn Maxson*

Accreditation Standards and Curriculum

The publication, in 1940, of *How To Evaluate a Secondary School* [1] marked a relatively new era in the development of curriculum. Although accreditation was by no means a new idea, *How To Evaluate a Secondary School*, with the accompanying manuals, "Evaluative Criteria" and "Educational Temperatures," was the first major attempt at setting standards on a nationwide basis.

Prior to the Cooperative Study, begun in 1933, most accreditation was done by affiliation of secondary schools with universities. The first of these programs was begun at the University of Michigan in 1870, in an effort to replace college entrance examinations. [2] The agreement provided for the university to set standards for the participating high schools in return for allowing graduates of the school to be admitted without taking the entrance examination.

A series of suggestions between 1928 and 1933 led to the inception of the Cooperative Study. The first major step was taken when the National Association of Officers of Regional Associations passed a resolution proposing that the six regional accrediting associations join together in a cooperative study of secondary schools.

The work of the Cooperative Study continues with revised manuals published each ten years. Manuals for the evaluation of junior high schools and elementary schools have recently been developed and accreditation begun for these levels.

The influence of the Cooperative Study on the development of curriculum has been profound. While it did not lead to the development of a national curriculum as feared by some critics, it seems to have introduced elements of standards into several curriculum components. Experimental programs continue to be tempered by the evaluative criteria; curricular programs are examined for their effect on accreditation. Many state education agencies examine their policies for state accreditation in light of the evaluative criteria advanced by the Cooperative Study.

—*Larry L. Krause*

[1] Cooperative Study of Secondary School Standards. *How To Evaluate a Secondary School*. Washington, D.C.: the Study, 1940.

[2] Edward A. Krug. *The Shaping of the American High School*. New York: Harper & Row, Publishers, 1964.

4

Diversity and Conformity in American Curriculum

Ambrose A. Clegg, Jr.

Of the many values that operate in American education, perhaps no two evidence as much conflict or tension as do diversity and conformity. Diversity suggests conscious attention to differences, unlikeness, heterogeneity, and pluralism. Diversity implies a strong emphasis upon freedom, choice, and opportunity. In contrast, conformity suggests not only unity, but at its extreme, uniformity. It suggests some degree of control or coercion in relation to an accepted standard or norm. Conformity is also the avoidance of chaos or confusion that may arise when we accept a variety of options in the name of diversity. Indeed, we might say that a tension exists between the two in that we find examples of both operating simultaneously. It is no doubt a curious mixture of philosophic idealism and the pragmatic experience of our way of life that pulls us both apart and together at the same time. Or to say it somewhat more idealistically, we honor on the one hand the individual and make many attempts to allow for diversity, while on the other hand we ennoble the common good and justify curriculum decisions in the latter name.

The previous chapter has examined the philosophic dimensions of this problem, looking at the issues of conformity and diversity within the context of the larger historical picture of American education and the broader context of social and institutional developments of American society in general. In the following pages we shall look at a number of

Left: Nursery school playground, Robstown, Texas, 1942.

technical or operational aspects of school curriculum in terms of the extent to which they reflect the values of diversity and conformity. This will include such considerations as curriculum development and the decisions that affect it, methods of teaching, administrative concerns such as accreditation, consolidation of school districts, pupil testing and grade placement, psychological considerations such as maturation and readiness, and cultural considerations of ethnicity and multicultural education.

Curriculum Development

Perhaps no other area reflects so much of the tension between diversity and conformity as does the area of curriculum development and the decision making related to it. Because of the nature of the New England Puritan theocracy, interest in education was strong. The motive, however, was for training in religious and moral upbringing with a strong inculcation of Calvinist theology. The limited number of books, together with the fact that most teachers in the earliest days were themselves clerics, produced a considerable degree of conformity in the school curriculum. The Bible, the *Bay Psalm Book*, and the *New England Primer* all served as major sources of knowledge. They stemmed directly from the orthodox views of Calvinism and inculcated a strong sense of obedience to authority, particularly the authority of parents and elders. Since the child's nature was considered to be inherently evil, it was important that an emphasis be upon control, instilling a fear of breaking God's law and the dreadful consequences of sin. Thus, obedience, discipline, and fear were important elements of the school curriculum. They influenced not only the choice of subject matter but also teaching methodology which emphasized rote memory, rigorous discipline, and memorization of assigned texts. Early statutes in Massachusetts in 1642 and 1647, such as the well-known "Old Deluder Satan Act," set minimal regulations for the establishment of schools in towns of the colony.[1]

Town selectmen and school committees in Massachusetts and Connecticut early began to set standards for the regular operation of the schools. For more than two hundred years, until nearly 1850 in Massachusetts, the local minister or a board of visitors appointed by the town meeting would examine the pupils regularly to determine their mastery of the catechism, the Bible, and the secular branches of knowledge. Clifton Johnson, writing in 1904, noted that "the ministers had much to do with the public schools in all places, large and small. Their super-

---

[1] Nathanel B. Shurtleff, editor. *Records of the Governor and Company of the Massachusetts Bay in New England, II, 1642-1649*. Boston: Press of William White, 1853. pp. 6-7, 203.

vision was constant and vigilant." The function of visiting schools as a representative of the town meeting "continued to be the duty of the ministers in our rural towns [of Massachusetts] until the middle of the last century."[2]

As state legislatures and state boards of education became more powerful, they asserted increasing control over local education. In the years after 1850, many aspects of the school curriculum were regulated. The length of the school day, the number of days in the year, and important subjects such as reading, history, mathematics, spelling and grammar, were prescribed frequently by state law. Even today many highly specific areas of the school curriculum are mandated by state legislatures or identified in approved guidelines from state departments of education. These have included such special topics as the dangers of alcohol and tobacco, the merits of the American capitalistic system, the evils of communism, and more recently education in drug abuse and multicultural understanding. All of these topics have found their way into the school curriculum as a result of strong pressure by special interest groups or lobbyists for particular causes. Prohibitionist groups, for example, saw to it during the 1920's that the evils of alcoholism was a required subject in many states, especially in the South. During the period of the Cold War, right wing Americanism groups in Florida insisted that schools teach about the evils of communism in the high school social studies program. Within the past few years many minority groups have combined forces in states such as California to require a searching review of school text materials to ensure that institutionalized racism is removed from the schools and a stronger, positive program of multicultural education is substituted in its place. Thus, the regulatory power of the state is sometimes used by powerful pressure groups or lobbies to provide a controlling influence on the schools' curriculum and to bring about a certain degree of conformity regarding certain value positions.

Perhaps less obvious is the activity within school districts to provide a system-wide, centralized curriculum. Much can be said in favor of such an approach. It provides unity throughout a school district. It also makes for a common foundation for all children in the district and provides for close integration between the various units—primary, intermediate, secondary, and so on. Teachers have reasonable expectations of what is intended for pupils to learn and, if good records have been kept, of students' prior learnings as they move through a graded structure. A well-coordinated curriculum in a school district also represents a consistent application of a local school district's educational philosophy.

---

[2] Clifton Johnson. *Old Time Schools and School Books*. New York: Macmillan and Co., 1904. p. 24. Reprinted with permission.

What is done in the name of unity often results in uniformity. General philosophic goals are translated into broad educational objectives. Yet when it comes to the reality of the day-to-day operation of a particular school this often means the uniform purchase of identical textbooks and the common expectation that all students have progressed and covered the same content materials. There is also pressure among teachers that each one teach essentially the same material and not depart substantially from what the neighbor down the hall is doing. While minor variations are often permitted, tolerated, or even encouraged in the name of unity, and in the avoidance of uniformity, they are just that, relatively minor variations in content and theme. It is only when a novel curriculum is labeled experimental and supported strongly from the top with administrative approval that a substantially or radically different program is able to flourish. The recent experience of alternative schools, storefront academies, and various types of free schools within existing school situations has not been encouraging. For the most part, their existence has been relatively short lived. While many administrative reasons could be cited for their demise, their very own diversity was their Achilles heel. All too often they tended to operate somewhat outside existing administrative arrangements and did not have a direct supporting system within the regular administrative channels. In many ways their diversity was too threatening to the model of conformity found in the more traditional program. It almost seems that American educators have been more enamoured with the appearance of diversity (or should we say novelty!) than with the hard task of creating and sustaining a truly different educational program.[3]

Another new source of control of curriculum development has been the influence of the federal government in education. The history of federal aid to education has been one of increasing centralization and control. The long history of federally funded agricultural and vocational programs has brought with them a high degree of bureaucratic uniformity in curriculum development, standards for teachers, the provision of school facilities and in classroom materials. Ironically, each of these major moves for federal aid was built on the premise that there would be no federal control, or that the federal controls which were to be exerted would be minimal. Much more recently the decade of the 1960's produced an overwhelming amount of federal aid under the various titles of the National Defense Education Act (1957), the Elementary and Secondary School Act of 1964, and other school aid bills. Almost all these

---

[3] For an excellent analysis of the alternative school today, see: Allan A. Glatthorn. *Alternatives in Education: Schools and Programs.* New York: Dodd, Mead, 1975.

were highly prescriptive, categorical funding programs. While their aims were almost universally judged excellent, they produced a new kind of conformity and served to reinforce only too well the adage, "He who pays the piper calls the tune." Although Title III funds could be expended for innovative and creative projects in education, the degree of innovativeness and creativity was determined by a panel of field reviewers meeting in Washington, D.C.

Evaluation models often followed a rigorous statistical design for experimental research, a model which often could not be implemented in a local setting, nor within the limited funding available under the grants. A consequence of the funding was that what was funded became "innovative" even though it may have been commonplace elsewhere or abandoned as unworkable or worse in another time and place. Thus, the policy of restrictive and categorical federal grants often denied the opportunity for diversity and individuality to those school districts which might otherwise have been funded under broader, more general grants that could have been tailored to meet differing local conditions or where financial need was much greater. Is it any wonder that teachers and administrators soon became cynical in recognizing that the rich only got richer?

The most successful project-getters were those school districts that hired specialists who could read federal regulations carefully and write proposals which clearly met those specifications. Project administrators learned to respond to the changing whims of federal guidelines and even to anticipate new directions before they officially appeared in the *Federal Register*. Grantsmanship became a major asset for anyone involved in curriculum development. All of this is not to decry many of the truly fine educational developments that were made possible only under the availability of federal funds. It is to point out, however, the exceptionally strong degree of federal control in the highly specific nature of the guidelines and the insatiable appetite for funds that has been whetted by such programs. Indeed, it has not been unknown for curriculum directors to turn to their federal project writers and ask, "What's going to be in vogue next year and how do we get the money?"

The history of curriculum development in private schools has been a relatively negligible one. All too often private schools, including religiously oriented ones, have tended to follow the directions and trends of public schools, rather than to pioneer in new directions. Too few today are distinguished by the fact that they differ substantially from or provide alternative models for the public school. If anything, they are characterized, not by curriculum innovation, but by an appeal to social eliteness, a more rigorous approach to the traditional academic disciplines, and the expectation of a closer, more personal relationship between teacher and students in an upper middle class, Waspish boarding school environment. There were, of course, clear exceptions to this. Some of the more illustrious include Francis W. Parker's schools in Quincy, Massachusetts, and later in Chicago; the Ethical Culture School, the Horace Mann and the Lincoln Schools at Teachers College, Columbia University, the City and Country School founded by Caroline Pratt, Margaret Naumburg's famous Walden School, and Helen Parkhurst's Dalton School, all in New York City. Harold Rugg mentions a number of these and discusses at length their contributions as pioneering schools in the progressive education movement.[4] Mention must also be made of the laboratory schools at the University of Chicago directed by John Dewey[5] and at Ohio State University by Laura Zirbes.

A more recent illustration might be the growth of the Montessori schools which have revived the early work of Maria Montessori, an Italian social worker and educator of the early 1900's. To some extent, the Montessori schools have been a rather successful rival for primary education in public schools, but they have not had a very substantial impact in changing the traditional practices of public education. Typically, Montessori schools tend to be found in white upper middle class suburban areas and have appealed to a moderate to wealthy clientele who can afford the tuition costs rather than the poor for whom the ideas were originally developed.

By far the largest number of private schools today are those sponsored by the Roman Catholic Church. Growing out of long-standing conflict between Catholics and Protestants in the eighteenth and nineteenth

---

[4] Harold Rugg. *Foundations for American Education.* Yonkers-on-Hudson, New York: World Book Co., 1947. pp. 569-70, 594.

An even more important source is the series of essays written by many of these same pioneers for the 1926 NSSE Yearbook *Curriculum Making: Past and Present*, edited by Harold Rugg. Regrettably, there is no similar book since then that documents as well the recent innovations in curriculum development.

The most extensive source for references to the people, schools, and curricular programs of the progressive period is to be found in the bibliographical note, "Pedagogical Pioneers" in: Lawrence A. Cremin. *The Transformation of the School.* New York: Vintage Books, 1961. pp. 371-74, 376-78.

[5] One of the best curriculum histories is to be found in: Katherine Camp Mayhew and Anna Camp Edwards. *The Dewey School: The Laboratory School of the University of Chicago, 1896-1903.* New York: Appleton-Century, 1936. Paperback reprint: Atherton Press, 1965. Both authors were directly involved in the work of the school and worked with Dewey on the plans and outline for this account. As Dewey wrote in the introduction, "The account of the Laboratory School contained in the pages that follow is so adequate as to render it unnecessary for me to add anything to what is said about its origin, aims, and methods." (p. xiii).

centuries, the private schools were conceived by the American Catholic bishops as a viable alternative to the common or public schools which were largely Protestant (and occasionally anti-Catholic) in their values and practices.[6] Yet these same schools, with few exceptions, tended to follow the patterns of the nearby public schools in all curriculum areas except religion.

The drive to conformity or Americanization took an interesting twist, however, in the early 1920's. During World War I, many midwestern states, feeling a strong spirit of patriotism and nationalism, became openly self-conscious about the number of communities in which the German language was still used as a language of instruction in the schools. In addition, a growing fear of Bolshevism, radicalism, and a general xenophobia combined to produce a series of laws throughout the Midwest requiring English to be the official language of instruction. In Oregon, a suit was raised in an effort to force compliance with a law requiring all children to attend the public schools. The famous decision *Pierce* v. *The Society of Sisters* (1925) spelled an end to this strong pressure for conformity and the notion that the public school was the only guardian of Americanism.[7] Curiously, however, foreign languages did remain in the parochial schools that served a large number of small ethnic neighborhoods and it was not unusual throughout the early 1930's and 1940's to find schools taught for at least half a day in French or Polish. In the steel and iron cities of the Midwest, Czech, Hungarian, Greek, and Italian continued to be present. Many upper midwestern agricultural communities persisted in the use of German and Russian. It is a curious anomaly that teaching of a second language began to fade out in the middle 1940's and through the 1950's. But under the urgencies of Sputnik, the National Defense Education Act, etc., the study of critical languages was brought back in the schools. How ironic that some students in the high schools and colleges received special instruction in the languages that their grandparents used with some embarrassment around their Americanized children.

[6] For a refreshingly different account of the early development of Catholic schools, see: Robert A. Carlson. *The Quest for Conformity: Americanization Through Education.* New York: John Wiley and Sons, 1975. pp. 49-57. Carlson casts the story in terms of the growing pressure to Americanize the increasing numbers of Irish, French and German immigrants whose popish doctrines and European-born hierarchy were in constant conflict with the more settled, predominantly Protestant culture. The simultaneous drives for conformity and for diversity are viewed as the result of action and reaction by those who supported the growing common-school movement with its nonsectarian Protestantism and the insistence of the Catholics that they must preserve their identity through separate parish schools.

[7] U.S. Supreme Court. 268 U.S. 510-36 (1925).

National Curriculum Development

One could hardly leave the subject of curriculum development without examining the phenomenon of a national curriculum. To some extent, we must consider the ever-present use of such standard books as Webster's "Blue-Backed Speller," the McGuffey *Eclectic Readers,* textbooks of Jedidiah Morse and others. These and others existed before the days of strict copyright laws and pirated editions or local reprints were not unknown. So standard were these books that they could well be thought of as a very early national curriculum.

In a somewhat different respect, the reform methods of the 1920's and 1930's, especially those of the American Historical Association, in its effort to revise the social studies curriculum provided a kind of national curriculum movement. Strong guidelines were established in these reports and their influence was substantial in the development of thought in the social studies field. Unfortunately, few if any of these designs were translated into school text materials and the movement may be more remembered for the philosophic and theoretical thought positions by Beard and others than for lasting effects in the schools. But perhaps most important of all was the effect of the launching of the Soviet space missile Sputnik which challenged American educational interests. How could it be that a nation seemingly as technologically limited as Russia could surpass the United States in the race into space? This event dramatically ushered in an entirely new era in curriculum development.

Large amounts of federal monies from the National Science Foundation and later from the National Defense Education Act made innovative developments possible. A number of private and quasi-public institutions pioneered in curriculum developments which had nationwide distribution and visibility. Late in the 1950's the National Science Foundation funded the efforts for major developments in "modern math" and in new curricula in the sciences. The work of the School Mathematics Study Group (SMSG) received rapid dissemination through a series of federally funded teacher workshops. Other groups soon sprang up in Maryland, Illinois, and elsewhere and developed somewhat similar approaches to the new study of mathematics. Bruner's summary of the 1959 Woods Hole Conference in his short book *The Process of Education,*[8] provided a new impetus for scholars in the academic disciplines to work in an uneasy triumvirate with teachers and curriculum developers. In retrospect it must be said that it was often the academic scholars teamed with curriculum entrepreneurs and grantsmen who called the

---

[8] Jerome S. Bruner. *The Process of Education.* Cambridge: Harvard University Press, 1960.

tune, rather than public school administrators or teachers. More often than not, classroom teachers were Johnny-come-latelies. Nevertheless, in a post-Sputnik era, American education made every effort to catch up with what was alleged to be a three or four hundred year gap between the scholarly advances in the academic fields and what the schools were in fact teaching.

The alphabet soup curricula soon developed, with the BSCS, the PSSC, and many more like them. Important "think tanks" such as the Educational Development Corporation in Cambridge, Massachusetts, took the lead in the pioneering efforts to develop new curricula and to build bridges between the academic scholar and the school teacher. Summer retraining institutes for teachers sponsored by federal funds under the National Defense Education Act were widespread across the country. As new curriculum materials were developed and tried out in limited pilot settings, editors from commercial publishing houses often camped on the doorstep waiting eagerly for publishable manuscripts of new school curriculum materials. Recognizing the bonanza that was to be had, many of the major publishers developed highly effective sales programs which served two purposes. First, they disseminated the new curricula rapidly on a national scale to key decision makers in the school districts. Second, the publishers provided short in-service workshops usually involving highly talented and capable representatives who knew the material extensively and could demonstrate its use very capably with almost any group of children. Thus, they disseminated the new curricula quickly on a national scale and succeeded in whetting the appetite of influential decision makers. Rather than emphasize a diversity that might meet individual needs, many of the programs were merchandised with a hard sell for the "new salvation." Inquiry, discovery, cognitive tasks, conceptually oriented, etc., were the watchwords.

Closely allied to this was the concept of a network of influential decision-making people who had attended the government-sponsored summer workshops. These workshops often reached key supervisors, principals, and classroom teachers who were in a position to make important decisions regarding the adoption of these materials. It was not long, then, before these materials were being advertised widely in the professional publications and curriculum developers and teachers engaged in the projects were presenting the results of their studies at professional meetings. One wondered sometimes whether the conference presentation was really a scholarly presentation or whether the audience was getting a smooth sales pitch for the new product. Regrettably, however, many of the new projects did not exist very long beyond the experimental pilot versions. Too few had the necessary follow-up assistance from the curriculum developers or their agents. Teachers who had difficulty tended to abandon the material quickly. Elaborate curriculum programs complete with visual aids, simulation games, and other materials were often found gathering dust in a closet because the older or more traditional curriculum could be implemented without the difficulties encountered with the new materials.[9]

Regrettably, the diversity that was to be found in the abundance of new programs soon gave way to an urge for conformity. Whole schools adopted a single curriculum, even though the curriculum designers, as in the case of biology and physics, designed several alternative forms that would appeal to different students and different interest groups. The blue, green, and yellow versions of the BSCS biology program each had a different conceptual approach to be used for different purposes with different students. Yet too many schools made a decision to lock in on a single program, rather than tolerate the "confusion" from a diversity of programs, although each in its own way would provide a unity of theme and a consistency in conceptual development.

Graded Materials

Another aspect of the tension between diversity and conformity may be seen in the graded materials provided for schools. We have discussed above the question of unity and uniformity in school district curricula. Closely related to this is the identification by grade level of the scope and sequence of materials. The psychological rationale is clearly designed to provide logical continuity within the frame of curricular unity. In fact, however, textbook materials all too readily become locked into a particular "suggested" grade level assignment. At best, a teacher ought to feel free to pick and choose from a variety of materials best suited to the needs of individual children from the school book room. At worst, however, teachers and administrators tend to hold books closely in reserve lest a teacher in a lower grade steal the thunder from the teacher in a higher grade by exposing a child prematurely to new and different materials. Thus, the thought that a classroom library can be enriched with diverse curriculum materials is thwarted by the desire to conform to a prescribed syllabus and scope and sequence chart, which originally was intended to be suggestive and illustrative only, and not to be a prison from which there was no escape.

[9] For an excellent analysis of the problems encountered in the development and dissemination of an innovative curriculum, see: Paul E. Marsh. "Wellsprings of Strategy: Considerations Affecting Innovations by the PSSC." In: Matthew B. Miles, editor. *Innovation in Education.* New York: Teachers College, Columbia University, 1964. Chapter 10.

Many of us can remember coded markers on the spines of books, whether circles, triangles, dots, or numbers, which indicated the intended grade placement for the books. These were thinly veiled efforts to prevent a child in a low reading group from realizing that he had a different text which might perhaps be better suited to his needs. Indeed, one company even published what it called classmate editions which were readers that contained the same stories with the same illustrations, even appearing on the same pages in companion books but written at different reading levels with different vocabularies. How strong the impulse to conform!

Individualized Education

One of the current catchwords is individualized education. Yet the topic is hardly new. Harold Shane identified some 35 or more various plans that have attempted to deal with individual differences in school programs. Included within the list were such familiar names as the grade level grouping, heterogeneous grouping, homogeneous grouping, departmental grouping, the Winnetka Plan, the Dalton Plan, the platoon plan, the ungraded unit, special grouping for the gifted, the opportunity room for slow learning or mentally handicapped students, and many variations of them.[10] A number of organizations or programs have sprung up within the past decade which have attempted to redeploy the resources and personnel of the school so as to better meet individual needs of students. Individually guided education (IGE) has been a major approach developed by the Kettering Foundation which has both organizational and curriculum components to it. Closely allied with such concepts as team teaching and flexible assignment of students, it attempts to develop programs and materials for individual children. While some schools have been very successful with this program, other projects such as Westinghouse's Project Plan have made use of computers and modern technology to provide a much more learner-directed self-paced approach to instruction. All too often, such programs tend only to vary the rate of individual learning. What the children study is essentially the same for everyone. Missing from such programs is the analysis of individuals and their differing learning styles and the development of curricula which may have common threads for some and very different strands for others. Even those schools which boast of being "open concept schools," more often fail to provide the great diversity which their name suggests. In the frenzied rush to jump on the band wagon to imitate the British

[10] Harold G. Shane. "The School and Individual Differences." In: *Individualizing Instruction.* 61st Yearbook, Part I, National Society for the Study of Education. Chicago: University of Chicago Press, 1962. Chapter III.

Infant School, too many teachers and administrators have failed to take time to develop the essential philosophic commitment to freedom of choice for teachers and students alike, the ready acceptance of diverse alternatives, and the limited use of external structures.

Prior commitment to such ideals is probably far more important to the successful development of an open school than all the efforts to eliminate walls, provide movable furniture, or cluster children in pods. Yet entire schools are built with great open spaces and flexible partitions while hardly a day is spent in in-service training, staff development, and long-range planning. The cult of efficiency compels us to well-organized sameness and conformity!

In summary, there has been much tension in the field of curriculum development between the two values of diversity and conformity. A number of pioneering efforts of the progressive education movement were cited. Curiously, however, the efforts to develop new and different curricula, whether in the open school concept, the individually guided education, or the alternative schools, are often swallowed up and allowed to die an untimely death by default, neglect, or the pressures of a community which cannot abide for very long schools which are radically different from those about them. Thus, the pressures which gave rise to diversity are counterbalanced by a pressure to conform to more established ways.

Methods of Teaching

An analysis of the many methods of teaching, whether intended for elementary, secondary, or collegiate instruction provides many examples of the tension between diversity and conformity. In our earliest educational history the principal method of teaching was the use of rote recitation. Every young scholar toed the mark on the schoolhouse floor and recited verbatim memorized lessons, whether from the *Bay Psalm Book*, Webster's "Blue-Backed Speller," or from the McGuffey *Eclectic Readers*. Each child was expected to recite without error or to repeat without elaboration the material in the text. Clearly the emphasis was upon conformity and correctness of the response, for all too often the schoolmaster had little knowledge beyond what was in the book.

While later developments in the nineteenth-century Normal Schools emphasized a growing science of pedagogy in the development of principles or techniques of teaching, teaching methods still emphasized a strong sense of conformity. As towns and cities grew in the early 1800's, the one-room schoolhouse with children at various ages and levels of instruction gave way to large group instruction in the Lancastrian School with its monitorial approach. But perhaps no single invention produced a greater movement toward conformity than the development of the graded school in Massachusetts in the 1840's. It was conceived as a means of increasing the teacher's efficiency and providing for the orderly progression of students through requisite content matter. Whatever opportunity was provided for diversity in the one-room schoolhouse, it was lost to the efficiency of the graded school. Carried to the extreme, large numbers of students were grouped into classes or sections on the basis of age or past achievement. It was not at all unusual in many cities to see as many as six or eight sections of every grade. Once labeled as a slow student in one of these sections, it was almost impossible for a child to escape from the caste into which he had been put, sometimes quite arbitrarily.

Despite the advances of the growing field of psychology, liberated from philosophy only in the late 1880's, there was little impact upon methods of instruction. The work of such early psychologists as Herbart, James, and Thorndike contributed substantially to the question of how students learn, but much remained of the formal discipline approach in the primitive psychology. Despite these developments in learning, methods of instruction still involved large-group instruction with little or no attempt to provide for individual differences or needs. It was not until the middle 1930's that developmental psychologists such as Gesell, Ames, and others did extensive work to identify specific individual differences and to suggest curriculum implications for them. Perhaps the most noteworthy was the concept of readiness in that certain tasks, whether intellectual or psychomotor, could most profitably be delayed to later stages of children's development. Abstract relational concepts such as time, space, and distance were difficult for children to deal with in the primary grades. Thus, the chronological teaching of history, or the use of reference coordinates in geography, such as latitude and longitude, ought best to be deferred until children were 10 or 11 years old and in the middle grades. To some considerable extent, these early concepts have been affirmed in Piaget's developmental stages. These stages have been useful for curriculum workers in that they have identified periods when children need most to work with concrete manipulable materials and when they can deal with abstract, hypothetical, and deductive thinking at a much later period of development. Still to be fully developed are the curriculum implications of psychologists such as Kurt Lewin's client-centered therapy, the nondirectiveness of Carl Rogers, and Arthur Combs' humanistic psychology.

An important aspect of the progressive education movement was its focus upon the development of the individual child and the growth of the child-centered approach to teaching. Kilpatrick's[11] activity movement provided the specific ways and techniques of putting into practice the educational principles espoused by Dewey. Teachers learned to develop centers of interest around which motivation could be developed and various learning activities, based on the interests of children, could occur. Even though the project method or the unit curriculum often provided a whole-class approach to a broad, single topic of study, there was ample room for all of the children to participate in varied ways, depending upon their own special needs and interests. Teachers were encouraged to capitalize upon such interests and to encourage students to use their talents in many diverse ways, all in the furtherance of a major theme. While diverse opportunities provided for individuals in these methods of teaching, emphasis was also given to the development of small-group work in the form of various student committees which explored different aspects of a topic of study.

In the 1930's and 1940's educators and psychologists were becoming aware of the factors of social psychology and relating that to the biological patterns of child and adolescent growth and development. They tried to establish links between the growth of the individual and the development of a social role with peers in small work and play groups. Thus, units of work in social studies were often organized around student interests and various parts of a topic of study were investigated by committees. Teachers helped children to learn socialization by assuming the roles of leadership and followership, task identification and problem solving through task assignments. Thus, a child had many opportunities throughout the school year to have diverse experiences, both as an individual and as a member of a group to help in organizing and planning his or her own learning. In some content areas where necessary skills are better identified, such as reading and mathematics, grouping was more often based upon prior achievement than on interests.

In summary, many of the teaching methods advocated in the progressive education movement placed high premium on the creativeness and independence of students, their ability to plan and direct their own learning, and to be responsible for the completion of various tasks leading to their learning goals. While the teacher still maintained an overall responsibility for the general direction of the class, students were freely encouraged to share in all phases of the curriculum planning, in the

[11] Among the most important of William Heard Kilpatrick's works are: "The Project Method." *Teachers College Record* 19: 319-35; 1918; and *Foundations of Method*, 1925.

evaluation of the learning outcome and the process through which they went. *The Child-Centered School* by Rugg and Shumaker [12] is a good example of how such methods were to be carried out.

Many of the methods of teaching described above represented outstanding models of teaching and learning. In many cases they were perhaps more talked about than practiced. Underlying the force of the progressive movement was a very large measure of conservativism in educational values. Conservative forces attacked the progressive social studies textbooks of Harold Rugg. Campaigns sponsored by the American Legion and the Chamber of Commerce challenged many of the radical positions found in Rugg's books. Many of the curriculum innovations were difficult at best to implement, even by the most skillful teacher. Ideas such as the activity program, unified, integrated, or core curriculum, required skilled teachers who had command of great amounts of knowledge and who were capable of synthesizing broadly ideas, facts, and concepts from several disciplines. For the poorly trained teacher, this was an almost impossible feat.

In a more general way, many of the broad social goals of the progressive era had been satisfied. Old shibboleths, such as the whole child and creative self-expression had begun to lose much of their luster. In addition, a group of deeply conservative educational critics emerged after World War II, who attacked the progressive schools at some of their weakest points. Albert Lind's *Quackery in the Public Schools,* Arthur Bestor's *Educational Wastelands,* Robert Hutchins' *The Conflict in Education,* and Paul Woodring's *Let's Talk Sense about Our Schools* all appeared in 1953. These books, together with the pamphlets published by the Council for Basic Education, founded in 1956 and headed by Mortimer Smith and Arthur Bestor, pointed up some serious deficiencies of public education and lampooned pious statements and foolish practices where they occurred. At about the same time, James B. Conant, former president of Harvard University, in his book *The American High School Today* (1959), proposed a return to the traditional curriculum of the 1930's and, as indicated in the following pages, was able to bring about a sweeping return to the traditional subject-centered curriculum in the American high school. Thus, the greatly varied methods of teaching that accompanied the progressive education period with their emphasis upon the differing needs and interests of students often fell victim to the more traditional demands for conformity and regimentation as many classrooms in the 1950's returned to a discipline-centered approach.[13]

[12] Harold Rugg and Ann Shumaker, *The Child-Centered School.*

[13] See: Lawrence Cremin's analysis of the collapse of the progressive education movement in: *Transformation of the School, op. cit.,* pp. 328-53.

Other Methods of Teaching

In more recent years there have been a number of outgrowths of the methods of teaching advocated during the progressive movement. One of the most widely known has been the core program. Another, based heavily on Dewey's writing, has been called problem solving. More recently inquiry or discovery teaching has attracted widespread attention. Value clarification is still another method of teaching that attempts to deal with feelings, beliefs, and attitudes. Each of these in differing ways provided opportunity for diversity and individualization of instruction. The core program, with its effort to develop a unified or integrated study of some problem based on students' interests, not teachers' interests, provided a very flexible approach for integrating many areas of learning in a holistic way. Like the activity movement and the project method that preceded it, there was great opportunity for individuals or small groups to pursue their own special interests and talents. Because it provided a psychological and logical base for integrating many curriculum areas, it was a very useful method of curriculum organization. Its vitality lay in the fact that new problems and new approaches to them could be considered as students' interests grew and developed. It could be as vital and fresh and stimulating as the concerns of the contemporary world. All too often, however, the program became stultified with a series of fixed problems which would be assigned to certain grade levels. Everyone studied the same subject in pretty much the same routine way. After a while a teacher became an expert on the life of the Indians or the pioneers or the problems of peacekeeping with the League of Nations or the United Nations. Dusty models of an Indian tepee or longhouse were taken out of the closet to be used once again in a ritualistic way. What was important was that the problem did not spring from the needs or interests of the children, but rather from the fixed plans of the teacher or the school district. This is not to suggest that good learning did not occur. But it is to suggest that the vitality that may have been present based on real interests of children yielded to the efficiency of repetition.

Dewey's problem-solving method was widely touted as an important development in the methods of teaching because it appeared to be so closely linked to the strong faith in scientism. Dewey had outlined a number of logical steps in his book, *How We Think*, first written in 1910.[14] Taken in the abstract, they provided an important understand-

[14] John Dewey. *How We Think*. Boston: D. C. Heath and Company, 1910 (revised 1933).

ing of the important intellectual process of problem identification, data gathering, testing or verification of proposed solutions, the drawing of conclusion, and the reformulation of theoretical thought. Exponents of this method often oversimplified Dewey's intellectual process and glorified it into what many teachers felt was a scientific method. They would then proceed in the most formula-like way or cookbook approach to the study of some problem, more frequently identified by the teacher than by the students. Too often this method gave undue attention to the development of great quantities of factual data and far less attention to the conjecturing of important questions to be solved or hypotheses to be tested, for which the factual data should provide some evidence.

Few schools provided any real opportunity to apply or solve realistic problems, even hypothetically. Too often the problem simply ended in a summary statement of factual data. In many respects, problem solving became a new orthodoxy with a rigorous conformity to the steps Dewey had outlined. In the 1960's the new orthodoxy would become inquiry. In the middle 1960's Hilda Taba's studies on children's thinking processes provided effective questioning strategies to apply principles or generalizations to new situations with questions such as "What would happen if . . .?" Anticipating a great variety of student responses, some highly creative, others limited and predictable, Taba urged teachers to look at the spontaneity of responses, the fluency of ideas, the logical development of thought, the imaginativeness of alternative solutions and the use of available data to support probable conclusions.[15]

Jerome Bruner's work on the study of concept formation in young children [16] led to an important essay on the role of inquiry or discovery as a cognitive process in learning.[17] The discovery approach became popularized in Bruner's book *The Process of Education*. His oft-repeated proposition became almost a password for curriculum developers:

We begin with the hypothesis that any subject can be taught effectively in some intellectually honest form to any child at any stage of development. It is a bold hypothesis and an essential one in thinking about the nature of a

[15] Taba's strategies were first developed in Cooperative Research Projects sponsored by the U.S. Office of Education in 1964 and 1966. They were widely tested in Contra Costa County in California, later developed more fully as inservice workshop training programs by the Northwest Regional Laboratory, and finally made available in: Hilda Taba, *et al. A Teacher's Handbook to Elementary Social Studies, An Inductive Approach.* Reading, Massachusetts: Addison-Wesley, 1971.

[16] J. S. Bruner, *et al. A Study of Thinking.* New York: Wiley and Co., 1956.

[17] J. S. Bruner. "The Act of Discovery." *Harvard Educational Review* 31 (1): 21-32; 1961.

curriculum. No evidence exists to contradict it; considerable evidence is being amassed that supports it.[18]

Simply stated, the idea was that students could study the various disciplines following the ways and processes of scientists. That is, they could learn to ask important questions, formulate hypotheses, develop factual data, derive insights and conceptualizations, and finally develop generalized principles. Closely tied to this was the notion that the scholarly disciplines of knowledge have an integrity and structure of their own and that each discipline has its own set of appropriate concepts and methods of investigation. The concept of structure was an important element because it suggested that there was an internal consistency and logic to the organization of subject matter. The structure consisted of central concepts and generalizations or theories that were the particular domain of that discipline. It remained for curriculum developers to organize appropriate content matter in such a way that students could formulate the essential concepts and discover relationships for themselves, rather than to be told in an expository manner the relationships between various concepts.

At first glance it appears that such methods of teaching would lend themselves well to the diversity of thought and individualization, but as curriculum developers prepared packaged materials, there appeared to be a rather strong guiding hand which would structure or manipulate the student to predetermined conclusions. Curriculum theorists and teachers alike have argued about the degree of subtle control over the students' learning processes with much of the inquiry material. Were children being led down a primrose path to a conclusion which had already been determined by the teacher? Was the learning process which tried to ape the scientific process merely a sham? Others argued in reply that it was foolish to try to reinvent the wheel or to spend great amounts of time in highly inefficient ways when a more straightforward (but manipulative) approach might be used. What was at issue was the rather strict control or limitation of materials all of which were carefully designed to provide the appropriate illustrations or exemplars for the concept to be studied. Excluded were materials that would often reflect divergent views or which would require a student to separate out extraneous materials before he could begin the process of concept development. It may be that this task of discrimination of relevant from irrelevant information is of critical importance.

Value clarification is another method of teaching which has had

[18] J. S. Bruner. *The Process of Education.* New York: Random House, Inc., 1960. p. 33.

much potential for diversity and individualization. Strategies developed by Raths, Simon,[19] and others have provided many opportunities for students to share in diverse and creative ways their expressions of beliefs, attitudes, and values. Indeed the key element of all value clarification work is expression of one's own individual positions and outlooks. Any effort to encourage students to conform to a particular viewpoint or to proselytize for any particular value (even for what one regards as traditional basic American values) defeats the entire purpose of value clarification strategies. This is the one area of the curriculum where teachers must be open to many possible responses, must be supportive of students' right to speak their views and to seek clarification of them. This is certainly not the place for dogmatic and authoritarian styles of teaching.

In contrast to many of the strategies and methods of teaching described above, a number of developments in recent years have tended to place a strong emphasis upon the value of conformity. One of these is in the area of performance or competency-based education, which attempts to specify rather precisely the student outcome or behavior. The concept of competency or performance-based education is not nearly as new as its recency suggests. One of the most ardent advocates of the scientific and industrial approach to education was Franklin Bobbitt. In his book *How to Make a Curriculum*[20] (Boston, 1924), Bobbitt likened the curriculum maker to a "great engineer." He held that the job of the curriculum designer was to classify in detail the full range of human experience and then build a curriculum that would prepare students for life in the real world. In setting curriculum aims, he specified and quantified what could be measured with precision. His views reflected a dominant Watsonian behaviorism of the 1920's. The same trend of thought appeared in Ralph Tyler's criterion that evaluation of the outcomes for the Eight-Year Study should focus on realistic observable behaviors or performances of students.[21] A similar philosophy can be seen in Tyler's model for the analysis of curriculum in terms of objectives and outcomes.[22] Most recently, there is the well-known work of

[19] Louis E. Raths, Merrill Harmin, and Sidney B. Simon. *Values and Teaching: Working with Values in the Classroom.* Columbus, Ohio: Charles E. Merrill, 1966.

[20] Franklin Bobbitt. *How to Make a Curriculum.* Boston: Houghton Mifflin, 1924.

[21] Eugene R. Smith, Ralph W. Tyler, *et al. Appraising and Recording Student Progress,* Vol. III in the series *Adventures in American Education.* New York: McGraw-Hill, 1942.

[22] Ralph W. Tyler. *Basic Principles of Curriculum and Instruction.* Chicago: University of Chicago Press, 1949.

Mager [23] on behavioral objectives, followed by Popham's [24] work on instructional objectives. The movement of behavioral objectives reached its high water mark with the catchy phrase "If an outcome is not observable and measurable, it's not worth talking about."

While the effort to focus the goals of teaching upon student performance or competencies makes for precision and greater accountability in identifying the outcome of learning, it also makes for a much greater sense of conformity to predetermined objectives. Too often the instructional goals which identify student outcomes do not provide for diversity of options, nor do they look for creative responses as the desired behavior. Carried to the extreme, competency measures tend to suggest that all students must pursue the same goal in quite similar ways. Each student must be able to demonstrate the outcome specified at least as a minimum behavior. Other outcomes may be added beyond that, but this is at least base level for all individuals.

At a time when schools have been charged with a failure to provide precise and specific information about the peformance of students, such specific outcomes help make the schools far more accountable for their teaching efforts. One finds it hard to argue with the notion of accountability. Taxpayers do pay for their children's education and we in the profession should find better ways of being able to report what has happened and if desired goals have not been achieved, then we should be able to explain why not. On the other hand, it is in the potential that every student must conform to certain predetermined outcomes that we raise serious questions about the issue of conformity regarding performance- or competency-based education. Too often the competencies that have been identified have been highly mechanical and often trivial. Lists of competencies have failed to identify some of the much more important cognitive thought processes or value clarification outcomes. They have tended not to place a premium upon diversity and creativeness of response. Our concern is that the competencies or the indicators of performance are not set at varying levels of excellence and quality, but at the minimum level of acceptable performance.

In summary, we have reviewed a number of strategies for teaching. Many of the earliest teaching methods required little more than rote memorization of materials. Even those students reciting individually

[23] Robert F. Mager. *Preparing Instructional Objectives.* Palo Alto, California: Fearon Publishers, Inc., 1962.

[24] James W. Popham. *Systematic Instructional Decision Making.* Los Angeles: Vimcet Associates, 1965. Popham revised and modified some of his earlier views in: *Instructional Objectives.* American Educational Research Association Monograph Series on Curriculum Evaluation, III. Chicago: Rand McNally, 1969.

conformed to the rest of the group reciting their lessons verbatim. A number of newer methods grew out of the progressive education period which incorporated diverse responses and individual participation by students. Unfortunately, some of these methods were handled ineptly and became dull, formal processes in which all students studied the same materials in nearly identical ways. Newer methods such as inquiry or discovery teaching, value clarification, and the use of performance objectives or competencies were also reviewed. Each has the potential for being highly creative and responsive to individual needs; each also has the potential for being badly misused, resulting in conformity of individuals to traditional practices.

Administrative Organization

One of the most obvious sources of the tension between diversity and conformity in education is in the administrative organization of schools. We have already discussed the graded-school pattern and the problem of alternative programs within established schools, such as storefront academies, house plans, and free schools. We have also seen that there is a strong tendency to unify the curriculum in each of the schools within a district. The argument is often made that the children who come from a group of elementary schools which feed into a common secondary school ought all to have a common background of learning experiences. While there may be some merit to the argument for unity, it also stifles the opportunity to develop a highly creative and individualized program within a school which may be more responsive to the needs of children in that area. This is especially ironic when we consider the concept of the neighborhood school, which in recent years has seemed to become a very hallowed concept. If the neighborhood school is to be more than a geographic identity, then it ought to have a unique existence of its own, differing from others that are nearby within the same school system.

This point was made very clearly in the controversies in New York City in the early 1970's to establish the independence of such schools as Ocean Hill-Brownsville. The right of parents, teachers, and administrators to determine what curriculum is most appropriate for different groups of children, especially those of different cultural or ethnic backgrounds, was strongly asserted and finally won. This same battle for decentralization and curriculum control has been waged in other large cities, but the arrangement often founders on the distribution of tax revenues from the central school district headquarters. The irony is that the movement for consolidation of school districts which began in the 1920's and 1930's as a means to eliminate small and inefficient districts has now produced an overwhelming sameness within each district. It is rare to find several schools within a school district each of which has its own unique character in its curriculum, program, or ways of operating. As we have discussed above, alternative schools are by far the exception and have had a very short-lived existence. Thus, we can see once again that the value of diversity in school programs is overshadowed by the drive to conform for reasons of increased efficiency.

Although such an arrangement might be utopian, what a unique opportunity it might be to have each elementary school in a school district uniquely different in some way from all its neighbors and if there were several high schools, then each of these could be uniquely different, too. Such a proposal might finally give true freedom of choice to residents of a community, who then should be able to pick and choose from among a great variety of options. This was the ideal envisioned by the advocates of the federally sponsored voucher plan a few years ago. One wonders what it would take before the genius of American efficiency would begin to make each one of the schools more and more alike as if they were branches of a large department store established at neighborhood shopping centers. Even in higher education, there is more similarity and uniformity among colleges and universities than there is dissimilarity. This is especially true with state colleges and universities. It is certainly a wonder that the many small private colleges of the nation, each with its distinctive appeal, have managed to survive as distinct entities for so long.

Another aspect of the organizational pattern of education that reflects the polarity of diversity and conformity may be seen in the movement for accreditation. The history of the American secondary school is replete with illustrations of the drive to provide unity of program and measurable conformity in so many ways. Commission after commission in the period from 1880-1920 gave strong recommendations regarding particular subjects which soon became required in each school. The Carnegie unit which fixed the number of hours of instruction in a class per week in any subject has become a universal measuring rod and has standardized the 40 or 50 minute period of instruction. It is, indeed, a curious phenomenon that the work of many of the commissions in this period produced a college preparatory curriculum, the successful completion of which would usually assure admission to a large number of cooperating colleges and universities.

The evidence of the Eight-Year Study, however, refuted all of the hallowed prescriptions for fixed curricula and required courses. The results of this study amply demonstrated that students who came from the innovative progressive schools, who had not studied the traditional curriculum, did as well or better in college as did the students who came from the traditional schools.[25] Probably because the results of this study appeared during the war years, these impressive results never had the impact that they might have had in laying to rest forever the stranglehold of the traditional curriculum.

It is certainly a curious phenomenon that only a few years later, in 1950, a former president of Harvard University, James A. Conant, should argue persuasively for the introduction of a highly traditional and fixed pattern of academic subjects. In his report on the American comprehensive high school[26] he argued for such standards as four years of one language, three years of another, four years of mathematics and science, and English, etc. It is strange, in this writer's opinion, how educators and lay public alike could ignore the findings of the Eight-Year Study so completely and leap on the bandwagon for a program which returned the schools to the 1890's. In addition, Conant strongly argued for the elimination of many of the thousands or more of very small high schools and urged the establishment of major comprehensive secondary schools. Perhaps no single document was as powerful as the Conant report in the early 1960's in justifying and legitimizing the reshaping of the structure of the American secondary school and producing a high degree of structure and conformity to an outmoded ideal.

Conant argued, of course, that the comprehensive school, because of its size, had the opportunity to offer many courses that would not otherwise be available in smaller schools, especially in advanced courses in the sciences and mathematics. Once again, creativeness, diversity, and individuality were sacrificed to efficiency and economy. Nowhere in

---

[25] Wilford M. Aikin. *The Story of the Eight-Year Study.* New York: Harpers, 1942. Other reports in the five volume series published between 1942-43 included H. A. Giles, and others. *Exploring the Curriculum;* Eugene R. Smith, Ralph W. Tyler, *et al. Appraising and Recording Student Progress;* Dean Chamberlain, and others. *Did They Succeed in College?* and a final volume, *Thirty Schools Tell Their Story.*

[26] James B. Conant. *The American High School Today: A First Report to Interested Citizens.* New York: McGraw-Hill, 1959. Conant's second report, *Education in the Junior High School,* Princeton: Educational Testing Service, 1960, made similar recommendations. A later report, *Slums and Suburbs: The Commentary on Schools in the Metropolitan Areas,* New York: McGraw-Hill, 1961, recommended a less rigorous position than in his report on the high school. In the report on urban schools, Conant seemed to recognize the magnitude of social and economic conditions as they affect education for all citizens. Yet he provided no effective alternatives to existing programs and appeared to only grudgingly modify the rather stringent curriculum recommendations he had made in his earlier report on high schools.

the Conant report, which called so strongly for the return to a classical tradition of the liberal arts disciplines, was there any recognition of the innovative and creative programs of learning developed in the progressive schools and well documented in the reports of the Eight-Year Study. One can only wonder what values were operating so strongly in the minds of professionals and laymen alike that they would move so swiftly and so massively for the return of American secondary education to the traditions that existed at the turn of the last century.

Finally, we should make note of the influence of accreditation agencies at the college and university levels. Groups such as the North Central Association, the Middle States Association, and the American Association of University Professors, to name but a few, have had powerful influence in accrediting colleges and universities, both private and public. This is equally true among the professional schools where many organizations have sprung up that have vied for control by accrediting the graduates of professional schools. In the field of education, the National Council for the Accreditation of Teacher Education has had a major controlling influence in the recognition accorded to teacher education programs.

For the most part, accreditation agencies served to provide normative guidelines on such matters as faculty-student ratio, total number of books in the library, financial resources, and the nature and extent of program, resources available, etc. Accreditation visits (a gentler word than inspection!) usually came once every five or ten years. The institution typically was asked to prepare an extensive self-study report. The accrediting agency provided a rather elaborate guideline and set of checklists to be used in preparing the self-study. A visiting team would then visit the college and talk with a number of faculty and students in an effort to substantiate the data presented in the institution's own report. Its findings would be announced later, and if all had gone well the college would be considered accredited for another five or ten year period. In recent years a number of colleges and universities have begun to challenge the concept of regional or professional accreditation. Serious thought must be given to whether the tremendous amount of time invested in making the preparation for the self-study and the visit by the accrediting team is worth the costs involved. Too often the report from the visiting team yields little insight or evaluative comment that the members of the local institution did not already have available. More important, the normative quality of the accreditation guidelines has tended to produce greater uniformity and less diversity. The institution that has a unique program or that does not meet most of the traditional established standards will have a tough time in being accredited. The

Left: Bilingual Czechoslovakian-English instruction in New York City, 1942.

Below: School-sponsored scrap iron drive, Roanoke, Virginia, 1942.

burden of proof appears to be with the institution being studied to defend its practices that differ from traditional norms. While there may have been a value at one time in recognizing a level of quality attested to by a regional accrediting agency and in weeding out inferior and substandard institutions, the uniformity that is encouraged by the system now seems to be a rather high price to pay. For the most part, the accrediting agencies seem more concerned with maintaining the established standards, practices, and vested interests of the status quo than they are with helping an institution to break the barriers to meet the needs of the year 2000.

To a lesser extent, the pressures of accreditation are also found in elementary and secondary schools. Almost every state has some form of school accreditation program, usually carried out by the state department of education. Most of these programs have been normative, like those at the college level. They tend to count the number of books in the library, verify that teachers have current certificates, compute the ratio of teachers to students, check on the auditing and bookkeeping procedures, visit classrooms, and look at lesson plans. For many years New York State· accredited its secondary schools, both public and private, through the system of state Regents examinations. These were statewide examinations conducted in various content areas. Pupils' scores were reported to the state office in Albany. High scores on the Regents examinations were necessary to obtain an academic college preparatory diploma and also to qualify for state scholarships. In a state as large and populous as New York, these examinations exerted a tremendous controlling influence on curriculum development. Students and teachers engaged in innovative programs would always have to keep one eye toward the Regents exam. Indeed, it was a common joke among most teachers that real teaching stopped early in May so that students could drill for the Regents examination in June. As for private schools, accreditation by regional agencies tended more often to be an item of prestige, but nevertheless exerted a similar kind of control over programs and curriculum content.

Closely related to the Regents exams are new external examinations which have similar impact. Most notable are the Scholastic Aptitude Tests (SAT) developed by the Educational Testing Service of Princeton, N.J., and the College Entrance Examination Board tests (CEEB), also of Princeton. These and other examinations like them are a source of great concern to youngsters seeking admission to college. Satisfactory scores on these tests often determine entrance into a favored college or university. Just as in the case of the New York State Regents examinations, they have a covert effect of teaching for the test. Classroom teachers, wise as to the way these tests have been constructed, often slant their program to prepare students for such tests. Almost every bookstore carries review books filled with practice exercises to help students prepare for these tests. Often the items included reflect obscure or very difficult factual knowledge. Vocabulary development is tested by the knowledge of analogies, imagery, metaphors, similes, synonyms, and antonyms, many of which have never been a part of the school curriculum, even as an incidental aspect of reading good literature just for its enjoyment. External examinations such as these, useful as they have been as indicators of ability, and presumed predictors of success with similar material in college, have nevertheless exerted a strong degree of conformity in the school curriculum.

In this section we have examined a number of facets of school organization which serve to control and limit the educational programs. Consolidation of schools, promoted in the name of efficiency, has tended to produce more conformity than it has diversity. Regional accreditation also served a useful purpose in that it helped to bring many institutions to a recognized level of quality, but in doing so, the normative standards often became the controlling influence. Programs and institutions which departed substantially from these norms more often found themselves on the defensive to justify their departure from the traditional practices.

Ethnic and Multicultural Education

What has been the pattern of schooling for children from different ethnic groups and cultural backgrounds? A rapid review of our educational history would suggest that culturally different groups have either been separated from the majority group or have been excluded almost entirely from participation. The history of educational programs for blacks in America is all too familiar. In our earlier history it was illegal in many states to provide any education whatever for slaves. From time to time slave owners took it upon themselves to educate their slaves in the rudiments of reading and writing and ciphering, but education beyond that point was rare indeed. During the Reconstruction after the Civil War, the Freedmen's Bureau began major efforts to develop educational programs for blacks. By the 1880's whites had reestablished the control of power in most southern states and Black Codes were enacted which soon brought about an almost completely dual society of blacks and whites. Both legislation and custom combined to create virtually two different school systems in every community with a dual system of teachers and administrators. The concept of separate but equal was reinforced in the famous *Plessy* v. *Ferguson* decision of 1896. But the reality all too often was that the schools were separate but seldom, if ever, equal. It has been well documented that schools for blacks were generally inferior in physical equipment and resources, in enforcement of attendance regulations, and in the quality of instruction. The *Brown* decision of 1954 was a major breakthrough in efforts to eliminate the dual system for it declared that separate facilities were inherently unequal.

In northern cities, racial segregation was more a matter of geographic and residential separation than legislative restrictions. Blacks attended schools with whites but up until World War I their number was comparatively few. The movement to the northern cities of a large number of blacks during the World Wars I and II produced major changes in residential patterns. Some neighborhoods became predominantly black, and by the middle 1950's the term ghetto, originally a European Yiddish word used to define a restrictive neighborhood for Jews, was being used to describe the neighborhood where blacks lived. As more and more whites fled to outer parts of cities and to the suburbs, the concentration of blacks increased in many schools and a clear pattern of separation and isolation had begun to develop. The resulting effect of cultural separation, whether enforced by law or by preferential housing patterns, was essentially the same.

The educational pattern for other ethnic groups was quite similar. Color was also a barrier for the Orientals on the West Coast, including Chinese, Japanese, and Filipinos. Enforced legal segregation was also the lot of the Native American whose educational program under the federal Bureau of Indian Affairs was limited almost exclusively to schools on the Indian reservations.

Ethnic and cultural groups whose language was not English also experienced the problem of separation and isolation. Successive waves of immigration of Jews from central Europe who spoke Yiddish, Polish, or Russian, often congregated in urban areas. While they brought with them a rich educational heritage and cultural life, they perceived that one of their principal tasks was to become assimilated into the dominant English-speaking culture if they were to participate fully in the life of a thriving metropolis. Other groups, such as French, Germans, Poles, and Czechs often maintained their own language in newspapers and as a medium of instruction, even in public schools until World War I. At that time, fear of Germans, Bolsheviks, Socialists, and foreigners in general gripped America and a series of laws were passed in many states which mandated English as the language of instruction. It was not uncommon, however, for many groups, especially in parochial schools, to continue to use their own languages in schools well into the 1940's.

Indeed, Roman Catholic and Lutheran schools staffed by religious and clergy from European countries did much to maintain the ethnic heritage in neighborhood enclaves. These schools were reinforced in the hundreds of Little Italies, Germantowns, and similar ethnic communities by local radio programs, newspapers, church services, and social organizations that used the native languages almost exclusively.

To what extent can we say that the American schools provided opportunity for cultural enrichment and diversity or that they tended to enforce a model of conformity to the majority culture? It is probably fair to say that, almost until the middle 1950's and early 1960's, the well-established melting-pot theory [27] of American democracy tended to submerge the values of differing ethnic groups. To be fully American was to be assimilated into the white community that spoke and read English. It was also an important element of the democratic faith that every person, no matter what his origin or nationality, had an equal opportunity to participate in the American democratic society. It was common to find public schools teaching classes in English and citizenship for foreigners. Learning English was the first step in becoming a naturalized citizen and in becoming eligible to vote. How historic an irony it is that in the middle 1960's thousands of college students received National Defense Education Act scholarships to study "critical foreign languages," usually Russian, Polish, Czech, Chinese, Japanese, and later the less well-known languages of developing nations of the Third World, such as Hindi, Urdu, Swahili, and other tongues. And it was only in 1975 that the Voting Rights Act of 1964 was amended to require, as a corollary to the prohibition of English literacy tests, that voting information be published and ballots issued in the local language of the citizens.

In a quite different vein Barbara Sizemore has argued that many American institutions, such as the church and school, have perpetuated the melting-pot theory which she regards as a functional myth for those in power. She holds that it is potentially harmful and psychologically

---

[27] The term "melting pot" appears to have come from the play *The Melting Pot*, by an English-Jewish writer, Israel Zangwill, which was first performed in New York in 1908. The central theme of the play was that America was God's crucible, the great melting pot in which all ethnic differences would amalgamate and a new man would emerge from a kind of ethnic synthesis. While the theme of assimilation represented a popular American ideology at the turn of the century, it remained far from reality. See: Nathan Glazer and Daniel P. Moynihan. *Beyond the Melting Pot: The Negroes, Puerto Ricans, Jews, Italians and Irish of New York City.* Cambridge: MIT Press, 1970. Interestingly, Zangwill later became an ardent Zionist, the very antithesis of the melting-pot prototype. He devoted much of his energies to the Zionist cause and changed his earlier views on racial and religious mixture. (*Ibid.*, p. 290.)

detrimental to powerless and minority groups, for it forces them to give up their unique culture.[28]

By the early 1950's a number of ethnic groups had begun to reexamine their own cultural heritage and find strong reasons to be proud of that heritage and to seek opportunities in schools for different educational offerings. The movements to produce racial identity and self-awareness resulted in the introduction of courses in black or Negro history, black literature, and similar topics. By the middle of the 1960's most colleges and universities had begun to provide special programs for black students in their history and culture. Black studies programs in colleges soon acquired status as interdepartmental programs and in some cases acquired independent departmental status on their own. The movement soon followed in the high schools. New courses in black literature and black heritage were widely introduced. One of the problems was that white teachers were often found teaching courses in black culture and black literature, because there were so few black teachers in many of the predominantly white schools.

Some real problems began to emerge and they may be thought of as the mirror image of the melting pot theory. How do we encourage educational diversity on the one hand, and yet acquaint all students with the cultural heritage and background of various ethnic and cultural groups of the society? Should all students be enrolled in black history courses? To the minority student, who has had no choice in the study of the predominant white culture, perhaps the answer is all too obvious. Are we building in a new sense of conformity if everyone is expected to study the cultural heritage of various groups? Or if we recognize the value of studying one another's cultural heritage, do we return to one of the earliest justifications of the value of conformity, that is, the common good? [29]

An important curriculum aspect of studying ethnic cultures is that the materials used must clearly reflect the point of view of that subgroup of society. There are too few curriculum materials readily available in schools today which show any sensitivity to the reaction of native

[28] Barbara Sizemore. "Shattering the Melting Pot Myth." In: James A. Banks, editor. *Teaching Ethnic Studies: Concepts and Strategies.* 43rd Yearbook. Washington, D.C.: National Council for the Social Studies, 1973. Chapter 4.

[29] One of the most useful sources dealing with ethnic and multicultural education is: James A. Banks, editor, *Teaching Ethnic Studies* (cited above). It is an excellent combination of background essays on cultural pluralism, racism in America, social justice and minorities, the melting pot myth and ethnic content in the white curriculum. Other chapters deal with the teaching of ethnic minority cultures, the Asian-American, black studies, Chicano experience, Native Americans, Puerto Ricans, white ethnic groups, and women's studies.

Americans to the white settlement of America. Only recently have poignant accounts become available written by Japanese-Americans about their own forced relocation early in World War II. Such materials can portray, if only in a vicarious way, the sensitivity of feelings and the viewpoint of the members of the non-majority culture. For one man's progress is another man's plunder. One man's triumph is another man's agony. One man's conquest of new lands becomes another man's captivity and enslavement. If such feelings are to be brought out in the studies of the cultural groups, then there must be great latitude or diversity and individualization in curriculum design, in teaching methods, and in freedom for students to respond to these new understandings with sensitivity and acceptance.

In contrast, the history of the past has been one of conformity in which the model of culture taught by the school was the predominant white culture. The day is over when schools can ignore the cultural contributions of minority and ethnic groups which have enriched the heritage of America. This is especially true in large cities where blacks, Chicanos, and Puerto Ricans may make up a very sizable proportion of the school population. Less obvious is the problem of the more affluent white suburbs, the great stretches of middle America and the rural areas of Appalachia, and the more remote portions of the South and West. It is in these predominantly white communities that the problem goes largely unnoticed and where cultural awareness is still to be raised. There are many communities where there are children and adults who have no contact at all with members of minority groups, except through television which presents limited vignettes of blacks, Chicanos, and other groups.

To a lesser extent, many of the communities mentioned above do have some experience with white ethnic groups, either currently today, or in the historical past. The influence of these cultural groups can certainly be studied, and their contributions to the town and the city can be explored. What is important is that the white paternalism that was so much a part of the melting pot theory not be used as a mask for examining the sensitive and provocative questions. One must ask how power, authority, and influence were used, through economics, social class structure, and political activities to control or hold sway over minority groups. But at the same time students must also be exposed to the sensitive and uniquely human qualities of the ethnic groups and their value positions on life, the acquisition of wealth, peace and harmony, violence and strength, the role of the family, the respect for elders, the love of children, the place of authority and similar value positions. For it is often on such matters as these that value positions are most divergent and about which there is the greatest ignorance and mis-understanding.

In this section we have looked at the problems of ethnic and multi-cultural education from the points of view of diversity and conformity. Our history has been filled with examples in which the culturally differ-ent child bowed to the majority culture. He abandoned his language, changed his style of dress, food, and folk ways to accept those of the dominant majority. A challenge for the future is to use those goals as opportunities for diversity and individualization in the study of diverse cultural backgrounds and heritage in our American society.

Educational Research, Testing, and Evaluation

Perhaps no other aspects of education reflect more the value of conformity than do research, testing, and evaluation. We should say right at the outset that this is not to condemn the past efforts in research and evaluation but rather to say that we have employed a particular mode of investigation that has looked at the performance of groups of students rather than the progress of individuals. To a very large extent, we have been held captive by the psychological model of research in carefully controlled experimental conditions which has focused heavily upon the establishment of the group norm and the comparative perform-ance of one group versus another.[30] In contrast, studies conducted in naturalistic settings using other methodologies such as ethnography, or which focus upon the individual rather than the class as the unit of analysis, have been given little attention until only quite recently. These latter approaches, which will be discussed more fully below, appear to have considerable potential for exploring the effects of diversity and individuality in the curriculum.

The earliest research studies, often conducted by state superintend-ents of instruction, tended to be normative surveys which sought to establish the how much and how many of the educational scene. School buildings were compared in terms of size, square footage, numbers of classrooms, wealth per pupil, etc. Means and medians for school districts of various sizes were calculated and determined. State agencies and even the U.S. Office of Education helped to compile this massive set of descriptive research. Especially in large cities, such as New York, Chi-

---

[30] For a hard-hitting review of the very limited impact educational research has made upon teaching, see: Geraldine Jonçich Clifford. "A History of the Impact of Research on Teaching." In: R. M. Travers, editor. *Second Handbook of Research on Teaching.* Chicago: Rand McNally, 1973. Chapter 1.

cago, and St. Louis, these normative surveys served as useful guides for providing a certain degree of unity and even control in school districts.

One of the earliest "researchers" in education was Joseph M. Rice, a physician turned educator-journalist, who had spent two years between 1888 and 1890 studying pedagogy at Jena and Leipzig. Rice made a firsthand appraisal of American public education by visiting classrooms, talking with teachers, attending school board meetings, and interviewing parents from Boston to Washington, and from New York to St. Louis. He visited some 36 cities and talked to more than 1,200 teachers. His lively and pungent criticisms of ignorant and inefficient practices as well as exciting schools and inspired and enthusiastic teachers, appeared in a series of articles in the New York *Forum* from October 1892 through June 1893. These were republished as *The Public School System of the United States* (New York: 1893). Rice had stirred up a hornet's nest and provoked vigorous replies from the supporters of the public schools. He persisted in his studies and in 1897, using evidence from tests on 33,000 school children, demonstrated that there was no significant correlation between the amount of time devoted to doing spelling homework and achievement in spelling.[31]

Probably the most significant force in the entire testing movement was Edward L. Thorndike, whose work in psychology of learning, statistics, and measurement was monumental. Thorndike wrote a number of monographs on construction of tests, devised tests of his own including tests of oral and silent reading, English usage, spelling, reading, and reasoning. In addition, in seeking to transfer his laws of learning, he strongly advocated the use of practice, exercise, or drill with rewards, and the measurement of progress through frequent testing, especially standardized tests, to develop reliable estimates of learning.[32] Early studies in spelling, arithmetic, and reading often compared results on city-wide achievement tests, using newly developed scales and standardized tests. Thorndike and his students, for example, had developed scales for measuring achievement in arithmetic (1908), handwriting (1910), spelling (1913), drawing (1913), reading (1914), and language ability (1916).[33] Statistical data were frequently calculated in terms of frequency distributions, ranges, means, and medians to show the performance of various schools throughout a school district. By 1918, Walter

[31] Joseph M. Rice. "The Futility of the Spelling Grind." *The Forum* 23: 163-72; 1897.

[32] For a critical account of Thorndike and his contributions, see: Geraldine Jonçich. *The Sane Positivist: A Biography of Edward L. Thorndike.* Middletown, Connecticut: Wesleyan University Press, 1968.

[33] See: Walter W. Cook. "Achievement Test." In: Walter S. Monroe, editor. *Encyclopedia of Educational Research.* New York, 1941. pp. 1283-1301.

S. Monroe reported over 100 standardized tests designed to measure achievement in elementary and secondary school subjects.[34]

Certainly no account of the research and testing movement would be complete without mention of the work of J. Wayne Wrightstone, who for many years was director of the Bureau of Research in New York City. Under his direction thousands of students and hundreds of teachers were involved in tests of the activity program and other aspects of the progressive school program. Schools in every borough of the city were set up as paired for control and experimental groups and actively involved in attempting to assess the impact of the progressive reforms and to weigh that against conventional achievement.[35]

In a closely related development, the French psychologists Alfred Binet and Theodore Simon began to work on scales to assess intelligence. While there were many refinements of the original Binet scale, the most important was the Stanford revision, described by Louis Terman in the measurement of intelligence. It was Terman who also developed the notion of the intelligence quotient (IQ), a number expressing the relationship of an individual's mental age to his chronological age.

Close upon the heels of these developments came the efforts during World War I by a group of psychologists who offered their services to the Army to try to construct a group intelligence test for Army recruits. In 1917 under the direction of Robert Yerkes, then president of the American Psychological Association, the group developed a number of instruments, the most important of which were Army Scale Alpha, a group test for recruits who could read and understand English, and Scale Beta, a nonverbal group test consisting largely of pictures and diagrams with directions in pantomine for recruits who could not read or write English. The tests were used for a variety of purposes, particularly to classify recruits for a range of tasks within the Army on the basis of presumed intelligence.[36] One of the most important aspects of

---

[34] Walter S. Monroe. *The Measurement of Educational Products.* Seventh Yearbook, Part 2. The National Society for the Study of Education, 1918.

[35] See for example such works of Wrightstone as: "Measuring Social Performance Factors in Activity and Control Schools of New York City." *Teachers College Record* 40: 423-32; February 1939; "Evaluation of the Experiment with the Activity Program in the New York City Elementary Schools." *Journal of Educational Research* 38: 252-57; December 1944. More comprehensive analyses are presented in such volumes as: *Appraisal of Experimental High School Practices.* New York: Teachers College, Columbia University, 1936; and *Appraisal of Newer Elementary School Practices.* 1938.

[36] Clarence S. Yoakum and Robert M. Yerkes. *Army Mental Tests.* New York, 1920. Also: Robert M. Yerkes, editor. *Psychological Examining in the United States Army.* Washington, D.C., 1921.

the testing program was the development of tests that could be taken by large groups of men in a relatively short time. This was a major improvement over the individually administered Binet and Terman IQ tests. Out of this would develop in the 1920's and 1930's a whole gamut of intelligence and achievement tests that could be administered in a relatively short time by a teacher to an entire class of students. Indeed, whole schools and school districts could be tested in only a few days.

It is clear to us now, in retrospect, that these tests have in fact been measures of achievement of the majority culture. We have come to see that such tests have been unfairly discriminatory in that they have failed to tap other fundamental ways of learning and elements of a culture which do not appear on the standardized tests. Many efforts in the past decade have been made to try to develop culture-free tests. Nevertheless, the point to be made here is that the tests were developed and that normative scales were established. At the same time we learned a good deal about the growing science of statistics. The concept of the normal curve of distribution with its characteristic bell shape, was a very useful concept for describing the distribution of the data as it grouped around a theoretical mean of a group. The concept of a standard deviation as a measure of how far a score departed from the mean, the percentage of total scores within a standard deviation, above or below the mean, became an extremely useful way of labeling subdivisions of data. It was not very long before intelligence scores could be identified as within a normal range, above average, very bright, and genius; correspondingly, below average, educable, trainable, and moron.

The same concept of standardized testing and the use of a normal curve of distribution to describe the data became an important yardstick for judging school achievement. In the 1920's and 1930's as standardized educational tests were developed, the Iowa Test of Basic Skills, California Tests of Mental Maturity, the Metropolitan Reading Readiness Test, and others were widely used as devices not only for judging the quality of instruction, but also for grouping of children. Scores on these tests were considered nearly infallible and a great aura of mystery surrounded them. Few would doubt or challenge their validity and many administrators would make irrevocable decisions for grade assignment, curriculum placement, etc., based on these scores. Few teachers or administrators understood the related concept of standard error of measurement which was so important in understanding that these scores were not fixed and finite values, but had a built-in range of plus or minus a number of score points. Yet with great precision and finality, students were assigned to classes for the gifted or relegated to classes for the slow or retarded learner based upon the scores on these tests.

This is not to devaluate entirely the efforts to assess intelligence and academic achievement. Rather it is to recognize and to decry the abuses which occurred in the name of scientism and to point out the tremendous degree of conformity which resulted from the application of such normative and standardized measures. The rise of the testing movement promised more precise identification of needs, talents, and shortcomings of individual students. It also promised the possibility of more specific personal curriculum adaptation. Both things have failed us so far. We are unable to identify or predict with great confidence outside of cultural settings. In addition, test results typically provide more data than anyone can use. The promise of testing is prostituted by the utter necessity to group pupils for manageability. And to date, we have not been able to manage the great variability that the test data have identified.

Educational research also progressed well beyond the data-counting stage. As our knowledge of statistics increased, vast numbers of correlational studies were completed to try to determine how one factor was associated with or related to another, and whether that relationship was strong or weak, positive or negative. From these clues it was hoped that further studies could be done to determine the effects of such a relationship. Other statistical measures, such as the t-test and Fisher's analysis of variance allowed experimenters to compare performance of groups of students, usually on pre- and post-tests of performance or achievement. What is important to point out, however, is that the unit of measurement was the entire class. Individual students were seldom, if ever, the unit of analysis. To increase the generalizability of the research, investigators studied large numbers of classes, sometimes involving almost entire school districts to increase the unit of measure. The mean of the experimental group, compared with that of the control group, was the paradigm of investigation. Only recently have curriculum developers and administrators been able to translate the statistical jargon to recognize that a large amount of variance means a great amount of diversity within the classroom. The smaller the variance, the less the diversity in achievement.

It is really amusing to think about the extent to which educational researchers have gone to mask or "account for" individual differences. A rather sophisticated technique, called the analysis of covariance actually manages to compensate for, or adjust for, initial differences in scores on pretest measures that may otherwise affect post-test achievement. It only serves to point out how strong is our desire to look at the performance of the total group as the unit of measure and to hold constant those extraneous things that would affect post-test achievement. In recent years we have tended to hallow or hold as sacrosanct the use of parametric statistics which imply a normal distribution of some trait such as achievement. Other statistical measures, such as nonparametric statistics, which do not assume a normal distribution of some trait, have been decidedly less favored by researchers. Researchers have created an orthodoxy that favors the parametric statistical model. But in the area of special education where the individual is the unit of measure and not the large class, the nonparametric statistics have been used to great advantage.

Efforts to assess and evaluate student performance also reflect a normative approach. At the most direct level, the schools have typically issued report cards to parents that use A, B, C, D letter grades or numerical standards based on 100 per cent. Each of these was based upon the theoretical normal curve of distribution and carried with it very much the same standards of conformity described above. At the elementary school level, progress has been made with much more descriptive reports about individual student progress, informal techniques of reporting through parent conferences, and other measures. But little progress has been made in the secondary schools and in the colleges which adhere so tenaciously to the norm-referenced approach.

Efforts to report progress in terms of instructional objectives and competency measures have been discussed above. These also fall victim to the same pressures of conformity to the lowest common denominator.

Most recently, efforts have been made to develop some form of national assessment of educational progress. While it is undoubtedly useful to try to determine just what is the state of our educational programs, the spectre of the misuse of such data is frightening indeed. Already one has heard of reports that this or that school district is above or below the mean in the acquisition of certain information and thought processes. But what reaches the national and local consciousness is not the uniqueness and diversity of students but rather the extent of their conformity to others in similar groups.

Just as in the case of the New York State Regents exams, SAT and CEEB exams mentioned above, the National Assessment of Educational Progress has the potential for becoming a national curriculum. The great efforts to achieve consensus upon objectives prior to the beginning of testing have certain commendable features in terms of identifying common learnings and probably common outcomes. But at the same time it sharply limits the degree of individuality and diversity that might otherwise exist. In one of the early reports of the description of some of the objectives Lawrence Metcalf wonders about the responses a black ghetto family might make to the descriptions of the objectives. He notes that the poor, the black, the radical, and the violent were absent from or *unrepresented* on the various reviewing panels. The most radical group mentioned was the League of Women Voters. "It is no wonder, then," Metcalf complained, "that descriptions of good civic behavior and the family read like exemplars from Dick and Jane readers."[37]

At the beginning of this article we suggested that other methodologies held considerable potential for exploring the effects of diversity and individuality in the curriculum. An ample body of research methodology is currently being developed which offers new approaches to the problem of educational research but which does not make use of the tightly controlled model of psychological research.

Shaver and Larkin[38] have pointed to the use of ethnography as a viable research tool for examining classrooms in naturalistic settings. Work by Jackson[39] in his observation of Chicago schools, and Smith and Geoffrey[40] point to the value of this mode of research in helping formulate more appropriate hypotheses for further investigation.

In quite another direction, Brophy and Good[41] have focused attention over a number of years on the relationships of teachers to individual students and have looked at the individual student as the unit of analysis for research. Their work represents an important departure from the traditional models described above since it seeks to avoid the concept of representing "typical" teacher behavior by some general index of indirectness, use of student ideas, or acceptance of feelings. Rather, such research seeks to determine how a teacher initiates or responds with individuals or small groups on the basis of appropriate feedback of data about the student. "Given the increasing curricular emphasis upon mastery learning, individualized instruction, learning centers, modular instruction," Brophy and Good contend, "we suspect that more and more teacher behavior in elementary classrooms will be directed toward individual students and subgroups of students rather than the entire class."[42]

[37] Lawrence E. Metcalf in: "Observations and Commentary of a Panel of Reviewers." Related to Report #2. *Citizenship.* National Assessment of Educational Progress, a project of the Education Commission of the States, July 1970. p. 25.

[38] James P. Shaver and A. Guy Larkin. "Research on Teaching Social Studies." In: Robert M. Travers, editor. *Second Handbook for Research on Teaching.* Chicago: Rand McNally, 1973. pp. 1254-58.

[39] Philip Jackson. *Life in Classrooms.* New York: Holt, Rinehart and Winston, 1968.

[40] L. M. Smith and W. Geoffrey. *The Complexities of an Urban Classroom.* New York: Holt, Rinehart and Winston, 1968.

[41] Jere E. Brophy and Thomas L. Good. *Teacher-Student Relationships: Causes and Consequences.* New York: Holt, Rinehart and Winston, 1974.

[42] *Ibid.,* pp. 5-6.

While studies of the types described above are still too few, it seems that the pendulum might be swinging toward greater attention to the diversity of individual students and less toward conformity to the performance of the group as the norm in research and evaluation. If so, the change is welcome and long overdue.

In this chapter we have reviewed a number of aspects of American education from the point of view of diversity and conformity. These two values have tended to coexist simultaneously in tension with each other. The pressures to conform are balanced by the pressures to provide for the individual in varying and diverse ways. Correspondingly, the pressures for diversity are counterbalanced by those that seek unity or more often uniformity in the name of efficiency, order, or even Americanization. We have examined some of the technical concerns of schooling such as curriculum development, methods of teaching, school organization, and educational research, testing, and evaluation. In each of these we have seen examples of the competing values. It has probably been one of the great saving graces of our pluralistic society that these two values have operated together to provide an essential unity within the context of cultural diversity.

BICENTENNIAL VIGNETTES

Hilda Taba, Curriculum Worker

". . . learning . . . is an interrelational process, the three important determining elements of which are: (1) what in this connection may be called the learning materials (that is, environment, stimulation, teaching, books—in fact, everything with which the learner comes in contact and to which he reacts); (2) the nature, abilities, and interests of the agent of learning; and (3) the structure, form and sequence of the process of learning itself together with its results." [1]

By thoughts like these, Hilda Taba first became known in the "educational" world.

Hilda Taba was born in Estonia. She earned a Bachelor's degree in 1926 from the University of Tartu and a Master's degree in 1927 from Bryn Mawr. In 1932, she was awarded a Ph.D. from Teachers College, Columbia University, having been a pupil and protege of both John Dewey and William H. Kilpatrick. Also in 1932, Taba published *The Dynamics of Education*. While holding an assistant professorship at Ohio State University, she was assigned with Laura Zirbes to write a chapter for the first yearbook of the John Dewey Society (*The Teacher and Society*, 1937). It is understood that Taba wrote the chapter titled,

"The Teacher at Work." Later, she moved to an assistant professorship at the University of Chicago.

From 1945-1948, Taba was the director of the Center for Intergroup Education sponsored by the American Council on Education. This project led to the establishment at the University of Chicago of a center for the study of intergroup relations funded by a grant from the National Council of Christians and Jews. Hilda Taba directed the Chicago center from 1948-1951. Based upon the project implementation, she authored several books. Among them were *With Focus on Human Relations* (with Deborah Elkins, 1950), *Leadership Training in Intergroup Education* (1953), *School Culture* (1955), and *Teaching Strategies for the Culturally Disadvantaged* (with Deborah Elkins, 1966). In 1951, Dr. Taba became professor of education at

[1] Hilda Taba. *The Dynamics of Education*. London: Routledge & Kegan Paul, Ltd. p. 155.

San Francisco State College, and, at the time of her death, she was professor of educational administration there.

Beginning with the work with intergroup relations Taba used action research to test, to try out ideas. The foundations for her *Curriculum Development Theory and Practice* (1962) were begun with experiences related to the project. This field research continued, and in 1967, she published *A Teacher's Handbook for Elementary Social Studies*. Both of these works suggested curriculum practices which were implemented and found workable prior to publication. Since her death, Taba's influence has continued strong, particularly in social studies curriculum materials and in teaching strategies.

Judgments concerning the significance of contributions to a given area of study are often based on applicability, and continuing relevancy. The works of Hilda Taba stand favorably on each of these criteria.

The possibility of planning learning experiences to attain a wide range of objectives has never been well understood or practiced, partly because of a traditional separation of planning content for planning and learning experiences and partly because of the assumption that good content will bring about the development of thinking and other mental skills. The planning for effective attainment of a wide range of objectives requires several things. One of these is an awareness that the *different behaviors involved in different areas of objectives require different types of learning experiences to attain them.*[2]

[2] Hilda Taba. *Curriculum Development: Theory and Practice.* New York: Harcourt Brace Jovanovich, 1962. p. 279.

—*Patricia A. Moseley*

Life and Death of Building America

The doors have closed on *Building America*. Locked away, one of the most unusual and innovative programs of the century.

Sponsored by the Society for Curriculum Study, an organization concerned with curricular innovation and development, and arising out of worldwide economic and anxiety-producing crises, this curricular program attempted to deal with such urgent and deepseated problems involving American culture and society as "the present status and future possibilities of American agriculture, industry, commerce, mining, transportation, communication, housing, social and governmental institutions, etc." (p. 38).[1] *Building America* originated

[1] All references from Robert Ernest Newman, Jr. "History of a Civic Education Project Implementing the Social Problems Techniques of Instruction." Unpublished doctoral dissertation, Stanford University, 1961.

with and was sparked by Paul R. Hanna, then at Teachers College, Columbia University, later at Stanford University. His associates included C. L. Cushman, Edgar Dale, William S. Grey, Hollis L. Caswell, James Mendenhall, Harold Hand, Jesse Newlon, Paul E. Drost, and Clair Zyve. *Building America* became a series of picture texts dealing with social and economic life in the United States.

Spanning 13 years, each month from October to June a new issue appeared dealing with a particular phase of American culture and society. The first issue, October 1935, was entitled "Housing"; others included: "China," "Crime," "Family Life," "Food," "Fuel," "Politics," and "Power." Ranging from 24 to 32 pages in length, three-quarters of the space consisted of pictorial presentation. A short text accompanied these pictures to sharpen some of the issues and explain in more detail major points raised. Utilizing the two approaches in one publication, editorial board members believed that pupils would focus more attention on, and achieve a greater understanding of, the diverse solutions offered to the specific problem being examined.

Early years of publication were fraught with fiscal concerns. Hanna and Mendenhall realized they would need to publish at least 10,000 copies per issue before they could undertake the project. Funds donated by the Civic Education Press were not enough to cover expenses for the first year of publication. Concerned educators and editorial board members reached into their Depression pockets for the needed funds. Why during this time of financial squeeze would educators contribute to a fledgling and risky publication? Board members felt that early contributors were worried that, during this critical point, amid economic chaos, Americans could well make the wrong decisions. Hanna voiced the concern of these educators when he said (p. 52):

We need to reaffirm our fundamental faith in democracy in order to turn to human advantage whatever our ingenuity provides for using new material or spiritual controls.

Building America survived and grew.

The professed belief of the editorial board in the infinite worth of individual human beings, regardless of race or social class background, led to a publication that attempted to present, in as scholarly and objective manner as possible, facts, issues, and values involved in considering alternative solutions to social problems. Americans should, by right, have access to objective information concerning crucial social issues of the day in order to make sound decisions. Unwittingly, this premise seemed fated to bring about the publication's downfall.

In mid 1946, the California Society of the Sons of the American Revolution (S.A.R.) charged the series with undermining the principles of American government. In particular, the S.A.R. was concerned with two specific issues of *Building America:* "Civil Liberties" and "Our Constitution." Criticizing these issues for portraying many minorities as clamoring for rights denied them by the majority, and for protecting the civil liberties of many minority groups and individuals with extreme social philosophies, the S.A.R. accused the issues of being "written from the standpoint of a professional agitator and using class and race conscious methods" (pp. 237-38). Had the series itself been the only thing subject to critical examination and heavy protest, the course of events might have taken a different turn. The S.A.R., however, viciously accused several state officials and lay members of the State Board of Education as being affiliated with Communist front organizations. Near the end of the second year the Senate Education Committee cleared the officials and members, leaving the conflict to center only on the series. Powerful voices that had spoken out against accusations of the state's education system being managed by pro-communist sympathizers became much less vociferous. Public interest waned, and *Building America,* unable to regain adequate support, succumbed.

On October 15, 1948, editor Frances Foster closed the office doors of the *Building America* series for the last time. What had been founded "to help students freely discuss and study controversial issues, had itself been forced into the position of appearing to be a bitterly contested controversial issue—too controversial for use in the public schools" (p. 436). Yet the death of the *Building America* series did not diminish the voices of its ardent supporters. Many of them believed—and still feel—as Frances Foster, who wrote to the editorial board "I have never for a moment lost the belief that BA or something like it was greatly needed; I feel it is needed now more than ever" (p. 153).

—*Marilyn Maxson*

David Eugene Smith:
Father of Mathematics Education

Although best remembered for his monumental achievements in the study and documentation of mathematical history, David Eugene Smith (1860-1944) was a major contributor to the development and growth of mathematics and mathematics education. Phillip Jones, writing for NCTM, said "The history of mathematics education . . . probably should be dated from the period of David Eugene Smith's incumbency as professor of mathematics at Teachers College, Columbia University, 1901-1926."[1] His list of firsts in the teaching of mathematics and in curriculum is formidable. For example, Smith directed the first two doctoral theses in mathematics education at Teachers College in 1906. These

[1] National Council of Teachers of Mathematics. *A History of Mathematics Education in The United States and Canada.* Washington, D.C.: NCTM, 1970. p. 454. For additional information about Smith, see, especially: D. J. Brokaw. "Contributions of David Eugene Smith To The Teaching of Elementary Mathematics." Unpublished master's paper, University of Texas at Austin, Austin, Texas, 1929; J. Ginsburg. "Professor Smith's Literary Activities." *Mathematics Teacher* 19: 306-11; 1926; W. Reeve. "David Eugene Smith." An editorial in: *Mathematics Teacher* 37: 297-98; 1944.

theses were on the history of the teaching of arithmetic and geometry.

Born in Cortland, New York, in 1860, Smith graduated from Cortland State Normal School in 1881. After receiving an LL.D. from Syracuse University in 1884, he taught mathematics at CSNS until 1891. In 1887 he earned his Ph.D. from Syracuse. He was a professor of mathematics at the Michigan State Normal School at Ypsilanti from 1891 until 1898 when it conferred an honorary Master of Pedagogy degree on him. He became professor of mathematics at Teachers College in 1901 and later was named professor emeritus.

Smith was a member of the NEA's Committee of Ten and wrote the "Report of The Committee of Ten on Mathematics" which appeared in 1896. Later he served on the National Commit-

Right: One-room school, Ojo Sarco, New Mexico, 1943.

Facing page: Elementary school dance class, Washington, D.C., 1942.

tee on Mathematical Requirements.

Dr. Smith's study of teaching methods led to the publication in *Educational Review* of "Studies in Mathematics Education" in 1897. Earlier he had published one of the first studies on the role of sex differences in mathematics achievement which appeared in *Educational Review* in 1895.

Published in 1904, Smith's *Grammar School Arithmetic* was the first of the modern texts to appear in the first quarter of the century. For example, Smith's book was the first to use an "x" for "times" in multiplication.

Dr. Smith's concern for pedagogy resulted in the *Handbook To Smith's Arithmetic* in 1905. His influence in the changing patterns of arithmetic pedagogy was reflected in "Movements in Mathematical Teaching" and "The Old and New Arithmetic" both of which were published in 1905. In 1909 the *Teachers College Record* printed his "The Teaching of Arithmetic" as an article. The issue was in such demand that Teachers College issued the article as a small book. He wrote "The Teaching of High School Mathematics" in 1902 and a book, *The Teaching of Elementary Mathematics*, in 1905. This book was the first modern methods text in mathematics in this country.

His *The Teaching of Geometry* (1911) became a classic in geometry methods. It had a major impact and lasting effect on how subsequent geometry texts were written. For example, this methods text was the first to give a detailed explanation of "how to" present each major idea or proposition in plane geometry. Additionally, Smith was a member of the National Committee of 15 on the geometry syllabus and contributed significantly to its published report in 1911.

Smith co-authored one of the first junior high school mathematics textbook series. It was published in 1917 and became a model for junior high texts which followed. His methods text, *The Teaching of Junior High School Mathematics*, greatly influenced curriculum development. In it, he discussed how the curriculum is made and how objectives may be attained.

Many of Smith's works reflected the larger social or educational forces or movements of his day. He met the vocational movement head on with his text *Vocational Algebra* which was designed to be used in the shop and in commerce. He tried to echo the utilitarian theme with such articles as "Connecting Arithmetic with the Child's Everyday Experiences" and "Problems About War for Classes in Arithmetic." He contributed to the literature of the efficiency movement with such articles as "How May the Teaching of Mathematics Be Made More Efficient?" which appeared in 1909.

In summary, David Eugene Smith was a curriculum shaper and

mathematics educator of impressive note. He contributed textbooks at all levels of arithmetic and mathematics. He defended the teaching of mathematics. He developed a philosophy of teaching which influenced teachers and curriculum makers alike. He studied teaching. He wrote about teaching. He developed curriculum. He kept pace internationally. He led the way in new techniques and text content. He was a scholar and historian. David Eugene Smith has left his mark on mathematics education.

—*Merle B. Grady*

The Eight-Year Study

Hilda Taba calls attention to the far-reaching impact of the Eight-Year Study when she maintains, "The strategies of organizing and administering the work of curriculum development today are essentially extensions of methods employed when the task of the local school districts was to implement the designs established by . . . the Eight-Year Study."[1]

The 1942 five volume publication of the Progressive Education Association's Eight-Year Study, conducted from 1932-40, addressed itself to the question, How might the tenets of progressive education more effectively respond to the needs of secondary students than do traditional programs? Through the participation of 30 secondary schools, the following reforms did emerge: teachers asked why certain traditional subjects were taught; barriers between departments crumbled; schools reached out to communities; and outmoded lesson plans were replaced by innovative materials.

To determine the longitudinal effects of progressive education, Ralph Tyler undertook a follow-up study at the college level of 1,475 matched pairs (one student from an Eight-Year Study school and one from a traditional school). In some 20 categories, the graduates of the experimental schools surpassed their traditionally educated counterparts. The Eight-Year Study contributed a significant impetus to innovative practices at the secondary level.

The research associated with the Eight-Year Study assessed student interests and conceptualized an evaluation program which has remained a standard method for the analysis and classification of objectives. Finally, as an experimental study it accounted for experimentation with curricular patterns on the classroom level and the development of innovative conceptual schemes.

—*Elaine F. McNally*

[1] Taba, *Curriculum Development.*

SPELLING

LOOK CLOSELY AT THE FIRST WORD IN
YOUR LESSON AND PRONOUNCE IT ALOUD.
THINK OF A SENTENCE USING THE WORD
LOOK AT THE WAY THE WORD IS SPELLED.
CLOSE YOUR EYES AND TRY TO SEE THE WORD
WRITE THE WORD WITHOUT LOOKING
AT THE BOOK.
OPEN YOUR BOOK AND SEE IF YOU
WROTE THE WORD CORRECTLY
IF YOU WROTE THE WORD CORRECT
LY, WRITE IT THREE TIMES.

LANGUAGE

1. Make a plan.
2. Leave margins.
3. Indent.
4. Begin each staten
   with a capital.
5. Punctuate the en
   sentence.
6. Check your paper.

5

Sisyphus Revisited

David Turney

Each moment is the fruit of forty thousand years. The minute winning days, like flies, buzz home to death, and every moment is a window on all time.

—*Thomas Wolfe,* Look Homeward, Angel*

THIS CHAPTER is essentially a set of reflections on the panoramic views presented in preceding chapters of the development of our system of public education over the past 200 years. Some of the reflections have grown out of readings of the material presented in this Yearbook. Other statements have grown out of those highly charged discussions that take place when writers convene to discuss the development of a publication such as this. Some statements are based on deep personal conviction, which to some degree appeared to be supported either by the earlier chapters or by group consensus.

Many readers of this Yearbook will come to quite different conclusions and this will make the writing worth the effort so long as some fundamental issues are raised and dialogue is enjoined.

Left: Negro school, Veazy, Georgia, 1941.

---

* Thomas Wolfe. *Look Homeward, Angel.* New York: Charles Scribner's Sons, 1929. Reprinted by permission of Charles Scribner's Sons, copyright © 1929; renewal copyright © 1957; Edward C. Aswell, Administrator, C.T.A., and/or Fred Wolfe.

The Dilemma

The vitality of institutions is a variable factor that waxes and wanes across time. The value of a perspective which embraces 200 years is that the smaller fluctuations in vitality tend to level out and we can see more clearly those things we did well and those which were short of the mark or were regressions.

Working in a helping profession such as education has its own built-in frustrations. We work with people and mostly with young people. Because people are fallible, the experience of failure is a built-in feature of our work. As human beings, we and our charges work within limits. The more closely we approach these limits, the less stable our achievements become.

In the short range we do appear to resemble Sisyphus of Greek mythology, who was condemned to spend eternity pushing a boulder up a hill only to have it roll back down just before the top was reached.

The review of the past in the foregoing chapters is a history of the development of an institution continually expanding in size. Now in our bicentennial year, we look forward to a period of stabilization and a shrinking enrollment, already visible at the elementary school level.

We may well be approaching a watershed in the history of education where the drive to accommodate and encompass is replaced by greater qualitative concerns and by refinement of the ways we serve the needs of youth.

For the present, however, there are a number of problems which have not given much ground in the face of our repeated attempts at solution. Some of these problems are considered in the pages that follow.

Social Realities as Curriculum Sources

Early in the development of curriculum as a special field, three major sources for decision making were identified: the nature of society, the nature of the learner, and the nature of the learning process. Of these three sources, the first would seem to be the most affected by recent historical development. It makes good sense to say that schools should be responsive to the needs, aspirations, and mores of a community so long as real identifiable communities exist.

During the past thirty years, however, sweeping and basic changes in patterns and styles of living have virtually obliterated communities as we used to know them. The central cities are bloated and sick with wall-to-wall people. The traditional mechanisms for achieving social consensus have either withered away or have been destroyed by inept social planning, particularly in the housing area. Ever-increasing mobility of population has resulted in the new suburbia where neighborhoods of the kinds we used to know rarely exist.

Societal need has become harder and harder to specify because of these and related conditions. The true social reality of our present time appears to be that we will not be able to identify specific needs of a group of people until new social organizational forms emerge which will facilitate their expression. In these times, the curriculum worker, whose crystal ball has always been rather opaque at best, can only respond to broad social concerns articulated through larger units of government and the mass media.

Sequence Validity

Sequential organization is a part of how our world works. One occurrence does follow with considerable regularity on the heels of another and antecedent and consequence are observable daily. Because we are immersed in linked events of this type, it is easy to assume that learning has to proceed in the same fashion and that one thing must be learned before another simply because it usually occurs that way, was discovered in that order, or because there are progressive and linear relationships linking a series of occurrences. It is quite reasonable to assume, therefore, that learning will best proceed through use of natural or accidental sequences and consequently "sequence" has become a fundamental component of curricula.

This basic assumption has never been tested, except recently in a few situations, but there is much reason to believe that optimal learning experiences do not coincide with the patterns so easily observed in the materials to be learned.

At the peak of the experimentation with programmed learning one experimenter scrambled the item cards in a carefully sequenced linear learning program. Surprisingly, the participants achieved slightly better results when the sequence had been destroyed.

Gagné, who developed a hierarchical, systematic approach to scientific learning, got as good results when his units were presented in random order.[1]

What seems to be true at this time is that we do not really know what sequences, if any, are indispensable to effective learning. We have

---

[1] Robert Gagné. "Learning and Instructional Sequence." In: Fred Kerlinger, editor. *Review of Research in Education*, Vol. I. Itasca, Illinois: F. E. Peacock, 1973. pp. 3-33.

never really examined the problem—the value of sequences appeared to be obvious!

A good alternate hypothesis is that the ordering of elements to be learned is an important component of the process of learning—that those patterns the learner creates may, in many instances, be more viable for him or her than one imposed by the educator.

While learning by means of prefabricated sequences may not have the importance we have assumed, learning about sequences is surely of importance because skill in extrapolation depends on such understandings. Bloom ranks extrapolation as a thought process well up the middle of his taxonomy.[2] Since the bulk of our teaching appears still to be directed toward memorization and recall, the study of sequences and the logic embedded in them may well represent a useful goal for future curriculum emphasis.

Curriculum Development Problems

From the beginning, the actual determination of curriculum content has been closely linked to the means our society devised for production. Whether the materials of instruction appeared in printed form, pictures, or realia, they had to be produced or collected and made available before they could be utilized by teachers. Throughout most of our history, the major source of such materials has been through profit-making enterprises. Thus, a fundamental criterion for the availability and continued use of learning materials has been their salability. The importance of this fact has been recognized in many states and most schools through the development of sets of procedures for the selection of educational materials.

Continuous popularity of any curriculum material or learning device has depended ultimately on its appeal to a large proportion of the teachers who might be expected to use it. Publishing companies and other firms developing educational materials were quick to discover that the kinds of materials which were comprehensive enough to please most of the potential users, but not selective enough to greatly irritate many of them, would bring the greatest financial returns. As one publisher became successful with a particularly bland set of materials, others seeking to regain a share of the market, would modify their offerings in the same direction. This homogenizing effect, which has had similar consequences in popular music and literature, has produced a certain amount of uniformity in the education of youth which, granting the

[2] Benjamin S. Bloom, with Max D. Engelhart, Edward J. Furst, Walker H. Hill, and David R. Krathwohl. *Taxonomy of Educational Objectives, Handbook I: Cognitive Domain.* New York: Longmans, Green and Co., 1956.

amount of decentralization inherent in our system, could probably not have been achieved in any other way.

Educators were also quick to discover that this way of developing materials resulted in the teacher's serious dependency on a particular source of instructional materials.

The history of curriculum thought is shot through with diatribes against "textbook teaching."

Anyone who has spent much time teaching children and youth knows that the teacher must, perforce, use whatever is available, the requirements of teacher-pupil interaction leaving scant time for the development of any effective alternatives by the teacher.

This dilemma is at least one of the forces that produced the first great curriculum thrust which made its appearance in the 1930's and is most closely identified with Hollis Caswell.[3] Certainly at that time textbook writers were usually remote from the classroom setting and it was reasonable to assume that teachers in service would be in a far better position to decide what curriculum elements would be most useful and what kind of language or presentation would be most easily assimilated by pupils. Furthermore, reason suggested that the employment of many minds in the development process would ensure a better product.

Thus, we find appearing an approach to curriculum development centered on the employment of faculty committees led and directed by the curriculum specialist. Implicit in this approach was the intention of developing greater involvement by teachers in the decision-making process and consequently an enlargement of professional freedom.

Anyone who has worked with teachers in such professional groups can testify to the great power and creativity and ultimate good sense of such an approach. In the main, the curriculum guidelines and syllabi produced in this manner were of high quality and often came to grips successfully with some very difficult problems. Unfortunately, two major obstacles to the complete success of this approach soon became evident.

While curriculum committees were generally good at making the kinds of decisions essential to choice of content or the ordering of learning experiences, they were considerably less capable of producing under committee aegis viable learning materials. The consequence of this was that the carefully produced and reproduced guides languished in bottom drawers because materials essential to their proper implementation never materialized. Only the large and wealthy districts had the resources essential to the successful production of such materials and even in those,

[3] Hollis L. Caswell and Doak J. Campbell. *Curriculum Development*. New York: American Book Company, 1935.

such activity often received a rather low priority by school boards and administrators.

A further problem had to do with the dissemination and implementation of curricula generated by this approach. Within the curriculum field itself in this period, there was a strong feeling that teacher involvement in the production of materials to be used would guarantee the effectiveness of the teaching application. Actually, the pressures generated in classroom teaching tend to make any individual quite pragmatic as far as materials are concerned. Whatever shows some promise of meeting the educational needs of pupils will generally be pressed into service regardless of authorship.

The problem of dissemination of curriculum materials and their implementation in the classroom is still far from solution, as the focus of a number of federally financed research programs in the 1960's testifies. That this problem is a particularly human one was well known to curriculum workers as early as the 1940's. Alice Miel's statement that "Changing the curriculum means changing people," is still as true as the day it was written.[4] A major root of the difficulty lies in the fact that improved learning attributable to curriculum change is difficult to measure and demonstrate. This evaluation problem has been further complicated by the tendency to use group statistics as the basis of measurement rather than changes in the educational development of individuals.

The second major curriculum thrust emerged in the 1950's with the passage of the National Defense Education Act and the consequent massive marshaling of federal resources behind a variety of national curriculum revision projects.

In this case the working committees were composed of scientists and classroom science teachers with occasional involvement of professional curriculum workers. With the amount of resources available this work did progress rapidly past the identification and structuring of curriculum elements and began to show output in the form of teaching materials. This time the materials were field tested, revised, collated into sets of working materials, and further pilot tested.

It was easily apparent that these new materials would require teaching skills not currently possessed by many teachers in the field. Consequently, an implementation design utilizing summer workshops for science teachers was employed.

Again, unfortunately, effective dissemination appeared to require a marketing agency that was beyond the capability of the committees or at least not possible with the resources available. Ultimately the new

---

[4] Alice Miel. *Changing the Curriculum.* New York: Appleton-Century-Crofts, Inc., 1946.

curriculum resources were assigned to commercial publishers and the residue of this massive experiment now is available in textbook form. A basic goal of updating content in the sciences had been at least partially achieved at a tremendous cost, but the textbook remains at the center of the universe of curriculum materials.

The action that has not yet been linked to the curriculum development process is the establishment of a truly effective instructional support process within the system and possibly within individual schools where one attempts to initiate a new curriculum thrust.

Curriculum as a Controlling Element

One question new teachers often ask is "Do I have to follow the system or state curriculum guide?" This is a question which if one feels impelled to ask it, one had probably better. Clearly one of the intents of such documents is to ensure some measure of uniformity in the teaching process.

Unless the professional climate in one's building is *most* supportive, the freedom of the teacher to follow individual learning thrusts is circumscribed by a structured learning plan.

In a real sense this phenomenon identifies curriculum development as a tool which may be used to control the actions of teachers and to standardize the learning activities within the school. When viewed in this light, the curriculum becomes an ally of those forms of supervision which were designed to operate as a form of inspection.

Any honest attempt to individualize instruction requires a wealth of learning materials, a teacher wise enough to choose among them, and the professional confidence to do so. An educational leader who believes in this approach is also essential. We will never achieve maturity as a profession until teachers do assume full responsibility for the learning of the young people in their charge.

The Curriculum Specialist—Multilateral Dependency

Doyle suggests in his analysis of the development of educational professionalism that control of technical knowledge and process is a fundamental requirement. Because the actual work of the curriculum specialist in schools has not been carefully developed, the entire profession may be in considerable danger. In this respect the entanglement of staff development functions with those of program development has not been helpful; indeed, if one looks at the day by day commitment of the time and energy of curriculum workers in real school systems, one is likely to find increments of effort spread among administrative tasks, personnel tasks, funding activities, supervisory-inspectorial tasks, public relations activities, and a host of other kinds of duties which may be delegated from time to time by a chief administrator.

Frankly, the development of the instructional offerings of the school or system is fundamental and unless responsibility for this function is clearly fixed and discharged in a professional manner the entire operation is in serious jeopardy.

Of course, jobs have been vanishing in this area over the past decade. This is partly due to the diffusion of responsibility described earlier, but also a consequence of increased teacher militancy. As teacher organizations have squeezed out all "management" personnel and placed them in an adversary position, the curriculum workers begin to find basic curriculum decisions made through negotiations and political processes while at the same time as professionals they begin to occupy a no-man's-land somewhere between teaching faculty and administration. When these conditions pertain, such positions begin to be eliminated. Obviously, the independence of the curriculum worker has been severely circumscribed in ways that make critical curriculum decisions totally dependent on consensus of a variety of constituent bodies and agencies. In these circumstances, Parkinson's Law of Delay finds widespread expression.[5]

Self-Concept and the Multicultural Thrust

The twin human needs for self-respect and for affiliation with a group to whom we can give respect are both powerful and sometimes in conflict. Veneration of the past, satisfaction with one's genealogy, pleasure in group achievement, and veneration of group tradition often are pushed aside by the urgency of personal and individual needs. Tensions always exist to some degree between group mores and personal aspirations. Tightly knit groups with sharply defined goals can often successfully canalize individual self-development into group-approved outlets. Religious societies such as the Amish or Brethren are examples of such groups. But larger societies are rarely able to enforce such restrictions on the growth of individual self-concept.

All groups and organizations may properly be concerned with the quality of their public image and an individual member ought to be able to take pride in his or her group affiliation if he or she believes it is deserved. Certainly there is never any reason to be ashamed of an affiliation over which one had no control.

[5] C. Northcote Parkinson. *The Law of Delay*. Boston: Houghton Mifflin Company, 1971.

Waiting for the bell, Chicago, 1941.

One can, however, foresee possibilities of the drive for group identity and group pride constituting some obstacles to the freedom of development of individual members. Too strong an identity can be perceived as a handicap by the individual who may well hear other drumbeats and wish to take a different turn in the path.

A much greater obstacle to the achievement of a truly multicultural society is raised by the very nature of technology. The mass media profoundly affect the development of language and expression on a national base. Mobility of population shatters the neat boundaries of ethnic islands. The disenchanted youth of the 60's who wanted to "drop out" found that no existence was possible that did not depend to some extent on the establishment. The technological society holds rich material rewards for those who master its requirements; and because of mass communication all of our citizens know this regardless of their ethnic origin or identity.

Some years ago I visited the tiny Indian fishing village of LaPush on the seacoast of Washington State. Here was a small reservation where tribal identity was clear and powerful and members lived by fishing and production of traditional craft objects. There by the river-bank I saw a dugout canoe with an ornate carved prow identical to older examples now found in museums. On the stern of this canoe was an Evinrude outboard motor.

Surely the technological thrust of our larger society will modify and redirect our ethnicity in ways we were never able to accomplish through schooling. Given the present and anticipated future size of our population, we could not support this density at any reasonable standard of existence without our technology. Hopefully, we can maintain some of the richness of our multicultural heritage far into the future, but this will not be easy. Increasingly we will be forced to choose between such goals and those directed to the improvement of the quality of life for all citizens.

Fads and Furbelows

Real social change is painfully slow. It proceeds like a glacier whose movement is measured in feet per year. Educational and especially curriculum change is a part and parcel of social change and proceeds at about the same rate.

The minimum period of time to allocate to a basic change in education ought to be in the neighborhood of a decade. For change of this nature to become well established and persist it must not only be placed in operation with adequate support of all types required but it must be kept in operation until the actions of those involved become habitual.

The characteristics of the change itself must become a part of the tradition of the institution and be further reinforced by such ritual and pageantry as may be useful. Once firmly entrenched, the new pattern will become as resistant to change as the one it replaced; hence, we must be dead certain of the value of the innovation before we attempt to install it.

Most of our past effort at educational change has failed because we did not realize the magnitude of the task. Furthermore, a realistic appraisal of the difficulties would have warned us that we knew far too little about the possible consequences of our intended change to warrant a serious attempt to install it.

Clearly, serious proposals for educational change should be data based and be the result of lengthy and serious research and evaluation.

Currently our meager thrusts for modification appear to be more the result of advocacy patterns than of solid research findings. The examples we see in our recent past were largely born out of the enthusiasm of a few individuals who managed to convince others of the validity of their position. With massive support funds available to those who were politically effective and reasonably charismatic, the movement would get under way, at which time "Madison Avenue" techniques would take over.

In a few years when those involved began to realize that the task was harder and more complicated than they had believed, enthusiasm would dwindle, support funds would atrophy, and the brave new venture would disappear like an Indian sand painting at sundown.

In general, we behave toward innovation possibilities as if the history of curriculum development did not exist. Ideas that failed miserably in the past surface again and again, each time with new titles and new terminology. The information we need most is a taxonomy of past innovation coupled with penetrating analyses of the successes and failures that resulted, and as many clues as we can uncover as to why things failed or succeeded.

In general, the professional educational research establishment has developed an array of complex and involved procedures for evaluation without taking the time to identify and specify the problems which need study. One can always find a bundle of irrelevant variables to crank through a computer and the resulting printouts only serve to obscure further the real problems we should be addressing. There have been and continue to be a few real scholars in the educational research field, but far too often work in the educational research area appears to be based on a clear understanding of Woody Allen's maxim, "Take the Money and Run."

Some Benchmarks for 1976

A Bicentennial is a rather short period of time in the sweep of Western civilization, and yet during this period our nation has created an institution for servicing the educational needs of its people that is without parallel in recorded history. That this institution has not fulfilled all the hopes and aspirations that were held for it is not surprising, for schools are created and operated by people who are fallible and prone to error.

It is also clear that schools have been held in such high esteem that the society has delegated a multitude of functions to them usually with little concern for the cost of discharging adequately these pyramiding social responsibilities.

As Harold Benjamin was fond of saying, "The United States has never shot the works on its educational system. Instead it has shot two-bits and complained about the size of its winnings."

The central task for educators in this bicentennial year is to take stock of our achievements and failures, looking to the past for those substantial insights which can serve as benchmarks for future development.

What then can we identify as learnings from our past which can serve as solid foundation for the future?

Size and Leadership

One of the things we have not learned to do very well is to provide high quality service to large numbers of people. As our institutions grow larger we inevitably find ourselves managing rather than leading. As we burgeon in size, problems of control move us toward legalistic and regulatory processes and away from the informal and intimate. Moves toward decentralization of larger systems have thus far not been very helpful, partly because we have not identified which functions need to be decentralized and which are served best by a total institutional approach. A further problem involved in effective decentralization lies in the fact that it is fairly easy to delegate responsibility but difficult to delegate commensurate authority. The delegation of authority requires faith and the understanding that in the best of systems breaches of faith and consequent error will occur. Current concerns with accountability make it less likely that top leadership will risk the delegation of authority. The dangers of such action are so apparent that few will take the risk.

Leaders vary in their capacity to interact effectively with numbers of people. A very few seem able to influence and inspire large numbers. Most of us do our best work with 15 to 30 individuals, the rest we manage but do not lead. Someone has said that "an institution is but the lengthened shadow of the person at the head of it." If we are to improve the system, we must learn much more about the identification and development of leaders and evolve means of placing them in positions where they can breathe new life into the stagnant and decaying institutions that are so grievous to us.

Stability and Change

Stability and change are usually viewed as opposites and mutually antagonistic. The presence of one, we have felt, usually means the absence of the other. True institutional change, however, is more likely to occur in a stable setting than in a chaotic one. While it is true that one can upset the working of a system in the name of change and generate a plethora of modification activities, solid and lasting implementation always calls for persistent and concentrated administrative support.

For successful change to take place, principals, superintendents, and school board members must be convinced of the value of the change and be deeply committed to achieving the desired modifications. They must understand the cost and be willing to pay it. Such commitment can only arise in a leadership group whose members respect each other's capabilities and who have worked together long enough to trust each other. This situation seldom exists in today's schools. With the average tenure of superintendents down to about two years, such continuity of leadership that remains is found in the principalship and in school boards. The situation is further aggravated by teacher militancy and professional negotiations in which teachers are the adversaries of their boards and administrators. Under these conditions no innovation, however brilliant in conception, has much chance of bearing fruit.

No matter how much one sympathizes with teachers' grievances, and they are many, one is forced to the conclusion that the present design for the resolution of these problems results in serious damage to the educational advantages the schools offer.

The Timely and the Timeless

Adults have always resented the brashness of youth. They do not relish their children telling them that they have been doing things wrong, that the world has changed and the adults have been left behind, or that there are significant problems they have left unattended and should be addressing. Indeed, the resentment is usually deeper when the children are right.

Past and current violent eruptions of controversy over instructional materials used in schools appear related in part to this predictable reaction. Schools are often perceived as avenues for social change. Because schools have achieved a reputation for responsiveness to social pressure, we have been prone to address serious problems in the adult society through the introduction of content in the curriculum, often by statute, though the problems actually can only be resolved by the adults in the social order.

The bulwark of segregation is residential restrictiveness. Segments of the adult society and the courts have taken the position that the problem can be solved through manipulation of the composition of school populations in ways which adults are not willing to adopt themselves. There is ample evidence to support the generation of school populations designed for the purpose of maximum learning for pupils. The research of Jencks and Coleman supports this position and a good bit of earlier evidence pointed in the same direction.

The construction of populations to contain a balance of well-motivated pupils with those who do not take easily to formal learning may be sound professionally. This is different, however, from manipulating the composition of populations to solve social problems deeply embedded in the society itself. Well educated children can be expected to change their world as they become adults. This is perhaps the best that we should expect of schools.

The search for truth is the endless task of educated persons. Schools must deal with the truth as they are given to know it and they must inspire those they teach to continue this quest. Teachers and administrators have a legitimate concern with the social nature of the institution they operate and it should reflect the social truths they teach. The nature of the larger society is not the exclusive concern of any agency however much it may appear to need changing.

There is always much to be taught that has served us well in the past and has established its validity in a variety of ways. Such content serves to illuminate the present and to explicate present practices.

No educational system can ignore the present, indeed the past is usually helpful in understanding it. Ugliness and sordidness are as much a part of life as beauty and nobility of spirit. Proper balance in a curriculum must include elements of both our triumphs and our tragedies. Anything less than this is deceit.

Growing Up in a Technological World

We presently support a population of some two hundred and thirty million people in the United States and although the growth rate has slowed, there are likely to be still more people in the years ahead. Small mishaps in the functioning of our technological support system such as the Eastern seaboard power blackout of a few years ago serve to warn us of the fragility of our existence. Withdraw our technology and we die in massive numbers. We no longer generate large food surpluses. Agricultural production as we know it is basically dependent on power from petroleum, fertilizer produced through chemical processes, and insecticide to control crop damage. It is not within our power to run back the clock and return to simpler means of production. Natural or man-made catastrophe could return us to that level, but one cannot foresee other means of population control being employed deliberately for such an end.

Our world is a technological one and we must learn to live with it and in it because it is the only one we are likely to have. Such a world as this places certain requirements on its inhabitants as a price for the rewards it holds.

The more sophisticated technology becomes, the more vulnerable it becomes to sabotage or mismanagement. Power lines are easy to disrupt as the people in Portland, Oregon, learned in the spring of 1975. Transportation networks that deliver food and medical supplies are dependent on fuel allocations. The computer, a crowning achievement of technology, is the most fragile of all. Its memory can be wiped clean with the use of a ten-cent magnet.

As a consequence of the fragility of this marvelous creation that sustains us, we in turn must develop a society disciplined as we have never foreseen. In frontier days, horse thievery was a hanging offense because people's very lives depended on the availability of their mounts. In a similar way our own lives may depend on our understanding of, respect for, and protection of our technology; and for the development of this disciplined style of life we will most likely call again on our educational system.

Responsive Environment

Thus far, schools have been constructed and operated by adults for children. Through reflection, study, and much trial and error, we have established institutions that reflect how adults think children ought to live and learn. For the youth who go to school, the establishment has been a given. Occasionally, young people have been involved in shaping the school environment but always after the configuration has jelled and is resistant to change.

If the schools were viewed as experimental laboratories in which many alternative forms of living and learning could be investigated and tested, we might go about their design and organization quite differently. In physical terms a school could be designed for maximum flexibility and plasticity. Space configuration, traffic flow, seating and lighting, and color treatment of space could be modifiable by students according to needs and principles they identify. Students could also maintain their surroundings as part of their learning and institutional responsibility. Beyond this, the student body could be continuously involved in testing a variety of governmental principles. How should health and safety problems be handled? How will the school society arrange for protection of the weak from the strong? What regulations are essential and how should they be enforced? What responsibility does the school society have with respect to the attendance and learning difficulties of its peers? What assistance should the school society provide for the handicapped?

Conceived in this way, the school could become a dynamic setting for the discovery and rediscovery of those social skills so needed in the adult world. Furthermore, such an approach would teach by example that people *can* change the environment they inhabit and they *can* learn effective techniques for getting the job done.

Dedication

One of the good things about bureaucracies is that once set in motion, they tend to continue. They continue to deliver service at least at some minimal level, even in the absence of leadership, and continue grinding away even when staff morale is low. This is not to be admired but it is probably to be preferred to total collapse and total unavailability of service. In such circumstances, educators concentrate on holding the operation together and goals of institutional preservation become the only operational objectives. At this point we toil as Sisyphus toiled, rolling our boulder uphill.

In this bicentennial year we might be advised to sit on our boulder a while and consider what we really should be doing. This is easy to say and hard to do, particularly in view of the findings by Coleman and others that in the aggregate, teaching does not have the profound consequences we had believed.

In particular cases, however, we do understand the potency of teaching. We understand it in terms of the differences it has made in our own lives and we see daily in our schools the transformation of lives that is the essence of our craft.

We know in our hearts that people have always made a difference to people, and we have seen over and over again the consequences for the lives of others of the actions of dedicated people. The great schools in our past, and there have been many of these, were great because of the dedication of the people who worked in them.

If we in these days have lost some of our potency, it is because we have lost sight of our real reason for being. The great central purpose of the schools is the transfiguration of the individual. Society has a responsibility to evaluate us in terms of our success and needs to look closely at our mortality rate. Just as some of the physicians' patients die and as some individuals' lives end in tragedy, so educators will never be successful with all those they undertake to educate. Yet we must do our best for all and grieve for our losses.

Whatever the design of our institutions in the future, whatever shape curricula may take, however we may decide to resolve professional questions, these solutions must contribute to a reawakening of our dedication to young people and must serve to focus our attention on the individual's needs, potential, and future.

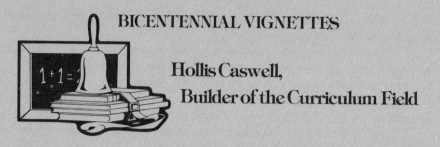

Hollis Caswell, Builder of the Curriculum Field

Influenced by George D. Strayer, his major professor, Hollis L. Caswell became involved in the wave of school surveys during the 1930's. These studies viewed a wide scope of school system problems ranging from school plant ventilation to the generalized functions of education to pupil achievement. Among the most important of Caswell's works was the Virginia State Curriculum Program which was a culmination of his experience in curriculum revision in Alabama, Florida, and elsewhere. Caswell's work in Virginia became a prototype for later work in other state studies. A landmark work that followed was the volume, *Curriculum Development* (1935), co-authored by his Peabody colleague, Doak S. Campbell. Because of the book's comprehensive treatment, it lent significant aid to the formation of the professional curriculum field. Caswell later employed principles developed in the state studies to curriculum improvement programs in public school systems.

Placing Caswell in any of the major schools of educational theorists is difficult at best. With a career spanning more than half a century of diverse experiences, including the presidency of Teachers College, Columbia University, Caswell denies that he ever "became really active in the Childs-Counts group, committed to using education as a means of reforming society—nor was I active in the Progressive Education group." Caswell recalls that during the 1930's the progressives thought him to be "too traditional," and that some thirty years later, Ralph Tyler found him to be "too progressive."

Caswell's alliance with the John Dewey Society was perhaps the answer to his concern that "the Progressive Education group at that time was going off on an extreme to organize education just for the immediate experiences of children." He feels that the Society was "more 'with it,' seeing the school as an agency with a program for the improvement of education." His dissatisfaction with extremes of the curriculum pendulum stemmed from the fact that "either the curriculum was child-centered exclusively, or subject-centered and ignorant of society."

Caswell notes further that the 1960's saw a swing to the "old subject-centered ideas, and now (1975) there's a demand for fundamentals again. We're getting away from looking at experience as the thing, jumping back to Bobbitt and Charters, and ignoring the thirties' and forties' state studies—overlooking their significance." Caswell further relates that "the Eight-Year Study was obviously far less influential than it was cracked up to be."

Stating those tenets of curriculum planning and development that are distinctly associated with his own "social functions approach," Caswell indicates that it is necessary to build a curriculum that is related to social problems and needs, and concerned with the immediate as well as potential interests of the child within a meaningful, systematic order of knowledge. Caswell's stance on curriculum making as an integrated

balance among these ideas is doubly interesting—not only for its renewed focus on curriculum responsibility for social education and action, but also for its application as a curriculum plan in firm alliance with Dewey's notions on education.

Caswell's first doctoral student at Teachers College, Dr. William M. Alexander, states that Caswell "saw firsthand the tremendous gap between the academic curriculum of the schools and the actual social and economic problems of the country . . . and he was adamant in the belief that social understanding (originating from a socially-oriented curriculum) would result in social action. . . . He had no peer. . . ."

—*Terry Hobbs Heller*

Major sources for the material in this essay are a telephone interview with Dr. Caswell on March 24, 1975, and a letter to the author from Dr. Alexander dated December 1, 1974. The author acknowledges these with grateful appreciation.

Segregation and the Supreme Court, 1896-1954

> . . . in the field of public education, the doctrine of "separate but equal" has no place. Separate educational facilities are inherently unequal.
> —*Brown et al.* v. *Board of Education of Topeka et al.,* 347 U.S. 483 (1954)

The *Brown* v. *Board of Education* decision sounded the death knell for constitutional segregation of the races in the nation's schools. In order to understand the *Brown*

decision, previous cases dealing with racial segregation must be recalled.

By its decision in *Brown* v. *Board of Education*, the Supreme

Court overturned its ruling in *Plessy* v. *Ferguson*, 163 *U.S.* 537 (1896) which had established the constitutional basis for segregation in this country. The *Plessy* case dealt not with educational facilities, but with a Louisiana law mandating "equal but separate accommodations for the white and colored races" on railroads. The Court ruled that such a law was a necessary exercise of the state's police power in maintaining peace and order. It rejected the argument that forced segregation of blacks and whites "stamps the colored race with a badge of inferiority."

In the decades immediately after the *Plessy* v. *Ferguson* decision, the Court tended to enforce the "separate" provision of the decision while ignoring its requirement for "equality." An example is found in *Cumming* v. *County Board of Education*, 175 *U.S.* 528 (1899) in which the Court found no violation of equal protection of the law as a result of Richmond County's operation of a high school for whites while refusing to provide the same opportunity for blacks. The Court's stand on this matter gradually shifted and, by 1938, it insisted on a strict interpretation of "separate but equal" in *Missouri ex rel. Gaines* v. *Canada*, 305 *U.S.* 337. Lloyd Gaines, a Negro, was refused admission to the University of Missouri Law School after graduation from Lincoln University, the state's black university. Under existing Missouri law, the state offered to pay Gaines' tuition to the state university in any one of four adjoining states. The Supreme Court ruled that this was a clearcut violation of the "separate but equal" doctrine and ordered Gaines admitted to the University of Missouri.

The Supreme Court made an important change in its position on the concept of "separate but equal" in *Sweatt* v. *Painter*, 339 *U.S.* 629 (1950). This case has added significance because it hinted at what the Court would do four years later in *Brown* v. *Board of Education*. Sweatt applied for admission to the University of Texas Law School in 1946 and was rejected because he was black. He took the matter to court claiming the state was violating his right to equal protection under the law. At that time, Texas did not have a Negro law school although such a school was established before the case was finally settled in 1950. The Supreme Court, in reversing lower court decisions, ruled that the new Negro law school was clearly unequal to the University of Texas law school in terms of measurable attributes such as the size and quality of the faculty, variety of courses, library facilities, and scholarship funds. More significantly, the Court ruled that the white law school

... possesses to a far greater degree those qualities which are incapable of objective measurement but which make for greatness in a law school. ... The [black] law school ... excludes from its student body members of racial groups which number 85% of the population of the State and include most of the lawyers, judges and other officials with whom petitioner will inevitably be dealing when he becomes a member of the Texas bar. With such a substantial and significant segment excluded, we cannot conclude that the education offered petitioner is substantially equal to that which he would receive if admitted to the University of Texas Law School.

The stage was thus set for the decision handed down in *Brown* v. *Board of Education*, 347 U.S. 483 (1954). An important difference in this and the *Sweatt* case is that the Court found black and white schools to be approximately equal with respect to facilities, course offerings, and qualifications and salaries of teachers. The Court based its decision on segregation's effect on black youngsters:

To separate them from others of

similar age and qualifications solely because of their race generates a feeling of inferiority as to their status in the community that may affect their hearts and minds in a way unlikely ever to be undone. ... We conclude that in the field of public education the doctrine of "separate but equal" has no place. Separate educational facilities are inherently unequal.

After 22 years of eliminating segregated schools with "all deliberate speed," many of the nation's schools are still composed primarily of a single race. The reasons are varied but include resistance to integration on the part of some school officials and parents, "white flight," and lack of genuine open housing. Until this nation can eliminate "institutional racism" and fully integrate its schools, it probably can expect to continue to alienate many minority students and shackle them with the failure syndrome which burdened their parents and grandparents.

—*Richard L. Simms*

Sputnik Launches NDEA

Sputnik, the first artificial satellite to orbit earth, was launched by the Soviet Union on October 4, 1957. This event seemed to confirm the fears of the American public that the free world was losing the science and technology race to the communists. The nation's defense was seen at stake. The rapid advances of Russian tech-

nology seemed to have surpassed that of the United States and threatened to gain more ground in the future. What had happened to bring about this alarming condition? More important, who was to blame and how could the situation be corrected?

After initial explanations provided little comfort, President

Eisenhower directed the nation's attention to the deficiencies in the American educational system. The "progressive education" theories of John Dewey, as well as teachers and schools in general, came under vicious attack, not only by well informed individuals, but also by those who had previously given little thought to educational theory. American education was deemed too easy, especially in those areas that would develop scientists to direct the nation's technological development.

Numerous proposals were made to upgrade the educational system. The curriculum in science and mathematics had to be revised. Exceptionally talented children had to be identified and encouraged to continue their education. More emphasis was put on subject matter in teacher education. An increase in both the quantity and quality of scientific equipment in the schools was needed for better instruction and increased student interest. Finally, improvement of faculties and facilities in colleges and universities was needed. Since these changes were necessary for the nation's security, federally funded programs to achieve these goals were deemed both proper and necessary.

The American furore raised in response to Sputnik led directly to the passage of the National Defense Education Act (NDEA) of 1958. Over $1 billion in federal aid was authorized by a coalition of Democrats and Republicans to carry through the various programs of the NDEA. Although the stated goal of the act was to provide every young person an opportunity to develop his or her gifts to the fullest, the obvious impact was to be in the area of improved in-

High school algebra class, Washington, D.C., 1943.

truction and the encouragement of high ability students to enter the fields of science and technology and foreign languages. Clearly, NDEA was an act legitimizing schooling—at least in science, mathematics, and foreign languages—as a part of the national defense.

—*Pat Simpson*

On the Meaning of Education: LBJ[1]

MR. MCKAY: Getting down to more current matters, what do you consider to be the major problems in public education that you would like to see solved and how?

THE PRESIDENT: The provision—the existence of an economy that would make it possible for every child to financially stay in school as long as he needs to—to take all the education that he was capable of taking and with that—the economic ability of the child to stay in school and not have to drop out and quit to go to work—with that provisions of adequate facilities in the way of (a) teachers and (b) books and reference material and libraries and buildings to permit that to happen. If every child born could acquire all the education that their intelligence quotient permitted them to take, and to financially stay in school—God only knows what our gross national product would be—and the

strength that we would add to our nation, militarily, diplomatically, economically is too large even to imagine. And there is no investment that we could make that would return such high dividends. If we could just assume when a child is born that that child was going to be trained until it reached the point that it could no longer profit from that training and that if the economic situation in the individual family did not exist, that the government would provide the scholarship for the loan or grant whatever you want. To see that this was brought about, you would eliminate your slums, and largely your crime and certainly your poverty programs and things of that nature. Because all of these things that we frown upon and that give us problems in this country, ultimately are traceable to the dropout or the lack of education or to environment or to health problems or something else which could be cured by giving to every person the right to acquire all the education that he or she could take.

—*Charla McCoy*

[1] From an unpublished interview with President Lyndon B. Johnson, conducted by Mr. Robert E. McKay, May 21, 1965, in the President's Oval Office. Presidential papers. Lyndon Baines Johnson Library, Austin, Texas.

6

Sources for Curriculum History

Walter Doyle and Gerald A. Ponder

History's queerly strong perfumes
rise from the crook of this day's elbow . . .

What, in fact, happened in these woods
on some obliterated afternoon?

—*Adrienne Rich,* "Readings of History" *

THE CURRICULUM FIELD has been a practical one, concerned more with the technical problems of selecting content and deriving objectives than with analysis and introspection. Consequently the field has produced few histories, since history is not a "practical" art, really. It rather attempts to recount, to explain, to interpret. The contributions of histories lie more in the realm of understanding, of adding perspective, than in the procedural. Yet recently curriculum specialists have begun to exhibit a substantial degree of self-consciousness about the past, to mediate the pervasive ahistoricism that Herbert Kliebard and others have suggested as a characteristic of the curriculum field. And histories of the curriculum field have begun to appear.

Left: Japanese-American school children join their classmates in pledge of allegiance. The next day, they and their families were removed to detention camps for the remainder of the war. San Francisco, California, April 1942.

---

* Adrienne Rich. *Snapshots of a Daughter-in-Law.* New York: W. W. Norton & Company, Inc., 1967. Copyright © 1956, 1957, 1958, 1959, 1960, 1961, 1962, 1963, 1967, Adrienne Rich Conrad. Reprinted with permission.

This volume of interpretive essays contributes to that growing body of literature by explicating a number of tensions and themes which seem to account for many of the events and processes in the history of the curriculum field. Given the interpretive intent, however, it is hardly possible for these chapters to reflect the full range of scholarly activity related to or emerging from recent curriculum study. The following list of sources for curriculum history is offered, therefore, as both a supplement to the preceding essays and as a selective summation of current inquiry and promising directions. Hopefully this collection will assist scholars and practitioners to delve more deeply and fruitfully into curriculum issues of the past and present.

Early attempts to chronicle events in the curriculum field suffered, as did most educational history, from a narrow professionalism and isolationism. Many of these histories appeared as introductory sections in curriculum or supervision textbooks, telling their stories of progress and success, and harnessing history to show the causes for that success and the obstacles working against contemporary proposals. Further, curricular issues were treated in near isolation from broader directions and movements in schooling and American life. As the essays in this Yearbook suggest, the day for that kind of self-serving parochialism has passed. Curriculum history, if it is to provide understanding and inform decision making, must be written in the context of a more mature historical scholarship.

American educational history has in recent years witnessed a virtual renaissance that has increased both the quantity and the quality of investigation in that area. This renewed interest has seriously challenged orthodoxy in educational history. Modern historical scholarship has begun to incorporate a broader focus in selecting relevant educational issues as well as a greater reliance on interpretative frameworks to integrate chronological data. David Tyack's work exemplifies especially well this new line of inquiry in educational history. The works of Katz, Wiebe, and Hays also have proven particularly useful in understanding and interpreting events and issues related to the curriculum field. In addition, the institutional histories by Lazerson and by Kaestle have made important contributions to historical perspectives of curriculum and schooling.

But to suggest that recent histories have contributed needed perspective is not to say that the scholarship is fully mature or that curriculum history is now definitive. In her recent address at the American Educational Research Association, Geraldine Clifford argued convincingly for the need to go still further, to "people" educational history rather than simply to focus either on ideas or institutional arrangements.

Clifford's focus on the people who lived in educational institutions is especially relevant to histories of teachers and teaching, an area in which Finkelstein and others are beginning to establish foundations. Histories of pedagogical practice, some of which are cited in the following bibliography, can have important implications for curriculum history.

Historical studies in the curriculum field have begun to appear with increased frequency. In the past several years one or more sessions on curriculum history have been scheduled at the annual meetings of the American Educational Research Association. The last two annual conferences of the Association for Supervision and Curriculum Development have included exceptionally popular sessions on "Looking Into the Future From Out of the Past." And a similar interest in historical dimensions has been reflected in recent issues of *Curriculum Theory Network*, published by the Ontario Institute for Studies in Education. Scholars such as Vallance, Kliebard, and Walker have made important contributions to identifying and interpreting historical issues in the curriculum field. Finally, recent textbooks by Gwynn and Chase and by Tanner and Tanner devoted substantial portions to historical matters. These and other activities suggest that the future holds the promise of achieving the degree of historical awareness the curriculum field so badly needs. We hope that this list of sources encourages that awareness.

Sources

Arthur N. Applebee. *Tradition and Reform in the Teaching of English: A History.* Urbana, Illinois: National Council of Teachers of English, 1974. ED 097 703.

Bernard Bailyn. *Education in the Forming of American Society.* Chapel Hill: University of North Carolina Press, 1960.

Mark Beach. "A History of Education." *Review of Educational Research* 39: 560-76; 1969.

Arno A. Bellack. "History of Curriculum Thought and Practice." *Review of Educational Research* 39: 283-92; June 1969.

Michael V. Belok. *Forming the American Minds: Early School-books and Their Compilers (1783-1837).* Agra, India: Satish Book Enterprise, 1973.

Charles E. Bidwell. "The Moral Significance of the Common School." *History of Education Quarterly* 6: 50-91; Fall 1966.

Frederick M. Binder. *The Age of the Common School, 1830-1865.* New York: John Wiley, 1974.

C. A. Bowers. *The Progressive Educator and the Depression.* New York: Random House, 1969.

Henry A. Bullock. *A History of Negro Education in the South: From 1619 to the Present.* Cambridge, Massachusetts: Harvard University Press, 1967.

Joan N. Burstyn and Ruth R. Corrigan. "Images of Women in Textbooks, 1880-1920." *Teachers College Record* 76: 431-40; February 1975.

John Calam. "A Letter from Quesnel: The Teacher in History, and Other Fables." *History of Education Quarterly* 15: 131-45; Summer 1975.

Daniel H. Calhoun. *Professional Lives in America: Structure and Aspiration, 1750-1850.* Cambridge, Massachusetts: Harvard University Press, 1965.

Raymond E. Callahan. *Education and the Cult of Efficiency.* Chicago: University of Chicago Press, 1962.

Robert A. Carlson. *The Quest for Conformity: Americanization through Education.* New York: John Wiley and Sons, 1975.

Martin Carnoy. *Education as Cultural Imperialism.* New York: David McKay, 1974.

Charles H. Carpenter. *History of American Schoolbooks.* Philadelphia: University of Pennsylvania Press, 1963.

Hollis L. Caswell. "Emergence of the Curriculum as a Field of Professional Work and Study." In: H. F. Robinson, editor. *Precedents and Promises in the Curriculum Field.* New York: Teachers College Press, 1966. pp. 1-11.

Geraldine Jonçich Clifford. *The Shape of American Education.* Englewood Cliffs, New Jersey: Prentice-Hall, 1975.

Geraldine Jonçich Clifford. "Saints, Sinners, and People: A Position Paper on the Historiography of American Education." *History of Education Quarterly* 15: 257-72; Fall 1975.

Walter Cocking. *The Regional Introduction of Educational Practices in Urban Schools of the United States.* Institute of Administrative Research, Study No. 6. New York: Bureau of Publications, Teachers College, Columbia University, 1951.

David K. Cohen. "Immigrants and the Schools." *Review of Educational Research* 40: 13-27; February 1970.

Ronald D. Cohen. "The Gary Schools and Progressive Education in the 1920's." Paper presented at the Annual Meeting of the American Educational Research Association, Washington, D. C., 1975.

Sheldon S. Cohen. *A History of Colonial Education: 1607-1776.* New York: John Wiley, 1974.

Sol Cohen. "The Industrial Education Movement, 1906-1917." *American Quarterly* 20: 95-110; Spring 1968.

Jill Conway. "Perspectives on the History of Women's Education in the United States." *History of Education Quarterly* 14: 1-12; Spring 1974.

Lawrence A. Cremin. *The Transformation of the Schools: Progressivism in American Education 1876-1957.* New York: Knopf, 1961.

Lawrence A. Cremin. *The Wonderful World of Ellwood Patterson Cubberley: An Essay on the Historiography of American Education.* New York: Teachers College Press, 1965.

Lawrence A. Cremin. *American Education: The Colonial Experience, 1607-1783.* New York: Harper and Row, 1970.

Lawrence A. Cremin. "Curriculum-making in the United States." *Teachers College Record* 73: 207-20; 1971.

Lawrence A. Cremin. "The Family as Educator: Some Comments on the Recent Historiography." *Teachers College Record* 76: 250-65; December 1974.

Michael C. Diamonti. "Charles W. Eliot and the Theory of Mental Discipline." Paper presented at the American Educational Research Association Annual Meeting, Washington, D.C., 1975.

Walter H. Drost. *David Snedden and Education for Social Efficiency.* Madison: University of Wisconsin Press, 1967.

Daniel L. Duke. *The Re-Transformation of the Schools.* Chicago: Nelson-Hall, 1975.

Harold B. Dunkel. *Herbart and Herbartianism.* Chicago: University of Chicago Press, 1970.

Elliot Eisner. "Franklin Bobbitt and the 'Science' of Curriculum Making." *School Review* 75: 29-47; Spring 1967.

Elliot Eisner and Elizabeth Vallance. *Conflicting Conceptions of Curriculum.* Berkeley, California: McCutchan, 1974.

Ruth M. Elson. *Guardians of Tradition: American Schoolbooks of the Nineteenth Century.* Lincoln: University of Nebraska Press, 1964.

Barbara Finkelstein. "Schooling and Schoolteachers: A Selected Bibliography of Autobiographies in the Nineteenth Century." *History of Education Quarterly* 14: 293-300; Summer 1974.

Barbara J. Finkelstein. "The Moral Dimensions of Pedagogy: Teacher Behavior in Popular Primary Schools in Nineteenth-Century America." *American Studies* 15: 79-89; Fall 1974.

Barbara J. Finkelstein. "Choose Your Bias Carefully: Textbooks in the History of American Education." *Educational Studies* 5: 210-15; Winter 1974-75.

Barry M. Franklin. "American Curriculum Theory and the Problem of Social Control, 1918-1938." Paper presented at the Annual Meeting of the American Educational Research Association, Chicago, 1974.

Colin Greer. *The Great School Legend: A Revisionist Interpretation of American Public Education.* New York: Viking Press, 1972.

Ronald K. Goodenow. "Progressive Education in the South: The Depression Years." Paper presented at a Conference of the History of Education Society, 1974.

Ronald K. Goodenow. "The Progressive Educator and Racial Tolerance: Intercultural Education, 1930-1941." Paper presented at the Annual Meeting of the American Educational Research Association, Washington, D. C., 1975.

Patricia A. Graham. *Community and Class in American Education, 1865-1918.* New York: John Wiley, 1974.

Patricia A. Graham. "So Much To Do: Guides for Historical Research on Women in Higher Education." *Teachers College Record* 76: 421-29; February 1975.

Edgar Gumbert and Joel Spring. *The Superschool and the Superstate: American Education in the Twentieth Century, 1918-1970.* New York: John Wiley, 1974.

J. Minor Gwynn and John B. Chase, Jr. *Curriculum Principles and Social Trends,* 4th edition. New York: Macmillan, 1969.

Louis R. Harlan. *Separate and Unequal: Public School Campaigns and Racism in the Southern Seaboard States 1901-1915.* Chapel Hill: University of North Carolina Press, 1958.

Samuel P. Hays. "The New Organizational Society." In: Jerry Israel, editor. *Building the Organizational Society: Essays on Associational Activities in Modern America.* New York: The Free Press, 1972. pp. 1-15.

Jurgen Herbst. *The History of American Education.* Northbrook, Illinois: AHM Publishing, 1973.

Jerry Israel, editor. *Building the Organizational Society: Essays on Associational Activities in Modern America.* New York: The Free Press, 1972.

Erwin V. Johanningmeier. "Assessing the Impact of Research on Schooling: A Problem in History of Education, Its Difficulties and Approaches." Paper presented at the Annual Meeting of the American Educational Research Association, Washington, D.C., 1975.

Clifton Johnson. *Old-Time Schools and School-Books.* New York: Macmillan, 1904. Reprinted Gloucester, Massachusetts: Peter Smith, 1963.

Phillip S. Jones, editor. *A History of Mathematics Education in the United States and Canada.* Washington, D.C.: National Council of Teachers of Mathematics, 1970.

Carl F. Kaestle. *The Evolution of an Urban School System: New York City, 1750-1850.* Cambridge, Massachusetts: Harvard University Press, 1973.

Clarence Karier, Paul Violas, and Joel Spring. *Roots of Crisis: American Education in the Twentieth Century.* Chicago: Rand McNally, 1973.

Michael B. Katz. *The Irony of Early School Reform: Educational Innovation in Mid-Nineteenth Century Massachusetts.* Boston: Beacon Press, 1968.

Michael B. Katz. *Class, Bureaucracy, and Schools: The Illusion of Educational Change in America.* New York: Praeger Publishers, 1971.

Herbert M. Kliebard. "The Curriculum Field in Retrospect." In: Paul W. Witt, editor. *Technology and the Curriculum.* New York: Teachers College Press, 1968. pp. 69-84.

Herbert M. Kliebard, editor. *Religion and Education in America: A Documentary History.* Scranton: International Textbook, 1969.

Herbert M. Kliebard. "Historical Scholarship: Persistent Curriculum Issues in Historical Perspective." In: Edmund C. Short, editor. *A Search for Valid Content for Curriculum Courses.* Toledo: University of Toledo, 1970. pp. 31-41.

Herbert M. Kliebard. "The Tyler Rationale." *School Review* 78: 259-72; February 1970.

Herbert M. Kliebard. "Bureaucracy and Curriculum Theory." In: Vernon F. Haubrich, editor. *Freedom, Bureaucracy, and Schooling.* 1971 Yearbook.

Washington, D.C.: Association for Supervision and Curriculum Development, 1971. pp. 74-93.

Herbert M. Kliebard. "The Rise of Scientific Curriculum Making and Its Aftermath." *Curriculum Theory Network* 5: 27-38; 1975.

Malcolm S. Knowles. *The Adult Education Movement in the United States.* New York: Holt, Rinehart and Winston, 1962.

Edward A. Krug. *The Shaping of the American High School.* New York: Harper and Row, 1964.

Edward A. Krug. *The Shaping of the American High School, 1920-1941,* Vol. II. Madison: University of Wisconsin Press, 1972.

Marvin Lazerson. *Origins of the Urban School: Public Education in Massachusetts, 1870-1915.* Cambridge, Massachusetts: Harvard University Press, 1971.

Marvin Lazerson. "Revisionism and American Educational History." *Harvard Educational Review* 43: 269-83; May 1973.

David Madsen. *Early National Education, 1776-1830.* New York: John Wiley, 1974.

Robert M. McClure, editor. *The Curriculum: Retrospect and Prospect.* Seventieth Yearbook of the National Society for the Study of Education. Chicago: University of Chicago Press, 1971.

Raymond A. Mohl. "Alice Barrows and the Platoon School, 1920-1940." Paper presented at the Annual Meeting of the American Educational Research Association, Washington, D.C., 1975.

Robert A. Morgart and George Mihalik. "The Treatment of the Working Class in American Educational Historiography." Paper presented at the Annual Meeting of the American Educational Research Association, Washington, D.C., 1975.

Gregory J. Mullen. "History and Analysis of Curriculum Thought, 1940-1974." Paper presented at the Annual Meeting of the American Educational Research Association, Washington, D.C., 1975.

National Society for the Study of Education. *The Foundations and Technique of Curriculum-Construction.* Twenty-Sixth Yearbook, Parts I and II. Bloomington, Illinois: Public School Publishing, 1926.

John A. Neitz. *Old Textbooks.* Pittsburgh: University of Pittsburgh Press, 1961.

John A. Neitz. *The Evolution of American Secondary School Textbooks.* Rutland, Vermont: C. E. Tuttle, 1966.

Michael R. Olneck and Marvin Lazerson. "The School Achievement of Immigrant Children: 1900-1930." *History of Education Quarterly* 14: 453-82; Winter 1974.

Gary L. Peltier. "Teacher Participation in Curriculum Revision: An Historical Case Study." *History of Education Quarterly* 7: 209-19; Summer 1967.

Henry J. Perkinson. *The Imperfect Panacea.* New York: Random House, 1968.

Gerald A. Ponder. "The Curriculum: Field Without a Past?" *Educational Leadership* 31: 461-64; February 1974.

Robert C. Pooley. *The Teaching of English Usage.* Urbana, Illinois: National Council of Teachers of English, 1974.

Frederick M. Raubinger, Harold G. Rowe, Donald L. Piper, and Charles K. West, editors. *The Development of Secondary Education.* New York: Macmillan, 1969.

Diane Ravitch. *The Great School Wars: New York City, 1805-1973.* New York: Basic Books, 1974.

Mary Louise Seguel. *The Curriculum Field: Its Formative Years.* New York: Teachers College Press, 1966.

Theodore Sizer. *Secondary Schools at the Turn of the Century.* New Haven: Yale University Press, 1964.

Douglas Sloan. "Historiography and the History of Education." In: Fred N. Kerlinger, editor. *Review of Research in Education,* Vol. I. Itasca, Illinois: F. E. Peacock, 1973. pp. 239-69.

Timothy L. Smith. "Immigrant Social Aspirations and American Education, 1880-1930." *American Quarterly* 21: 523-43; Fall 1969.

Timothy L. Smith. "Protestant Schooling and American Nationality, 1800-1850." *The Journal of American History* 53: 679-95; March 1967.

Joel H. Spring. *Education and the Rise of the Corporate State.* Boston: Beacon Press, 1972.

Ron Szoke. "Science vs. Philosophy in Education: The Kelley-Kilpatrick Debate of 1929-31 as a Moment in the Development of Educational Analysis." Paper presented at the Annual Meeting of the American Educational Research Association, Washington, D.C., 1975.

Daniel Tanner and Laurel Tanner. *Curriculum Development: Theory into Practice.* New York: Macmillan, 1975.

David B. Tyack, editor. *Turning Points in American Educational History.* Waltham, Massachusetts: Blaisdell, 1967.

David B. Tyack. "New Perspectives on the History of American Education." In: Herbert J. Bass, editor. *The State of American History.* Chicago: Quadrangle Books, 1970. pp. 22-42.

David B. Tyack. *The One Best System: A History of American Urban Education.* Cambridge: Harvard University Press, 1974.

David B. Tyack. "Compulsory School Attendance and Progressive Reform in the Nineteenth and Twentieth Centuries." Paper presented at the Annual Meeting of the American Educational Research Association, Washington, D.C., 1975.

Elizabeth Vallance. "Hiding the Hidden Curriculum: An Interpretation of the Language of Justification in Nineteenth-Century Educational Reform." *Curriculum Theory Network* 4: 5-21; 1973/74.

Gordon F. Vars. "Curriculum in Secondary Schools and Colleges." In: James R. Squire, editor. *A New Look at Progressive Education.* 1972 Yearbook. Washington, D.C.: Association for Supervision and Curriculum Development, 1972. pp. 233-55.

Decker F. Walker. "The Curriculum Field in Formation: A Review of the Twenty-Sixth Yearbook of the National Society for the Study of Education." *Curriculum Theory Network* 4: 263-80; 1975.

Decker F. Walker. "Straining To Lift Ourselves: A Critique of the Foundations of the Curriculum Field." *Curriculum Theory Network* 5: 3-25; 1975.

Helen L. Wardeberg. "Elementary School Curriculum and Progressive Education." In: James R. Squire, editor. *A New Look at Progressive Education.* 1972 Yearbook. Washington, D.C.: Association for Supervision and Curriculum Development, 1972. pp. 206-32.

Ira Marc Weingarten. "Conceptualizing the Reconceptualists." Paper presented at the American Educational Research Association Meeting, Washington, D.C., 1975.

Rush Welter. *Popular Education and Democratic Thought in America.* New York: Columbia University Press, 1962.

Robert H. Wiebe. *The Search for Order, 1877-1920.* New York: Hill and Wang, 1967.

Robert H. Wiebe. "The Social Functions of Public Education." *American Quarterly* 21: 147-64; Summer 1969.

Epilogue: Invitation to Curriculum History

O. L. Davis, Jr.

THIS YEARBOOK CONCLUDES with an invitation. As a part of bicentennial celebration, the invitation is to participate in making possible and making curriculum history.

Every curriculum worker in every school may participate meaningfully. The field needs to collect the abundant sources available for study. With the present interest in curriculum history, many workers seem poised to initiate study.

What kinds of sources are needed? Everything. A few examples.

We need the artifacts of curriculum. The books used by pupils and teachers, record books, plan books, even diaries and letters. The minutes and reports of curriculum committees and study groups at every level of schooling. And the accounts of meetings, the suggestions for change and adoption and institution, and the commentary about curriculum in newspapers, journals, school reports, pupils' notebooks, copy books, diaries. Everything.

We need the photographs of curriculum making and curriculum confronted. Surely, caches of photographs may be uncovered in individual sites and schools. Drawings, cartoons, skits, and programs of pageants, concerts, and contests. Everything.

We need the personal accounts of the actors in curriculum. We need the tales of progress and the anecdotes of frustration. Planning a course, conducting a school evaluation, writing a text or manual, setting

Left: Going home from school, Minnesota, 1939.

objectives. We need the accounts, in writing or recorded, of and by teachers, consultants, experts, everyone who has participated.

And we know we will not have all we wish for. But we can begin to amass some sources and everyone may help.

Repository for such materials should not be difficult to find and certainly, no immediate cause for reluctance to collect is apparent. State and local museums, libraries, and collections and, increasingly, university special collections are open to and welcome such materials as expansion of present holdings or the initiation of new collections. Likely, new and quite sharply focused collections and acquisition policy will follow the increased interest in curriculum history. The invitation, thus, is not only to collect but also to provide access.

Studies in curriculum history are needed in every concern and dimension of the field. None is exempt. To list some suggestions as illustrative is personal and gives in no way an adequate impression of need. Clearly, examples do not serve as inventory, however otherwise useful. So, some examples.

We need accounts of teachers, pupils, and principals in the commonplace and the exceptional. Of early Black Freedom Schools, both North and South. Of the extent of religious content in schools public and private. Of a variety of kinds of hidden curriculum. Of teachers and supervisors, of parents and pupils involved in the Eight-Year Study. Of curriculum development activities in the community schools of Hopeville, Alabama, and Flint, Michigan, and communities throughout the nation that tried to use these models.

We need studies of adoption-adaptation patterns. Of the McGuffey readers, Morse geographies, and other texts. And BSCS, SMSG, ESCP known at local district levels.

We need to know the curriculum history of individual schools and systems and in specific eras. Of vocational education at schools like Hume Fogg Tech in Nashville, Tennessee, and Timken Vocational in Canton, Ohio. Of the development of music instruction in Waco, Texas, from one itinerant teacher who led singing in school assemblies to a comprehensive program of vocal and instrumental music. Of the development of middle schools in Solon, Ohio, and junior high schools in Indianapolis, Indiana. Of foreign language instruction in Cincinnati, St. Louis, and New Braunfels during American peace and war. Of curriculum in black schools of rural south Georgia; Chicano schools in Zapata, Texas; Indian schools in Casa Grande, Arizona; Japanese schools in World War II resettlement camps; and more and more.

We need to know of the experiences of individuals and groups involved in curriculum development and acts. Of teachers released for curriculum writing in Denver. Of those who worked in school system and college experimental schools. Of members of curriculum councils in Spokane and Hot Springs. Of individual curriculum leaders whose books, speeches, group work, and conversations touched the lives of so many of us and influenced so powerfully our field. Of curriculum leaders who never wrote an article, spoke to a regional conference, or were officers of a professional association but whose work was steady and constructive for children and youth. Of textbook authors and editors and salesmen whose work brought us the materials basic or routine to daily classroom life.

We need small-scale studies and comprehensive investigations. We need studies of ideas and studies of people. As curriculum history is produced, the promise of increased understanding is enhanced.

And each of us can participate . . . in some way . . . to some extent.

Thanks.

Welcome.

Notes About the Authors

AMBROSE CLEGG is a Professor and Chairman of the Department of Elementary Education at Kent State University. Dr. Clegg has had extensive classroom teaching experience in the public schools of New York City, in Great Neck, New York, and at the college level in North Carolina, Massachusetts, and in Washington. He has been associated with the Tri-University Project (now TTT) at the University of Washington, where he directed an experimental program in teacher education, and is a member of the Social Science Education Consortium in Boulder, Colorado. He has been active in ASCD, the National Council for the Social Studies, and the American Educational Research Association. A number of his articles have appeared in educational journals, and he has co-authored a book, *Teaching Strategies in the Social Studies* (Addison-Wesley), with James A. Banks.

O. L. DAVIS, JR., Chairperson of the 1976 Yearbook Committee, is Professor of Curriculum and Instruction, The University of Texas at Austin. He has taught courses in several aspects of curriculum, analysis of textbooks and printed materials, teaching of the social studies, and research. He has contributed to numerous professional periodicals, and has been Editor-at-Large of the *American Educational Research Journal*. He is the author of several textbooks in the social studies. Active in many educational organizations, Dr. Davis has been on the ASCD Board

CLEGG   DAVIS   DOYLE

of Directors, the Executive Council, and was Associate Secretary from 1958 to 1960. He is presently a member of the ASCD Review Council. In 1975 Dr. Davis received the Exemplary Research Award of the National Council for the Social Studies, the first such award ever presented.

WALTER DOYLE is Associate Professor of Education at North Texas State University, Denton. He has taught in the Indiana public schools and at the University of Notre Dame where he also directed the Master of Arts in Teaching Program. His research concentration is in the areas of teacher behavior and classroom processes. He is the author of *Supervision: Key to Effective Teaching* (Dayton, Ohio: Pflaum Press, 1969) and articles in various professional journals.

Since 1966, FRANCIS P. HUNKINS has been at the University of Washington, Seattle, where he is Professor of Education, teaching in the area of general curriculum. He is the author of several books, including *Involving Students in Questioning* (Allyn and Bacon, 1976), and is co-author, with Patricia F. Spears, of the ASCD booklet *Social Studies for the Evolving Individual* (1973). Dr. Hunkins is active as a curricu-

HUNKINS   PONDER   TURNEY

lum consultant, serving school districts around the country as well as advising various companies.

GERALD A. PONDER is Assistant Professor of Education, North Texas State University, Denton. Dr. Ponder has been a history teacher at secondary schools in Arkansas and Louisiana and at Loyola University in New Orleans. He is currently the director of a professional semester program designed to help prepare teachers for inner-city schools. His research interests include the areas of curriculum history and development and social studies education.

DAVID TURNEY is Dean of the School of Education at Indiana State University, Terre Haute. Dr. Turney had taught courses in curriculum, supervision, and teacher education at George Peabody College for Teachers, Kent State University, and Indiana State University before assuming the deanship of the School of Education at Indiana State. He has written extensively for professional journals, and has contributed to books published by the National Education Association, the U.S. Office of Education, and the Association for Supervision and Curriculum Development.

Contributors of the Vignettes

CHARLES BURGESS, Professor of Education, University of Washington, Seattle

MERLE B. GRADY, Assistant Professor of Curriculum and Instruction, University of Dallas

TERRY HOBBS HELLER, Teaching Associate, Secondary Education, The University of Texas at Austin

EARL KENYON, Teaching Associate, Elementary Education, The University of Texas at Austin

LARRY L. KRAUSE, Teaching Associate, English Education, The University of Texas at Austin

SANDRA M. KUHLMAN, Chairperson, English Department, Clear Creek Intermediate School, Houston, Texas

ERIC C. LUNDGREN, Teaching Associate, Secondary Education, The University of Texas at Austin

MARILYN MAXSON, Teaching Associate, Elementary Education, The University of Texas at Austin

CHARLA McCOY, Projects Administrator, Special Projects Bureau, State Department of Public Welfare, Austin, Texas

ELAINE F. McNALLY, Doctoral Student in Curriculum and Instruction, Kent State University, Kent, Ohio

TIMOTHY H. MORISSEY, Department of Education, College of St. Thomas, St. Paul, Minnesota

PATRICIA MOSELEY, Assistant Professor of Education, North Texas State University, Denton

CHARLES RUSSELL, Principal, Belton High School, Belton, Missouri

PAT SIMPSON, Biology Instructor, Temple Junior College, Temple, Texas

RICHARD SIMMS, Associate Professor of Education, North Texas State University, Denton

KAREN SOLID, Doctoral Student in Curriculum, College of Education, University of Washington, Seattle

ASCD 1976
Yearbook Committee Members

O. L. Davis, Jr., *Chairperson and Editor*
Professor of Curriculum and Instruction
The University of Texas at Austin

Ambrose A. Clegg, Jr.
Chairperson, Department of Elementary Education
Kent State University
Kent, Ohio

Walter Doyle
Associate Professor of Education
North Texas State University
Denton, Texas

J. Merrell Hansen
Associate Professor of Education
Washington State University
Pullman, Washington

Francis P. Hunkins
Professor of Curriculum and Instruction
University of Washington
Seattle, Washington

GERALD A. PONDER
Assistant Professor of Education
North Texas State University
Denton, Texas

B. R. SMOOT
Director of Secondary Education
Austin Independent School District
Austin, Texas

DAVID TURNEY
Dean, School of Education
Indiana State University
Terre Haute, Indiana

ASCD Board of Directors

Executive Council, 1975-76

President: DELMO DELLA-DORA, Professor and Chairperson, Department of Teacher Education, California State University, Hayward

President-Elect: PHILIP L. HOSFORD, Professor of Education and Mathematics, College of Education, New Mexico State University, Las Cruces

Immediate Past President: GLENYS G. UNRUH, Assistant Superintendent for Curriculum and Instruction, School District of University City, Missouri

MITSUO ADACHI, Associate Professor of Education, University of Hawaii, Honolulu

JOSEPH BONDI, Associate Professor of Education, Department of Curriculum and Instruction, University of South Florida, Tampa

BARBARA DAY, Coordinator of Early Childhood Education, University of North Carolina, Chapel Hill

SARA M. DAVIS, Professor, Elementary Education, University of Alabama, University

GERALD FIRTH, Professor and Chairperson, Curriculum and Supervision Department, University of Georgia, Athens

267

DONALD R. FROST, Curriculum Director, Leyden High School, Northlake, Illinois

JAMES E. HOUSE, JR., Consultant, Secondary Education, Wayne County Intermediate School District, Detroit, Michigan

CHARLES G. KINGSTON, JR., Principal, Thomas Fowler Junior High School, Tigard, Oregon

JAMES B. MACDONALD, Distinguished Professor of Education, University of North Carolina, Greensboro

BETTE W. TREADWELL, Project Director, National League of Cities, Washington, D. C.

Board Members Elected at Large

Leslee J. Bishop, University of Georgia, Athens (1976)

Julianna Boudreaux, New Orleans Public Schools, Louisiana (1977)

Gwyn Brownlee, Education Service Center, Region 10, Richardson, Texas (1979)

Joseph W. Crenshaw, State Department of Education, Tallahassee, Florida (1977)

Ivan J. K. Dahl, University of North Dakota, Grand Forks (1979)

Lawrence S. Finkel, Northeast Bronx Education Park, Bronx, New York (1979)

Edward A. Karns, Parma City Schools, Parma, Ohio (1977)

C. Glen Hass, University of Florida, Gainesville (1976)

Lucille G. Jordan, Atlanta Public Schools, Georgia (1978)

Milton Kimpson, Community Relations Council, Greater Columbia Chamber of Commerce, Columbia, South Carolina (1977)

Chon LaBrier, Dulce Independent School, Dulce, New Mexico (1978)

Barbara T. Mason, Queens College, City University of New York, Flushing (1976)

Norman V. Overly, Indiana University, Bloomington (1978)

James A. Phillips, Jr., Kent State University, Kent, Ohio (1977)

James Raths, University of Illinois, Urbana (1978)

Vincent R. Rogers, University of Connecticut, Storrs (1976)

Mary-Margaret Scobey, Educational Consultant, Eugene, Oregon (1979)

Dolores Silva, Temple University, Philadelphia, Pennsylvania (1978)

Unit Representatives to the Board of Directors

(Each Unit's President is listed first; others follow in alphabetical order.)

Alabama: J. Murray King, Covington County Schools, Andalusia; Mildred Ellisor, Auburn University, Auburn; Dorthea Grace Rockarts, University of Alabama, University.

Arizona: John A. Black, Public Schools, Phoenix; Carl B. Furlong, Kyrene School District, Tempe; James J. Jelinek, Arizona State University, Tempe.

Arkansas: Jim Williams, Public Schools, Dumas; Calvin G. Patterson, Public Schools, Fort Smith.

California (liaison): Arthur L. Costa, Sacramento State University, Sacramento; Lewie Burnett, California State University, Hayward; Jon Slezak, Public Schools, Pleasanton.

Colorado: Bob Taylor, University of Colorado, Boulder; Robert C. McKean, University of Colorado, Boulder; P. L. Schmelzer, Public Schools, Ft. Collins.

Delaware: Henry C. Harper, Appoquinimink School District, Odessa; Catharine Y. Bonney, Public Schools, Newark.

District of Columbia: Inez Wood, E. A. Clark School; Bessie D. Etheridge, Spingarn Instructional Unit; Lorraine H. Whitlock, Woodson Senior High School.

Florida: Emmett L. Williams, University of Florida, Gainesville; Harry F. McComb, Broward County Schools, Ft. Lauderdale; Patrick F. Mooney, Dade County Public Schools, Miami Springs; Mabel Jean Morrison, Okaloosa County Schools, Crestview; Evelyn Sharp, Bethune-Cookman College, Daytona Beach.

Georgia: James W. Lay, Public Schools, Calhoun; Harold T. Johnson, Georgia Southwestern College, Americus; Sue Jordan, University of Georgia, Athens; Joe Murphy, DeKalb County Public Schools, Decatur.

Hawaii: Virgie Chattergy, University of Hawaii, Honolulu; Elmer Dunsky, Chaminade College, Honolulu.

Idaho: Claude A. Hanson, Public Schools, Boise; David A. Carroll, Public Schools, Boise.

Illinois: Mildred Hindman Phegley, Public Schools, Collinsville; Louise Dieterle, Illinois State University, Normal; R. Kim Driggers, Public Schools, Centralia; Raymond E. Hendee, Public Schools, Park Ridge; Mary Kay Huser, Illinois State University, Normal; Blanche Martin, Public Schools, Rockford; Donald W. Nylin, Public Schools, Aurora.

Indiana: James H. McElhinney, Ball State University, Muncie; Clive Beattie, Public Schools, Portage; Charles E. Kline, Purdue University, South Campus Courts, West Lafayette; Sister Elaine Kohn, Central Catholic Education Complex, Indianapolis.

Iowa: Millard Grell, Public Schools, Sioux City; Horace S. Hoover, Community School District, Dubuque; Frank Nugent, Johnston Community School, Johnston.

Kansas: Roy W. Browning, Jr., Public Schools, Topeka; Walter L. Davies, Public Schools, Kansas City; Harlan J. Trennepohl, Kansas State University, Manhattan.

Kentucky: Juanita K. Park, Western Kentucky University, Bowling Green; William Bolton, Clark County Public Schools, Winchester; J. R. Ogletree, University of Kentucky, Lexington.

Louisiana: Rita M. Ducamus, Public Schools, New Orleans; Darryl W. Boudreaux, St. Mary Parish Schools, Morgan City; Edwin H. Friedrich, New Orleans; Katye Lee Posey, Caddo Parish Schools, Shreveport.

Maryland: John A. Soles, Howard County Department of Education, Columbia; Robert E. Hess, Public Schools, Frederick; L. Morris McClure, University of Maryland, College Park; Janice Wickless, State Department of Education, Baltimore.

Massachusetts: C. Lois Cedrone, Public Schools, Westwood; Gilbert Bulley, Public Schools, Lynnfield; Paul V. Congdon, Springfield College, Springfield; Julian Demeo, Jr., Public Schools, Braintree.

Michigan: James L. Leary, Walled Lake Consolidated Schools, Walled Lake; William Cansfield, Mt. Clemens Community Schools, Mt. Clemens; LaBarbara Gragg, Public Schools, Detroit; David Newbury, Public Schools, Hazel Park; Virginia Sorenson, Western Michigan University, Grand Rapids; Jack Wickert, Public Schools, Kalamazoo.

Minnesota: Thomas Myhra, Independent School District 14, Fridley; Donald J. Christensen, Independent School District 196, Rosemount; Stan Gilbertson, Independent School District 271, Bloomington.

Mississippi: Barnes M. West, Jackson State University, Jackson; Norvel Burkett, Mississippi State University, State College.

Missouri: Kenneth Lackey, North Kansas City School District, Kansas City; Richard King, State Department of Education, Jefferson City; Howard Lowe, Public Schools, Springfield; Patricia Rocklage, Normandy District Schools, St. Louis.

Montana: Royal G. Barnell, Missoula County Schools, Missoula; Lloyd B. Ellingsen, Public Schools, Billings.

Nebraska: Ronald L. Becker, State Department of Education, Lincoln; Gerald Bryant, Public Schools, Grand Island; J. Jay Planteen, Public Schools, Omaha.

Nevada: Mel Kirchner, Washoe County School District, Reno; William K. Moore, Clark County School District, Las Vegas.

New England: Edward G. Hunt, Rhode Island Health Science Education Council, Cranston; Ashley Gray, University of Maine, Orono; Joan D. Kerelejza, Public Schools, West Hartford, Connecticut; Philmore B. Wass, University of Connecticut, Storrs.

New Jersey: Nicholas J. Sferrazza, Gloucester Township Public Schools, Blackwood; Kathryn M. Cooper, Public Schools, Ridgewood; Mary Jane Diehl, Monmouth College, Witong Branch; Alma Flagg, Public Schools, Newark; Arnold D. Tversky, Public Schools, Dover.

New Mexico: Mary Jane Wood, Public Schools, Las Cruces; Patricia Christman, Public Schools, Albuquerque; Zella M. Hunter, Public Schools, Roswell.

Wisconsin: Myron Anderson, Public Schools, Whitefish Bay; Jim E. Claude, Public Schools, Black River Falls; William Ernst, Department of Public Instruction, Madison; Ronald Sime, Public Schools, Plattville.

Wyoming: Reuben K. Jolley, Public Schools, Douglas; Lawrence A. Walker, University of Wyoming, Laramie.

ASCD Review Council

ASCD Headquarters Staff

Executive Director: Gordon Cawelti
Associate Director; Editor, ASCD Publications: Robert R. Leeper
Associate Director: Geneva Gay
Associate Director: Charles A. Speiker
Business Manager: John H. Bralove
Administrative Assistant: Virginia O. Berthy

Staff Assistants:

Elsa Angell
Sarah Arlington
Elizabeth A. Brooks
Barbara H. Collins
Anita Fitzpatrick
Caroline M. Grills
Dodie E. Hubbell
Teola T. Jones

Polly Larson
Frances Mindel
Iris L. Morton
Nancy S. Olson
Alice Powell
Barbara J. Sims
Myra K. Taub
Colette A. Williams

Acknowledgments

Final editing of the manuscript and publication of this yearbook were the responsibility of Robert R. Leeper, Associate Director and Editor, ASCD publications. The production was handled by Elsa Angell, with the assistance of Nancy Olson, Teola T. Jones, and Polly Larson, with Caroline Grills as production manager. The cover and design of this volume are by Peter A. Nisbet. The photographs are from the Library of Congress Photographic Collection.

ASCD Publications, Spring 1976

Yearbooks

Balance in the Curriculum (610-17274)	$5.00
Education for an Open Society (610-74012)	$8.00
Education for Peace: Focus on Mankind (610-17946)	$7.50
Evaluation as Feedback and Guide (610-17700)	$6.50
Freedom, Bureaucracy, & Schooling (610-17508)	$6.50
Leadership for Improving Instruction (610-17454)	$4.00
Learning and Mental Health in the School (610-17674)	$5.00
Life Skills in School and Society (610-17786)	$5.50
A New Look at Progressive Education (610-17812)	$8.00
Perspectives on Curriculum Development 1776-1976 (610-76078)	$9.50
Schools in Search of Meaning (610-75044)	$8.50
Perceiving, Behaving, Becoming: A New Focus for Education (610-17278)	$5.00
To Nurture Humaneness: Commitment for the '70's (610-17810)	$6.00

Books and Booklets

Action Learning: Student Community Service Projects (611-74018)	$2.50
Beyond Jencks: The Myth of Equal Schooling (611-17928)	$2.00
The Changing Curriculum: Mathematics (611-17724)	$2.00
Criteria for Theories of Instruction (611-17756)	$2.00
Curricular Concerns in a Revolutionary Era (611-17852)	$6.00
Curriculum Change: Direction and Process (611-17698)	$2.00
Curriculum Materials 1974 (611-74014)	$2.00
Differentiated Staffing (611-17924)	$3.50
Discipline for Today's Children and Youth (611-17314)	$1.50
Early Childhood Education Today (611-17766)	$2.00
Educational Accountability: Beyond Behavioral Objectives (611-17856)	$2.50
Elementary School Mathematics: A Guide to Current Research (611-75056)	$5.00
Elementary School Science: A Guide to Current Research (611-17726)	$2.25
Eliminating Ethnic Bias in Instructional Materials: Comment and Bibliography (611-74020)	$3.25
Emerging Moral Dimensions in Society: Implications for Schooling (611-75052)	$3.75
Ethnic Modification of Curriculum (611-17832)	$1.00

The Humanities and the Curriculum (611-17708)	$2.00
Humanizing the Secondary School (611-17780)	$2.75
Impact of Decentralization on Curriculum: Selected Viewpoints (611-75050)	$3.75
Improving Educational Assessment & An Inventory of Measures of Affective Behavior (611-17804)	$4.50
International Dimension of Education (611-17816)	$2.25
Interpreting Language Arts Research for the Teacher (611-17846)	$4.00
Learning More About Learning (611-17310)	$2.00
Linguistics and the Classroom Teacher (611-17720)	$2.75
A Man for Tomorrow's World (611-17838)	$2.25
Middle School in the Making (611-74024)	$5.00
The Middle School We Need (611-75060)	$2.50
Needs Assessment: A Focus for Curriculum Development (611-75048)	$4.00
Observational Methods in the Classroom (611-17948)	$3.50
Open Education: Critique and Assessment (611-75054)	$4.75
Open Schools for Children (611-17916)	$3.75
Personalized Supervision (611-17680)	$1.75
Professional Supervision for Professional Teachers (611-75046)	$4.50
Removing Barriers to Humaneness in the High School (611-17848)	$2.50
Reschooling Society: A Conceptual Model (611-17950)	$2.00
The School of the Future—NOW (611-17920)	$3.75
Schools Become Accountable: A PACT Approach (611-74016)	$3.50
Social Studies for the Evolving Individual (611-17952)	$3.00
Strategy for Curriculum Change (611-17666)	$2.00
Supervision: Emerging Profession (611-17796)	$5.00
Supervision in a New Key (611-17926)	$2.50
Supervision: Perspectives and Propositions (611-17732)	$2.00
The Unstudied Curriculum: Its Impact on Children (611-17820)	$2.75
What Are the Sources of the Curriculum? (611-17522)	$1.50
Vitalizing the High School (611-74026)	$3.50
Developmental Characteristics of Children and Youth (wall chart) (611-75058)	$2.00

Discounts on quantity orders of same title to single address: 10-49 copies, 10%; 50 or more copies, 15%. Make checks or money orders payable to ASCD. Orders totaling $10.00 or less must be prepaid. Orders from institutions and businesses must be on official purchase order form. Shipping and handling charges will be added to billed purchase orders. **Please be sure to list the stock number of each publication, shown in parentheses.**

Subscription to **Educational Leadership**—$10.00 a year. ASCD Membership dues: Regular (subscription and yearbook)—$25.00 a year; Comprehensive (includes subscription and yearbook plus other books and booklets distributed during period of membership)—$35.00 a year.

Order from: **Association for Supervision and Curriculum Development Suite 1100, 1701 K Street, N.W., Washington, D.C. 20006**